I0424165

A RATIONAL
APPROACH TO RACE
RELATIONS

A RATIONAL APPROACH TO RACE RELATIONS

◆

A GUIDE TO TALKING STRAIGHT ABOUT CONTEMPORARY RACE ISSUES

R. V. Roush

iUniverse, Inc.
New York Lincoln Shanghai

A RATIONAL APPROACH TO RACE RELATIONS
A GUIDE TO TALKING STRAIGHT ABOUT CONTEMPORARY RACE ISSUES

Copyright © 2008 by R. V. Roush

All rights reserved. No part of this book may be used or reproduced by any means, graphic, electronic, or mechanical, including photocopying, recording, taping or by any information storage retrieval system without the written permission of the publisher except in the case of brief quotations embodied in critical articles and reviews.

iUniverse books may be ordered through booksellers or by contacting:

iUniverse
2021 Pine Lake Road, Suite 100
Lincoln, NE 68512
www.iuniverse.com
1-800-Authors (1-800-288-4677)

Because of the dynamic nature of the Internet, any Web addresses or links contained in this book may have changed since publication and may no longer be valid.

The views expressed in this work are solely those of the author and do not necessarily reflect the views of the publisher, and the publisher hereby disclaims any responsibility for them.

ISBN: 978-0-595-49063-9 (pbk)
ISBN: 978-0-595-60953-6 (ebk)

Printed in the United States of America

To people of all races who want to get along, or just get ahead.

Contents

Preface

Most of us want a better life, more political power to bring about the changes that improve living conditions for ourselves and our families, and even for those who have similar demographic traits to ours. We want greater social benefits and services–good shopping, schools, families, housing, parks; safety, justice, the right to choose where we live and not have our neighborhoods destroyed. These desires transcend the biological fact of race, and in fact, are not related to race at all, nor gender, nor nationality, nor ethnicity. Our race has no bearing, nor should it, on most of what we want in our lives, though many wrongly believe that race continues to have a significant impact on what we're able to get and how we're able to get it.

Race is evident when we look in the mirror. We all have it. Though children of multiracial partners are increasingly blurring racial distinctions, racists have made a science of recognizing minute physical features that allow them to spew their senseless hatred.

Some of us consider our race to be our identity, the single factor that makes us different from other races. Racial identity in the 2008 Presidential Campaign became an issue for Barack Obama, for whom the country's race theatrics were a force that bound him to embrace strategies for appealing to apparently victimized blacks in America who wanted a candidate who would exploit white guilt for the historical exploitation of blacks, while seeming to remain a plausible and fair-minded candidate to white voters.

We can choose to feel superior based on our race, inferior, or equal in how others in society value us. We can choose to feel proud about the accomplishments of others of our race or angry about poor treatment we or others who belong to our race receive or received in the past. We can celebrate the difference and the perceived exoticism of our race, and we can value the cultural diversity of many races coming together. We can choose to believe, feel, and celebrate much about our race for which there is no supportive credible evidence or logical foundation and no relevance to race. We can choose to feel that others in our race betray our race, though racial betrayal is a metaphor; people can betray only people who've put faith in them; people betray the laws of their country; and people betray their own principles and values. People, not race, are betrayed.

We develop opinions based on associations we make with race—the culture and subculture of people belonging to a race as reported in the media and by our friends. Documented cultural attitudes prevalent among members of a race, including a culture's valuation of education, work ethic, or family cohesion, for instance, lead people to incorrect generalizations about the entire race. Cultural values as exhibited through clothing and hair style, walk and speech, vehicles and jewelry, tattoos and piercings, situations, religion, values, social mores, and geographic neighborhoods are readily confused with the race of the person who is seen to possess these characteristics.

Black teens who wear urban street fashion are presumed thuggish. To conclude potential danger based on clothing fashion that is typical of violent subcultures and taking avoidance and safety measures aren't racist responses. When associations and impressions based on culture are more broadly examined, most people are instead prejudiced, or biased, or bigoted, hating the things that they correctly or incorrectly associate with a race.

Racism is a specific category regarding race. Racial prejudice, stereotyping, and discrimination present far more widespread and harmful problems than does racism. Often misapplied, however, the label of racism gets more attention and jumpstarts more community action than allegations of lesser categories of racial injustice.

Racism, as used in this study, is defined as active, overt, and irrational hatred based on the false general belief that a different race of people is inferior simply for being a different race, often typified with an underlying desire to eradicate the race. Racist beliefs often influence the racist's decisions and actions, and sometimes these actions, though not the racist beliefs themselves, are illegal, such as with job discrimination and verbal or physical assaults.

Racists don't need to know the people that they hate, and maintaining racist attitudes is actually easier for them if they don't. Few people hate based solely on the single immutable physical trait of a stranger's race. Intimate knowledge of a specific person is assumed to precede hatred, which is a complex emotion, with multiple dimensions. Knowing people of different races, racists may find valid reasons to hate individuals that aren't based on race, and this study reveals that members of any race can be racist, even against others of their own race.

Very few people have such narrow mental boundaries that their hatred can be provoked by skin color alone. It is unlikely that people can be selectively irrational only in regard to skin color while concurrently being perfectly logical and highly functional in all other respects of their daily lives. Such people exhibit racism for practical reasons, most associated with succeeding in competition against another race. Currently, job competition has been the focus in the national discussion about illegal immigrant Mexicans, who have recently become a larger minority class than blacks in the United States.

Irrational beliefs regarding race are also dissected. Logic errors, racial double standards (such as those that allow hundreds of black rappers to publicly call black women HOs but punish a white man who does), hypocrisy, and race resentment are explained; bad laws made to appease narrowly focused activist groups who exert pressure on lawmakers are deconstructed; separatist and integrationist beliefs and how they affect race perceptions are examined; and the psychology of perpetuating and sustaining racial prejudice is also reviewed.

This study also reviews flawed arguments and deceptive strategies, many of which counter capitalistic tenets, that are based on the pretense that racism and discrimination exist where they don't in order to suppress race competition and extort social or economic concessions, rewards, or long-term advantage.

Potential solutions to poor thinking are also offered, as are suggestions for changing system structures and examining models of alternate ways to obtain social and civil justice. This approach is optimistic that good solutions can be found, but that many policies, laws, and practices aren't working. Further education about race issues, which is often slanted toward social tolerance, acceptance, and compromise, won't guarantee that people will think clearly and make good choices where race relations are concerned, but prejudice is within one's psychological control to change, even though it's unlikely that hardcore racists will be persuaded by rational arguments to more moderate viewpoints. It helps to see Individuals, talk of Individuals, and hold Individuals responsible. It is not helpful to hold race responsible.

Terms of the Study

No-Load Code

Neutral terms for members of races come into general use, but labels can quickly become unpopular (such as colored people and Negro), or are purposely loaded with negative emotions. Though race labels (black and white) may offend, special codes, such as Ph-B or Ph-W for phenotypically black or white, are themselves labels that can become connotatively defamed.

Race in this study is treated as a biological distinction. Color is one differentiating factor. Other factors include biological phenotypic dominance, that is, physical characteristics that place people on a continuum of belonging to an identifiable race. It is conceded that many see race as a role that people play and that designating a degree of racial identity with any certainty in the presence of mixed bloodlines is difficult even in genetic laboratories.

For those with predominantly Negroid racial outward appearance, the term black is used. For those with predominantly Caucasian features, white is used. Other races are identified as Asian, Hispanic/Latino, mixed for race of undetermined nature (which is how such races are often described in social settings), Middle Eastern, and Native American. The scientifically imprecise categorization criteria–color for blacks and whites but continent affiliation for other races and ethnic groups–may seem inconsistent, but since both African blacks and European whites have populated America for centuries, they are not considered recent immigrants from their native lands. Therefore, it is acknowledged that comparable terms are used–black and white–rather than the more distantly comparable African-American, which denotes continental citizenship, and white, which denotes race.

The choice of the terms white and black has no metaphorical implication nor poetic allusion to pureness, darkness, good, nor evil. It is understood that skin color is simply one factor that allows people to physically differentiate between other people and that many people are multiracial, not fitting snuggly into any single race category. Shades of brown don't make people more or less representative of a culture (though light brown skin has been and still is seen among some blacks as a factor in the attainment of social status). Some blacks, as a popular black comedian asserts, are "black from a distance." Black and white are used for the sake of simplicity.

People and groups in this book are presumed to be American citizens, unless otherwise stated, and reference to ethnic background is intended only to distinguish one minority from another or from a majority race or ethnicity. For simplicity, accuracy, and fairness in most instances, the terms African-American, Asian-American, German-American, Mexican-American, mixed-heritage/nationality-American, and other variations on hyphenated American affiliation will be avoided, except in quotations and when such hyphenation is factual. The patriotic allegiance, nationalism, pride, and emotional connection with multiple cultures as a pretentious affectation will be analyzed in depth elsewhere in this study.

Other Conventions Used

References to statistics are kept to a minimum, though statistical significance is not minimalized. Statistics are often used to support specific propositions and ignored or skewed by many authors if no supporting correlation for their hypotheses can be concluded from them. However, properly cited, statistics are important in describing hard realities in areas of crime, educational success, medical and health variations among races, and compositional percentages of a particular race in a field of endeavor. Metadata grouped by race and timeline show areas of failure and improvement. This study understands that facts are not subjective, but that individual explanations for them and their existence, what they mean and how they can be applied, and conclusions from them *are* subjective.

Opinion poll results are rarely cited in this study, except to deconstruct them and show them to be invalid. Opinion, no matter how widely held, isn't a factual representation of reality and is not evidence of racism, for instance, though a demographic population subset of people may agree with a loaded response choice on a poll that racism is prevalent and pervasive. It is unfortunate that knowledge of opinion poll results may spur people to action in an effort to correct misperceptions or negative conditions identified as a disproportionately important problem in the poll. Knowing poll results, people who want to be on the side of a winner will be influenced to take action that will let them define themselves as belonging to the group of winners.

Poll results are often skewed, especially when *only* the concept of racism, as opposed to other racial dimensions, such as racial discrimination in attainment of employment, is provided in the survey question. They're also skewed because the number and abstaining respondents and their reasons for tossing the survey in the trash aren't known, and neither is the impact their answers would have had on the results. Polls are also often wrong, a clear case being the polls in January 2008 that predicted that Barack Obama would win the New Hampshire primary election when, in fact, Hillary Clinton won overwhelmingly, stunning the pollsters.

Polls are floated during periods of high racial awareness and tension, such as during a jury trial in which a white police officer is charged with the murder of a minority, or in the aftermath of a race riot, with the hope that responses can serve as indirect or circumstantial evidence of racism by the officer or the rioters. The prevailing mood during such uncertain periods of momentary media saturation taints the results in ways that, though not newsworthy, sell newspapers.

A lot has been said about race. Extensive quoting could bog down the narrative, so quotes are kept to a minimum, and statements often will be consolidated and paraphrased to examine the illogical premises behind them.

The issue of race relations is examined from a rational point of view, rather than an emotional or altruistic or social one, examining why there is such a strong element of race resentment. The subject is approached from a Libertarian perspective and from the philosophy that people should take personal responsibility for their situation.

Any reader's intelligence should be insulted by the statement, "The author's a white dude, so this book's written from a white dude's perspective." Everyone has race in common. The objectionable assertion that no white person can legitimately discuss race issues is racially prejudiced and a bald attempt to discredit the source of information as a way of indirectly discrediting the information itself. A member of any race, with the right background knowledge and research, intelligence, empathy, and interest can objectively deconstruct and describe the emotional baggage heaped on race issues. It's a fallacy to believe that someone must live another's experience, be part of the experience and be intimately and completely involved and submersed in the culture of the experience, to know and understand it. There is an automatic presumption that only those who embody our gender, or our race, or our age can fully represent our interests, but if that were the case, only old white men would have chosen to live in the United States over the centuries. People can be fair to others of diverse backgrounds without having that diversity in common.

However, some people are wrongly convinced to assign greater credibility to the premises and statements and conclusions of people of such a background, lending greater thoughtless credibility to their illogical assertions. You can live an experience and still make bone-head assumptions and conclusions about the experience.

Deceptive methods and individuals who use them are attacked, not races. The issues are described without sensitivity to the needs of any group or race, without regard to protecting feelings, and with little concern for politically correct and indefinite language, though care is taken not to implicate entire races when describing the acts of individuals who are part of identifiable divisions in a group's political thinking. Observations and the inferences from those observations are stated without apology.

Breaks in the narrative to emphasize premises and observations look like this:

> **Premise:** Feeling/believing that you have been denied a product or service, employment, full equal representation, and fair treatment under the law *because of* your race doesn't mean that such slights were in fact based on your race, just as *feeling* safe from terrorist attacks doesn't mean that we *are* safe.
>
> Though you may think that a shadow in your bedroom will attack you, the shadow doesn't come to life. Though you may feel unsafe walking through or living in a multiracial neighborhood, you may be in no more danger relative to other neighborhoods. Emotional response doesn't depend on factual reality, even when the full particulars of the facts are known; when particulars aren't known with certainty but only suspected, emotions are guided by wild interpretations and speculation of the risks.

Generalizations and absolutes (describing things as all or none) are avoided, though slips may occur. Trying to simply a complex problem may lead to errors of omission, so any oversimplifications should be forgiven. Great diligence is used to identify and limit comments to those specific subgroups, such as black militant radicals or members of white Christian fundamentalist groups, who hold retro, regressive ideologies. Clear and plain language is intended, and snarky remarks will be made clearly evident with a smiley face (not really).

Though race relations between whites and blacks will be primarily addressed, other forms of racism will be discussed, such as profiling phenotypically Middle Eastern travelers at airports.

Projections, predictions, and speculation are avoided. For example, Henry "Skip" Louis Gates, in a special for PBS television, asked a black interview subject how life would be for blacks in 50 years. Such questions invite pure hopeful or despairing conjecture with little basis in reality, offering nothing to the understanding of race relationships. Gates also has a tendency to ask fraudulent, loaded, dichotomous questions that structure the response between two choices and presumes discrimination, such as, "Do you think you have been discriminated against more for your race or your gender." The question does not address other factors, such as skill level and ability, experience, age, talent, education, determination, and professionalism as possible measures for failure or success. It also assumes as fact that a person feels, or should feel, discriminated against, because they are racially discriminated against whether or not they believe they are.

Additionally, personal testimonials and anecdotes are included only if they introduce an opportunity to provide analysis; it is understood that testimonials are hearsay and not necessarily evidence of racism or racial discrimination.

Few historical cases involving racial conflict are discussed in detail, and readers are referred to further studies, which are numerous and extensive.

Introduction

Advancements in the financial, educational, employment, and political condition of traditionally disenfranchised races in America are an endorsement of democracy and capitalism. Now, more than ever, Americans are aware of the problems facing minorities and the historic discrimination and suppression minorities have endured. Whites who thoughtlessly relied on contemporary social custom to dismiss blacks in the past have been made aware of the negative impact of their racially prejudiced or discriminatory behavior. As a result of unified effort, predominantly black coalitions forced government legislators to draft and pass laws that ensured equal civil rights for all Americans.

Such progress does not come about flawlessly. Some of the methods used by a few minorities to gain headway led to racial antagonism, resentment, and volatile relations between whites and blacks.

Racism Defined

Depending on who provides the definition, racism can mean the overt hatred of a race and it's dominant or more aggressively visible culture, usually accompanied by violence and the intent to eradicate the race. Racism has been attributed to anyone who has the power to control certain societal rewards, such as employment, whether or not these people acknowledge that racism naturally colors their world vision and determines how they approach daily interactions. But racism has been claimed to manifest itself as the deprivation of a television cable station that a few blacks want in an area populated predominantly by whites. A coalition of black ministers calls for a boycott of a chain of grocery stores because they believe the closing of one grocery store in a poor black neighborhood is evidence of the owners' racism.

The word *racism* can conjure nasty images of victimization, job discrimination, unfair housing, legal precedents intended to reverse racism, substandard education, poverty, and a host of other indistinct negative correlation.

The salient trait of racists is that they supposedly hate people they don't know based on the race of those people. Generalized "hatred" of another race has its genesis in direct or indirect, and usually shallow and limited, encounters with people of the race, rather than in a belief in the ideology of superiority. However, by far the greatest influence on race perception is exercised by the media.

> **Observation:** There are many races in the United States, not just the black and white (and more frequently, Hispanic) you read about most.
>
> Pitting two traditionally wary and competitive races against each other lets newspaper editors, book publishers, and lecturers drum up controversy, interest, bitterness, and, most of all, sales. It's not just whites against blacks over issues of race and what race means in people's lives, but blacks against enterprising Korean capitalists, whites and blacks against Middle Easterners and illegal Mexican immigrants, and blacks against other blacks over drug sales territory, in which race is incidental to commerce.
>
> In a recent season of the television show, *Survivor*, teams were segregated by race, reminding viewers of legally enforced pre-civil rights segregation. *Survivor's* producers created controversy by being bold enough to admit to and exploit the racially separatist tendencies in their viewers, knowing that viewers would watch and root for same-race teams that "represented" them; the term, represent, is too often used interchangeably with the concept of having the same race in common, giving people the false impression that others of one's race are looking out for the interests of all members of the race they share. Tactics like this wouldn't happen in a racially neutral society because there would be no controversy in using them.

Racists are *not* confined to high-level power positions in social, corporate, religious, or political institutions. They aren't found only in the white race or only in the black race. They may verbally announce their senseless hatred, or they may hide it if revelation could conceivably subject them to allegations of racism and the bad public relations that come with such allegations. Racists may also hide their attitude to avoid legal punitive action for racial discrimination or personal reprisal.

> **Premise:** Racist thinking has no moral component, is not moral or immoral. Thought, and much speech, is legally protected. Illegal acts, whether motivated by racist thought, greed, anger, or chemical imbalance, are not protected.

Tolerant superiority among slaveholders meant that they didn't need to waste energy "hating" those to whom they felt superior. Racists don't really hate individual strangers; they simply disapprove of the attitudes, beliefs, values, culture, and lifestyles that they wrongly attribute to *all* members of the race that they select to shove. These simplistic feelings are reinforced every time the target race is reported in the media to demonstrate an act that reveals degenerate values, and this horrible tendency to generalize is understood by many in minority groups who publicly encourage their members not to give other races yet another reason to disapprove. Some minorities voice radical, seething, general hatred for other racial groups as often as whites make such ridiculous declarations. But it isn't the race that is attacked, but disapproval of alternate, repressive, even regressive, values held by a few members of the race; subjective associations and stereotypes are the adversarial link between whites and blacks.

Some people pretend to hate so they can justify their own racial discrimination to themselves and others. Hate, when it's deserved, reduces a sense of moral conscience about acts of discrimination and retaliation. But it's not hate that most people feel, and most people aren't racists, but prejudists. It's disgust or revulsion that people feel, disdain when a minority group demands that a majority share. It's resentment and mistrust. It's despair about the injustice of racially preferential treatment and the death of social values evidenced in the gangsta rap music of racial subcultures. Disagreement with the cultural practices and values of racial minority subsets can turn into fear that these values will be mainstreamed and etch away at one's own values and legal protections. For instance, Muslim populations in Rotterdam form a voting bloc that may oust Rotterdam's democratic incumbents and lead to totalitarian government policies, threatening through intimidation equality of the sexes, lifestyles, and freedoms. Unease around people of another race may be the result of generalizing to the entire race the objectionable activities of race subset groups. For instance, many Americans have developed a distrust of Islamic Arabs based on the terrorist actions of Islamic terrorists.

Contemporary arguments that blacks are inherently inferior (morally, intellectually, socially, and ethically) are less a product of racial hatred than of resentment that minorities are allowed to compete unfairly, whereas they were legally barred from any competition in the past. People resent changes to the status quo that remove their own unfair advantage. Extension of the right of minorities to compete is one of those changes. Extension of the right to compete with unfair advantage based on race feels like a slap in the face to many in the racial majority.

Racism is learned. Any generalized hatred is. Somebody teaches a child to hate, make fun of, oppress, and fear children of other races. Somebody teaches people that people who are different are bad or dangerous, just as somebody must teach children that some snakes and fire can be dangerous. In backward cultures, children and their teachers are plainly ignorant, having been taught their entire lives to automatically distrust other races and to generalize negative traits to them. A public figure's irrational statements are passed along to perpetuate irrationality. In an interview by Gates, white parents are reported to be irresponsibly teaching their children racial hatred: "My daddy told me not to listen to a black man," commented a white soldier charged with military insubordination to a black commander (Gates, PBS Special). Segregated, isolated within their own race and culture, children may have few opportunities for countervailing positive experiences with other races/nationalities. These racists-by-tradition may not be aware that the benefit of such thinking and consequent avoidance behaviors are intended to heighten personal safety or advance economically, for instance. Unlike Israelis and Palestinians in Jerusalem, who hate one another from tradition and knowledge of horrendous crimes that continue to be committed by each side, racists-by-tradition have no intentionality.

> **Premise:** Hatred is only one emotional response to racial diversity, though the most inflammatory one.

Few whites still truly believe that the white race is inherently and generally superior to other races. Widespread education has made such views inconsistent with reality. To hold beliefs of superiority is irrational in light of contradicting, and often daily communicated, evidence of the educational, intellectual, social, cultural, and political contributions by members of all races. The dramatically improving social and economic condition of blacks in general disputes faulty proclamations by speakers who overestimate how bad the lives of minorities are, how unjustly minorities are being treated as a race. "Forty percent of blacks are now comfortably middle class, compared with only 5 percent in 1940" (Charen, p. 86). Those brainwashed few within Nazi and skinhead extremist groups who still hold such beliefs, though conviction is flagging, usually are so ignorant that they fail to see the value in keeping their mouths shut, thereby forming a very verbal, but discredited, minority. Being racist gives these people a sense of purpose and identity.

Within the black community, the concept of black racial superiority goes by the name black, or racial, pride and esteem. A double standard exists, and whites are labeled racist if they announce their white racial pride.

The prevalence of white or black racism and racial discrimination isn't and can't be known (minority races also practice racial discrimination to maintain segregated workplaces and to gain a larger collective to hold power when the collective acts in concert). Proof of either racism or racial discrimination is difficult to gather. Unless racist thinking translates into acts that infringe on others' civil rights in a way that can directly be shown to be a result of racial discrimination, instances can't be known.

> **Premise:** Because racism exists doesn't mean that it exists rampantly everywhere in everyone in every instance.
> A worldview that revolves around the belief that racism is prevalent forces the viewer to see prevalence whether or not it exists. Interactions with other races are unrealistically framed with the presumption that others key on race in their daily activities and thoughts, and when they're introduced to members of another race. This is an ego-centered view of the world that doesn't reflect reality and results in habitual, though unfounded, distrust, anger, suspicion, offense, and frustration. Perceptions of mistreatment based on race burdens interactions between members of different races.

Colorism is an offshoot of racism by blacks against light-skinned blacks. When asked to rate how smart a person is in a photo, blacks more often indicate that a light-skinned version of the same person with darker skin is smarter, happier, and more successful–people with darker skin are rated more poorly by blacks. Colorism in America allegedly began during the slavery period because light-skinned blacks, often the offspring of unions between slave owners and slaves, received better treatment. They worked in the house and were beaten less readily. Being light skinned was associated with privilege. Dark-skin blacks were envious.

Light-skinned, mixed race people have straighter hair, narrower noses, thinner lips, in general, and are perceived by whites to be infused with fewer of the negative black cultural traits, though such perception is often baseless and relies more on self-reinforcing fairer treatment experienced by light-skinned blacks over the course of their lives that persuades them to reject degenerate cultural values. Self-important and superior attitude made it obvious that light-skinned slaves felt they were superior to dark-skinned blacks, and this attitude reinforced the hatred between mulattos and dark-skinned blacks. This dynamic still exists for some blacks, influencing some blacks to treat light-skinned blacks with as much derision as they do whites. Light-skinned blacks can't help their coloring. Some dark-skinned blacks will also attribute unfair advantage to every white person in the world. Self-pity and sour grapes make for a bad vintage whine.

Institutional racism is the term used to describe the practice by those in major societal institutions in education, business, and government of systematically discriminating against races. The term *institutional racism* condemns, in an overarching way, large groups of people of planning and premeditating racism, regardless of the race of those employed in these institutions. Some or many people in an organization or affiliated with an institution may be racist, but the institution or organization is not, just as brightly colored silk shirts aren't "gay," though the men wearing them to Broadway musicals may be. Inanimate objects can have no sexual preference, just as systems can have no racial preference. Policies and regulations can't be racist, though the people who created them as a means of racially discriminating and those enforcing them may be. There are a few reasons to label an institution or organization racist, rather than holding affiliated individuals responsible: in lawsuits, more monetary damages can be squeezed from organizations and corporations, and negotiations for concessions can often be granted more readily by organizations than by individuals.

Racism as practiced by individuals is a very specific concept. Its definition is limited. Discrimination based on race isn't racism. Stereotyping subpopulations of blacks or whites or Asians or Arabs isn't racism. Rejecting fallacious and malicious and self-serving allegations of racism isn't racist. Prejudice isn't racism. Racial profiling as practiced by law enforcement and airport security personnel isn't racism.

It is not racist that a white person doesn't care that other white strangers treated blacks poorly in the past, just as it isn't racist that a black stranger doesn't care about the hardships suffered by white strangers in the past; strangers aren't obligated to care about or to offer amends to other strangers, and it is hypocrisy to demand repayment from a stranger based on his race while explicitly refusing to acknowledge and honor the stranger's own ancestral hardships.

> **Premise:** Racism isn't illegal, but denying employment and public services based on provable racial discrimination is.

People are not connected by race unless they choose to be. We're not in this struggle together, though everybody has the right to attempt to convince others that everyone' fate is intertwined and that helping them somehow helps you. It doesn't. Each person of any race stands on his own and has the choice to form alliances either through deception or by acts that are mutually beneficial.

Differences between Racism and Racial Associations

Do people know the difference between racist thought and simple prejudice? This study presumes that most do, which implies intention in the commission of acts of racial injustice, such as racial profiling and job discrimination. To suggest that people know that they benefit from perpetuating racial injustice, infringing on civil rights, and slandering based on race also assumes that a rational–and practical–choice can be made, and has been made.

Emotional, intellectual, psychological, and financial options will always be factors in decisions to embrace racial stereotypes. *Perceived* benefits of racial stereotyping for both whites and black minorities include greater assurance of personal safety and security by avoiding those of a different race (black gangstas or skinheads), a more productive workforce that has more in common with others in the work place and more in common with customers, and exclusion of people who might bring along others of their race to compete for resources and housing. Benefits of racial stereotyping realized primarily only by whites include reduced business theft and gains in social status by association with other races (suburban white teens in black gangs, white politicians voicing concern for ailments allegedly peculiar to those in black communities, etc.).

To minorities who hear of successes and money made by alleging white racism, media attention and material concessions are perceived perks. For those who illegally immigrate to the U.S. and cite racial discrimination by majority populations, changes in immigration policy that relax enforcement of laws leads to real, rather than perceived, benefits.

People form opinions from the numerous perceptual associations they make between race and racial cultures and subcultures. Some black rappers are violent. Some teenage, gang-affiliated inner city black males kill to gain gang respect. Some southern rednecks drive pickup trucks with gun racks and have been known to harass minorities. Fear and caution and derision, rather than hatred, are more likely the more accurate descriptions of responses to people in these cultures.

Some people embrace a lifestyle and its associations for the sole purpose of acquiring an image–they want to be feared as thugs, hated, avoided, and they know that the acquired image is a big step in achieving that, based on the valid assumptions others will make. They affiliate with a gang whose reputation for violence is deserved and nurtured so that they can personally realize the benefits of the reputation, which include reduced retaliation and easier relinquishment of property by those whom they attack. In these instances, stereotypes applied by potential victims based on their attacker's group affiliation are valid and offer a protective physical advantage–people will give up their possessions rather than fight to keep them when they suspect that 50 gang friends have the lone gansta's back.

Identifying oneself as belonging to a culture and hoping to be judged precisely for that culture's associations gains the rewards of that affiliation. So, voluntary affiliation with a violent subculture paired with a demand *not* to be judged negatively based on purposeful associations leads to understandable resentment for the obvious hypocrisy and demanded double standard.

This same need for association applies to young white male suburbanites who assume black gangsta mannerisms, clothing, walk, attitude, talk, and friendships to get laid … and get laid. In the gangsta subculture, whites gain associative respect from the protective brotherhood they've infiltrated and are no longer perceived as easy targets, but as tough hoods with tough friends. In such cases, perception matters if alternate possible realities (other street hoods beating down clean-cut white boys in their neighborhood) are avoided.

Media Fire Fanning

Objective reports of negative incidents involving minorities–and the media invariably emphasizes the negative as newsworthy–are likely to give readers negative impressions about minorities in general. Liberal media outlets note the negative incidents, but excuse them, citing systemic racism or racial discrimination as the true demons. In Dayton, Ohio, media reports are racially partial toward blacks, a group that constitutes 43 percent of Dayton's population, according to the 2000 census.

An example of blatant race bias in the media is evident in the opening sentences of an article about a supply contract to General Motors: "After more than a year of trying to break in as a supplier to General Motors Corp., Beverly Bleicher made a shrewd business decision. She hired a white, male sales agent who was able to secure a $75,000 contract from GM.…" (*Dayton Daily News*, November 29, 1992). Aside from the bias of interviewing a black female who feels victimized because of her race (with whites rarely being interviewed for feeling victimized because of their race), the article doesn't address the possibility that Bleicher simply hired a good salesperson who just happened to be male and white. Perhaps the skill of the salesperson landed the contract, not the color of his skin nor his gender. Even the title of the article–"GM's minority suppliers worry"–presumes that white suppliers don't worry or don't need to. GM's total supplier base was 5,700 in 1992, and 1,480 of those suppliers were minorities, which is a generous percentage. Through the biased language of the article, the media is creating controversy, with the end goal to force GM to develop minority supplier programs to open up the bidding for contracts. Then, "Bleicher's $1.2

million manufacturing company has abandoned the automotive industry and now focuses on manufacturing engine parts for aerospace and defense industries...." According to Bleicher, fractured syntax intact, "'The fact that I am a black female, people have preconceived opinions of my inability of my soliciting the work. However, if I would send a non-minority person over, they were more warmly welcomed and receive more opportunity'" (*Dayton Daily News*, November 29, 1992).

Liberal media is typically duplicitous, siding with the black agenda. Another example of the slant in a report that fuels the issue of race is an article entitled "Race may be factor in fights" describing stabbings in a prison. Southern Ohio Correctional Facility warden Arthur Tate reported, "'The first incident involved a black man being stabbed by a white man. The second incident involved a white man being stabbed by a black man.... From that standpoint, race certainly is involved'" (*Dayton Daily News*). Prison investigators don't work hard to establish deeper motives.

> **Premise:** Sometimes crimes involving participants of more than one race aren't racially motivated.

Whether the story is about a white man who didn't get a job because of race quotas, or a black man who didn't because of racial discrimination, frequent reports about such possibilities make the injustice seem prevalent. People who read newspapers aren't interested in stories about job applicants getting turned away for their lack of experience. They want to read headlines like "Racial and National Divides" until they learn the story's about theater dramas being presented at a local university (*Dayton City Paper*, Jan 26–Feb 1, 2005). "Black men urged to lead the way at Think Tank" is a headline that presumes that black men need to be urged, implying that white men are currently leading, and that "thinking" may be an unfamiliar area for black men (*Dayton Daily News*, May 13, 2007). "Clergy discuss how to bridge a racial divide evident from failed school levy" is a subheadline that cites racism as evidence for a failed levy (*Dayton Daily News*, May 17, 2007). The article further insinuates that whites were actively racist in voting against the levy, though the funding was earmarked entirely for inner-city, predominantly black schools, forcing all local parents to pay a prohibitively high tax increase for schools that their children don't attend. Three separate headlines emphasize race in this article from the *Dayton Daily News* May 20, 2007 edition: "**DAYTON'S BLACK-AND-WHITE DIVIDE**: Race remains significant factor in city's elections: The vote map for the school levy mirrors the racial divisions seen in past mayoral contests." The prevalence of such alarmist headlines alleging race as a deciding factor in social injustice, and the statements by interview subjects in the stories claiming that racism is prevalent, inflames race as an imperative issue, though few think about race on a daily basis.

> **Premise:** The more sweeping the declarations of racial injustice, the more extensive and perversely slanted the mainstream liberal media coverage becomes.

If there's an extra dimension, such as the drama of social injustice, or the possibility that race played a role or that an employer is embroiled in a secret conspiracy to avoid hiring minorities, then there's an employer and a story worthy of attention by those who want to be appalled and indignant. We've all heard stories about minorities getting rude service in restaurants because the waiters are racist. Or not getting a job because the employer is racist. Not being promoted because of racist employment policies. Not being allowed to buy property in a white segregated neighborhood. Being singled out as a suspect based on race. The violence and riots by minorities. For some of these stories, the allegations are unproven, but for others, the truth is plainly written in policy and federal law.

Media distorts stories and focuses on exceptional cases rather than on average cases, giving people the impression that the exceptional case is the norm. Stories appear daily on television news, in the newspapers, and on talk shows in conversation about racial discrimination on the job or race-related hate crimes or unfair preferential treatment based on race. The news story doesn't discuss the rarity of the reported event or the expected occurrence rate in proportion to all such incidences. Checking the accuracy of facts and providing context aren't priorities for many reporters who know the importance of controversy and making deadlines. Sensationalism is interest, which reports must generate. Accentuating the negative lets do-gooders see problems and work on correcting them from their subjective points of view.

> **Premise:** The rate of racial discrimination isn't affected by someone's subjective evaluation, belief, and perception of its prevalence.

Popular media also makes bold, subjective, and unsupported claims. In season five's first episode of *History Detectives* broadcast on PBS in 2007, the detectives track down the origins of a rare recording of a live Amos 'n' Andy radio broadcast. Apparently, in 1931 at 7 PM, a third of the American population listened to a 15-minute Amos 'n' Andy story voiced by two white radio announcers, Free-man Gosden and Charles Correll. In the stories, the radio performers portray two uneducated southern blacks who've migrated north to live in the more sophisti-cated city environs and encounter "fish-out-of-water" difficulties, misunderstand-ings, and culture shock. "The racial stereotypes are degrading today," states *History Detectives* researcher Tukufu Zuberi of the offshoot television program in the 1950s, though no definitively offensive clips were shown on the broadcast episode as evidence. The researcher makes the value judgment on behalf of view-ers, not allowing viewers to make their own conclusions. Of minstrel-style carica-tures in both the radio program and the later television program, Zuberi states, "Of course, the caricatures of race and class were deeply offensive, and remain so." "As a sociologist who is African-American, researching Amos 'n' Andy is a tricky assignment." Stating such a bias is a clear indication of the story's slant and presumes that racist non-minority researchers conducting the same research wouldn't be as offended. The televised version of the Amos 'n' Andy show "only lasted two years," according to Zuberi, "because the African-American commu-nity rose up and protested and demanded that it be taken off the air," though no proof for this statement or proof that discounts competing or contrary reasons for cancellation are provided so that viewers can make their own conclusions. The radio show excluded African-Americans, the show's narrator alleges, "from par-ticipating on the stage," which presumably makes the leap of logic that the popu-larity of an allegedly racist radio program lasting 15 minutes a night made all competing entertainment outlets about blacks financially unfeasible in a compet-itive sense. No evidence is offered either of the numbers of stage shows during the height of the radio program's popularity, or the numbers of black theater-goers to black-organized stage performances. Nor was analysis offered regarding the attraction of a free radio broadcast to poor blacks and white who couldn't afford theater prices. "Some historians suggest that minstrel shows became popular as working class whites faced competition from African-Americans in the work-place," one of the researchers posits. During the Depression, a time that made work hard to find for everyone, though especially for minorities due to racial dis-crimination in hiring practices, did unemployed white factory workers decide to change careers, become actors, put on blackface, develop an act, and take it on the road? "For a couple of hours, the minstrel shows gave them their own sense of superiority." The media now has the ability to go back in time and read minds to fictionally dramatize a story.

Media seeks darlings. Many whites feel that a major sustaining factor of racist attitudes are statements from minority spokespeople that emphasize race as an inevitable factor in daily life. Some of these spokespeople seem to carry their podiums wherever they travel. Racial issues are discussed to the point of anger on college campuses. The interest is like watching a train wreck that diverts focus from other pressing problems. The undue emphasis also heightens the perception of the prevalence of race-related issues in society, when acts of racial discrimination and violence are actually quite rare. In fact, many of the maladies attributed to racism and racial discrimination occur across racial lines: poverty, poor job opportunities, job discrimination, fractured families, poor education, crime, violence, religious persecution, integration, miscellaneous hardships, medical problems, and life in inner cities. The races have everyone looking for racial discrimination where none could ever be proven, but the emphasis makes everyone who might be charged with it dread race issues, upsetting everyone who loathes any kind of treatment that is based on race.

Racial Stereotyping

Most people know that racial stereotypes are based on limited instances, but in their everyday thinking, they often forget this fact. Sometimes people have collected so little information about the diversity among members of a race or ethnic group that they don't know another viewpoint. Stereotypes may be positive, negative, or neutral. Negative stereotypes aren't inevitable. Data from one psychological study suggests that increased activity in the brain's amygdala, which registers wariness and vigilance, when subjects view faces from races other than their own might be a result of deep wired racial stereotyping. However, the longer the faces were viewed, the more that other parts of the brain, the prefrontal cortex and the anterior cingulate, regions associated with higher thought and control of reflexive responses, showed controlling activity. The researcher, William Cunningham of the University of Toronto, believes that "if people have a chance, they can modify or override the emotional response with the cognitive regions of their brain." (sciencejournal@wsj.com). From studies by psychologist Susan Fiske of Princeton University, category-based emotional responses generated by the amygdala can be overridden when viewers are forced to evaluate extraracial faces with a distinct purpose in mind, such as to determine affinity for carrots, making the faces more unique. Asked to determine age, however, subjects categorized based on racial stereotypes.

In another experiment designed by Anthony Greenwald of the University of Washington and reported by NBC's Dateline in a mid-May 2007 episode (dateline.msnbc.com), the word *good* or *bad* is paired with either a black or white face. Seventy-nine percent of whites showed preference for whites over blacks. Forty-two percent of blacks preferred whites, explained as a result of the media's more frequent coverage of incidents of blacks committing crimes, or as self-loathing based on race. Is it really news that people of the same race have a greater preference for others of their race? Since only two choices were provided in the experiment, the logic issue, or confounding factor, with this type of experiment construction is called forced response to extreme position response, which denies possible continuum responses.

The brain can't be rewired to be color blind. People are obviously different colors. It is human nature to discriminate between objects and people to form manageable patterns for the brain to handle. Figurative and symbolic color blindness is a bad metaphor that doesn't hold up under rational scrutiny. Personally practicing color blindness works only on a theoretical level removed from individuals in face-to-face interaction, and the concept is intended metaphorically for equal treatment in systems and law.

Uncertainty about people of other races and cultures is a psychological/educational dimension, though no amount of multiculturalism education can make anyone certain about individuals. However, people can have latent biases that can nevertheless be consciously eradicated by the individual. Bias is not entrenched, rigid, unchangeable. Some biases in attitude are automatic but individuals can deny their power to inform action.

> **Premise:** All members of the same race do not think alike, have the same tastes, have the same aspirations, make the same income, live in the same type of house, send their children to the same school, have the same educational background, think the same way about racial issues or heritage, or belong to the same political party.

Negative opinions about entire races invite people to confuse racial issues by implicating racism and its characteristic hatred. And though we must acknowledge that some people are racist, many transactions and outcomes involving two or more races should not be assumed automatically to be racist or racially focused. A capitalist factory owner who oppresses all employees regardless of race should not be said to be unequivocally racist because some employees are non-white minorities. People misconstrue the intent behind outcomes. Any member of any race can practice racial discrimination by denying earned and deserved power or reward, or civil rights to anyone based on race–black racism against whites ("expressions of rage" in post-Rodney King verdict parlance) is still racism;

worse, such acts constitute terrorism, defined as indiscriminate criminal and violent retaliation against innocent victims to instill generalized terror.

Conversely, insensitivity to what is depicted as another race's problems does not constitute racism. Insensitivity is most often due to the knowledge that poverty and crime and ill health, for instance, are part of the human condition and not exclusive to any particular race. Indifference to another race's stated need for racial pride and esteem or financial empowerment isn't necessarily racist. Acting in one's own best interests, though not directly benefiting others, regardless of race, perhaps even countering the interests of others as a by-product of self-advancement, regardless of race, may not indicate racism. Punishing those who abuse power, who commit unethical acts, or who are incompetent isn't a racist act only because the person being censured belongs to a racial minority. Emphasizing that dedication, tenacity, moral character, creative and original thinking, attention to detail, education, frugality, and hard work lead to success is not racist when deciding not to promote a racial minority who doesn't apply these values in his or her work.

Racial Discrimination as a Legal Distinction

Racial discrimination is a legal distinction for the practice of considering a person's race as an overriding factor in deciding *not* to sell goods to that person, not to provide services, to deny civil rights, or not to make employment available. Deciding *to* sell goods, *to* provide services, *to* extend the courtesy of civil rights, and *to* offer employment based on race is considered a positive outcome of discrimination and was not considered illegal. In this instance, a double standard is created based on perceived quality of the outcome of the discrimination; positive outcome, discrimination is okay, but negative outcome, and discrimination is illegal. However, a positive outcome based on race for one person is a negative opportunity cost for another who suffers when the resource becomes unavailable for fair competition.

Most frequently, racial discrimination is linked to unfairly favoring one race over another in hiring practices. It is a tool to oppress others. For instance, in Georgia in the early 1930s, all "the instruments of caste pluralism–social indignity, physical brutality, educational deprivation, and political exclusion–combined to keep the vast majority of blacks confined to the most menial kinds of work" (Fuchs, p. 103). Reverse discrimination laws attempt to reverse past discrimination against blacks, or a least balance the social justice scales, in essence by making the number of whites who experience racial discrimination equal to the number of blacks who have. These numbers aren't definitively tabulated or knowable, which makes the social engineering laws an exercise in presenting the *appearance* of doing something positive to correct past wrongs against minority races.

Attributing racism to an instance of racial discrimination aggressively assumes that an employer, for instance, has a deep racial hatred or is actively suppressing the equal rights of a minority job applicant. In fact, racial discrimination may simply reflect a racially insular employer's higher comfort level interacting with members of his own race, or the employer's beliefs, based on experience, that current employees are more productive working with others of their race, sex, and age. The employer may feel that his customers prefer to deal with employees of a specific race. Or the employer may hold little esteem for the credentials of the educational program from which the minority graduated. Or, more likely, employers don't want to hire the type of people who threaten to press false racial discrimination charges to extort jobs. But employers are not legally permitted to use any of these reasons for specifically denying qualified minorities career positions.

Business-based beliefs may coincidentally convince employers to withhold equal consideration for job candidates who happen to be of a different race, but it is presumptuous to attribute to the employer a deep-seated hostility toward minorities, or toward whites in the case of black employers who deny employment to qualified white applicants, for instance. Employer decisions and consequent actions are racially motivated, though not racist.

It is illogical for a job applicant to conclude that because he can think of no other reason that he wasn't hired, then it must be the interviewer's racism. The applicant's inability to generate reasons or to read the interviewer's mind doesn't indicate a default reason of racial discrimination. It doesn't matter if the applicant can think of five people who say that they *suspect* the interviewer was racist. The applicant may know a hundred or a thousand others who would give that reason for not getting a job, and that still doesn't make racism a controlling factor in why neither he nor they got the job.

In business, ability is less evident and less well defined than ability in sports, for instance, where the athlete can demonstrate talent or can't. Employers must rely on an applicant's reported past experience and develop faith in the applicant's educational background. Automatic presumption of racial discrimination is illogical. It also makes no sense to inductively conclude that a legal indictment of one business for racial discrimination in hiring practices is an indication that all businesses have a predisposition to racial discrimination; indictments often reflect the opinion of juries or judges, whose biased decisions are overturned daily. Even if the final verdict in the single instance is guilty, such a verdict is not grounds for labeling an entire business as guilty of general racism. An instance of discrimination doesn't prove systematic racial discrimination.

> **Premise:** Racial discrimination may not be a key reason in someone's failure to gain employment. Every failure by a non-white person cannot correctly be said to be caused exclusively by someone else's racism.
>
> Because some people falsely attribute their failure to get a job to discrimination does not imply that all people who make similar arguments are doing so falsely.

Racial Prejudice

Just as racial discrimination has a specific meaning that differs from the concept of racism, the concept of racial prejudice also has a less inflammatory meaning. Prejudice is the habit of harboring associations about strangers based on unrelated reports and experience. Prejudice is most often a comfortable reaction which reduces risk to one's personal safety in unfamiliar situations, an unthinking dependence on the ubiquitous negative publicity that members of a specific race receive, or on the warnings of parents about the violent predisposition of a race. Prejudice is unfair only if it is incorrect for a given person or situation, and only if acted upon in the suppression of another's civil rights. If the person who is prejudged does intend to mug you, having a gut prejudice lets you anticipate and decide to quickly release your valuables rather than let your pride and indignation at the insult get you killed.

> **Premise:** Informed opinions about other races, whether firmly or loosely held as beliefs, suffuse and often dictate one's actions.

Often, prejudice is an attempt to preserve one's narrow ignorance, because remaining narrow is easier and takes less energy than approaching every new situation with zero preconceptions, and thus no direction for proceeding in the interaction. Prejudging may lead to lapses in good and true judgment, and a prejudiced employer may fail to analyze a job applicant's skill levels, job experience, and other intangible qualities like honesty and desire to perform beyond expectations, which may effectively constitute illegal discrimination based on race. But prejudice, exclusively, does not presume hatred, hostility, or the idea that one race has a privileged superiority over another–all components behind the actions of a racist.

Statistics on race give more weight to general negative conclusions. Blacks, based on their percentage of the population, commit a disproportionate number of violent crimes, though in absolute numbers, whites exceed (Charen, p. 15). Crime rates for 1992 show that 1,360 blacks per 100,000 were arrested for a violent crime; "Though they represent only 12 percent of the adult population, ... in 1993, blacks comprised 44.2 percent of all inmates in jails and prisons ..." (Charen, pp. 20–21). Barring the exceptional cases of wrongful imprisonment, that's quite a safety concern, making associations of violence with the people who live in black communities understandable. Blacks are 325 times more likely to engage in gang attacks on whites than whites are to take part in pack assaults against blacks. Interracial rape is overwhelmingly black on white; black men rape white women 30 times more often than white men rape black women (Williams, *Dayton Daily News*, December 15, 1993). Whites choose black victims 2.4 percent of the time, whereas blacks select white victims in over half of the crimes they commit. However, "ninety-three percent of black victims are killed by other blacks, and 85 percent of the murders committed by blacks are of other blacks" (Charen, p. 25). Leonard Pitts, Jr. laments the murder of Washington Redskins football player, Sean Taylor, and other blacks of Sean's age and younger comprising 40 percent of murdered blacks. He cites that 92 percent of the 3,303 murdered blacks in 2006 whose assailants are known were killed by other blacks (*Dayton Daily News*, December 2, 2007). Some states, such as Iowa, incarcerate blacks at a rate more than double the national average: 309 whites to 4,200 blacks for every 100,000 people in their population, blacks being incarcerated more than 13 times the rate of whites ("Study shows minorities jailed more than whites," *Dayton Daily News*, July 19, 2007).

These numbers are the motivating force behind the excessive attention police give to young black males, but they're not an indication that police forces are racially biased or racist. Police know that heredity does not cause crime.

Frequent reports of blacks committing violent crimes, such as car-jacking and murder for clothing, and knowledge of the statistically and disproportionately high percentage of members of the black race committing violent crimes and hate crimes against whites cause a generalized fear and leads whites to insulate themselves against the risk of physical harm.

Group Dynamics

Racial harmony is harmed by generalizations that reinforce the division of *us* from *them*, though such division often enhances internal group cohesion. Superficial similarities of a class lets its members more easily refer to and identify other groups' members. An *us* against *them* attitude presents a clear, simplistically defined enemy. When people think of others as belonging to either us or them, the *them* quickly becomes depersonalized, a faceless group of people who don't share the world view of those in the *us* group. Insiders experience we-ness based on similar physical characteristics, language, and religion. Accepting the linguistic and cultural differences of others outside one's group may cause group disunity.

Within the group of them, however, are factions of even more specialized subgroups with their own political goals and perhaps differing methods of achieving those goals. The cohesiveness of the smaller groups depends on more narrowly defined commonality, such as race, age, sex, and opinions about the value of black and white segregation and integration, for example. Fear of blacks unites groups of whites just as a shared, denigrating attitude about women unites sexist, redneck males who want to maintain their male power hold. People within a specific age range, for instance, support others in the age range because they may inexplicably see themselves and their hopes residing in others of their own age.

Generally, women band together because they feel that if they don't, no other group will look out for their interests as well as they would. Races more actively promote their own members into positions that allow the race as a group to acquire more rewards. Some special interest, black subgroups encourage newly well off members of the black race to return their profits to the disadvantaged within their race so that the lifestyles of others in the race might, theoretically, be improved. The existence of special interest subgroups, ironically, increases the likelihood that outsiders may make dangerous and inaccurate generalizations about the whole racial group based on the behavior and activities of the subgroups.

We live in a society in which interest groups struggle in conflict with other groups: racial and ethnic groups, religious groups against atheists, unions against employers, men against women, the haves against the have-nots, pro-choicers against anti-choicers, homosexuals against heterosexuals. And every "insurgent group has fought its own fight, largely alone ..." (Katz, p. 34). The conflicts are based in each group's sense that it is "singular, bounded, and independent, and that it must stick up for its rights, privileges, and well-being in the face of an opposing group" (Gergen, p. 63).

Within a larger group, members lose their individual identity and are cloaked in whatever identity the group has. The accomplishments and contributions of individual members may be lumped together and credited to the group when those contributions are communicated outside of the group. Frequently, outsiders may view a group negatively because of the statements or actions of the group's chair or spokesperson. Vocally opinionated members of groups who have outrageous ideas receive the greatest amount of sensationalist-motivated media attention, though those members and their philosophies may be the remote minority within the group and may even be denounced by members of the larger group. Limited views bring those views to the forefront of awareness, enticing outside observers to form negative opinions of the whole group, generally.

Speaking of Race

No matter how outrageous the accusation, most forms of speech and racial slurs and counter speech are still protected, though employers have ways of penalizing those in their organizations for speech. The inflammatory speech laws were intended to curtail the vocal rights of people if they used language to incite violence, infringing upon the constitutional right of free speech of others. A high visibility instance of the law's equivocal interpretation was when former Cincinnati Reds owner Marge Schott's guaranteed right to speech was overridden by her obligation not to provoke anger within her self-policing business organization. Schott was censured by the sports industry and asked to attend a cultural sensitivity class for referring to Reds General Manager Jim Bowden as "my boy" (*Dayton Daily News*, November 25, 1992). Frank Allison, then President of the Cincinnati Chapter of the NAACP, stepped in. It didn't matter that Bowden is white. Allison told Schott "'the way you speak and refer to people can be offensive. I said, 'If you had referred to me—or any African-American male—as 'boy,' we would have taken offense.'"

Comedian Michael Richards, most well known for his Cramer character on the sitcom, *Seinfeld*, slandered racial groups publicly in a comedy routine and was expected to apologize, which he did, half-heartedly, on *Late Night with David Letterman* in December 2006. Senator George Allen from Virginia made a similar error in the November 2006 election campaigns by referring to an Asian Indian student reporter in derogatory terms. Don Imus was fired in April 2007 from his radio program for referring to college female basketball players as "nappy-headed HOs." A month later, CBS cancelled a shock jock radio show on WFNY-FM because its hosts Jeff Vandergrift and Day Lay made prank phone calls on the air that were rife with offensive Asian stereotypes (*Dayton Daily News*, May 13, 2007).

In such penalties, it is hoped that the manifestations of racism–violence and verbal slurs that could lead to violence–can be reduced while token re-education attempts are made to simultaneously adjust racist attitudes.

Hasty general statements regarding race may or may not reflect true prejudicial thinking. The necessity of public officials to convey messages in 30-second sound bites makes simplification and generalization appealing. If he had unlimited time and no chance of losing audience interest, a sports analyst might be more precise, saying that untrained white males who have no interest in basketball can't make jump shots with the kind of grace that other skilled basketball players admire and emulate (rather than the more concise but factually wrong generalization, white men can't jump). He could go on to quote statistics about the percentage of white basketball players versus black players who play on professional basketball teams, or whose famous fluid moves on the court lands shoe endorsements.

Often, speakers don't have a facile grasp of the English language. They have an imperfect ability to state how they feel, and so they lapse into sloppy generalizations in their speech that don't necessarily reflect their thoughts. Even when language is used to intentionally berate, such as a white calling a black a "knuckle-dragger," for instance, the name-calling insults and provokes anger, or intentionally tears down self-esteem for easier future subjugation whether or not the name-caller believes his derogatory remarks to be true. In August 1992, the Ohio Supreme Court declared that a 1987 state law prohibiting ethnic intimidation was unconstitutional and violated guarantees of free speech, seeking to penalize speech in addition to proscribed acts. Intimidation laws, though unconstitutional because they seek to punish thought and speech, are meant to reduce symbolic affronts against entire segments of society. Though intimidation laws have been struck down, training courses continue to be based on the premise that people need to be made more aware of words that may offend minorities. For instance, in January 1993, the Ohio Peace Officers Training Council required state academy students to take 24 hours of cultural and racial sensitivity training.

However clearly freedom of speech is supported by laws, hate crime legislation has overridden freedoms by categorizing name-calling and similar expressions as evidence of the advocacy of racial superiority, invalidating any defense that a white name-caller was simply jockeying for personal dominance over a specific individual, though not physically violating or depriving another of his constitutional rights, which is the former standard for defining crime. It is a telling double standard that blacks who use racial pejorative when calling out other blacks aren't cited for racism, though it's possible for blacks to hate their own race (see the King of Pop, Michael Jackson, as an example of a man who seems extremely uncomfortable in his black skin).

"Some universities, among them the University of Cincinnati, have student handbooks that say, and professors who teach, that blacks are incapable of racism. Therefore, media people see the Howard Beach and Bensonhurst incidents—where whites murdered and beat blacks—as racist and view situations where blacks do the same to whites as simply crimes" (Williams, *Dayton Daily News*). At Stanford University, some black students wore T-shirts proclaiming "Black by Popular Demand," but eyebrows raised when white students wore Ts stating that they were "White by the Grace of God." Though a number of college campuses have black student unions, white students at Temple University who organized a White Student Union created a controversy (Williams, "Crisis of 'racism' ...," *Dayton Daily News*). Black students can petition universities for special black culture centers, though whites are frowned upon for petitioning for WASP and southern plantation lifestyle centers. Blacks can have rallies in open public places about what blacks perceive as injustices that continue to be perpetuated by white-controlled institutions, but whites can't hold rallies protesting entitlements for which only blacks are eligible.

"Within the last decade or so, we have seen a rise in racial conflict and resentment. Especially unsettling is that much of this resentment is among our youth on college campuses" (Willams, "Kindling for the racial bonfire," *Dayton Daily News*). Black racial equality organizations, according to Walter Williams, are "little more than race hustlers championing a racial spoils system." Blame for the resurgence of racial resentment rests with otherwise decent people who tolerate and implement racist demands. Among these are college administrators who give in to black student demands for racially exclusive campus facilities or subsidize a black student union and intimidate a white student union; employers that have one set of performance standards for whites and another for blacks; and union agreements where, should layoffs become necessary, higher seniority whites are laid off before lower seniority blacks in the name of racial balance (Williams, "Kindling for the racial bonfire," *Dayton Daily News*).

Speech should be protected because self-reports of the intent of one's words where race is concerned are unreliable, and the self-reports of criminals are notoriously suspect. Criminals may report that they attacked someone because of that person's different race, but such statements should not be used as proof of the attacker's intent. The statement may be motivated by the attacker's plan to gain future acceptance in a race-based protective gang in prison, or to become a media whore so that he can later repent and be seen as amenable to reform and a second chance, or to obtain attention as a good cause or as a victim himself by his parents who pounded racist ideas into him all his life, somewhat mitigating his recent egregious actions. Self-reports also suffer from recall bias (people don't recall accurately the circumstances in a given past situation), lack of appropriate case controls, inadequate objective measurements, and uncontrolled and unevaluated confounding variables. The truth in verbal expressions about race can't be known precisely.

Every Kind of Diversity

In race relations, emphasis is generally placed on the differences between the races and ethnic groups rather than commonality. People remark about things they see in others that are different from what they see in themselves. Children who don't wear glasses make fun of other children who do. They make fun of other children who wear clothes that are different than their own. They make fun of people whose skin color is different than their own. Boys make fun of girls. Christian children make fun of Jewish children for their differing beliefs. Perhaps people hope that those they ridicule will rebel and enlighten them about the purpose of the difference, or perhaps by making fun of others, people are boosting their own self-esteem for how they are different and somehow better for the difference. For some, there may be an underlying hatred or fear of things that are different.

It's easy to find a minority or ethnic group to ridicule in America. America is still a melting pot, a metaphor that sees all people assimilating into one big goulash of sharply defined American culture, all cultural diversity melding into part of the overall culture. One American in four is of German ancestry, according to the 1990 Census Bureau. Germans make up the nation's largest ethnic group. The Irish are next, 1 American in 6; followed by the English, 1 in 8; blacks, 1 in 12; and Italian, 1 in 17. One American in twenty considers him or herself to be just plain American. The results came from a long version of the 1990 census form about ancestry, which went to one household in six. New data places the number of Hispanics living in the United States at 41 million, making Hispanics the new largest minority, or 13 percent of the population.

In the patchwork quilt metaphor, however, each ethnic group is separate, and the boundaries between them and other ethic groups are clearly defined. Members of ethnic groups and people outside the groups fear that assimilation of American systems and integration will weaken the ethnicity of the races. So, the patchwork quilt metaphor seems to depict how ethnic groups want to be, perhaps with a little pressure from others in society who want to segregate them so that it may more readily apply negative labels to the group, thereby oppressing it and differentiating the group's problems from society's problems. The Salad Bowl metaphor assumes that each ethnic group in the salad retains its unique culture and characteristics, and people recognize that they have a double-belonging, which means having a subculture while recognizing larger, American culture.

The melting pot metaphor, if true, contributes the most to building a unified America, whereas the patchwork quilt reflects the reality of American life more accurately, with the added dimension that ethnic groups appear to want to impress their cultures upon others for profit.

Regardless of the metaphor used, it's impossible to meet the needs of every individual in an ethnic or minority group. Group organizers, like the federal government who must abide by the wishes of groups that vote them into power, must accommodate as many people as possible, and it doesn't have enough budget to do this on an individual basis. It is difficult to make arrangements that benefit the greatest number of people while inconveniencing the fewest. However, if preferential treatment isn't offered, spokespersons for the excluded, special needs groups object. Their objections usually fail to take into consideration that making special arrangements for one group could infringe on the rights of everyone else for fair and equal treatment.

1

A Brief History of Racial Discrimination as Strategy

In democratic systems, being in the minority's a bitch. In a fight for special rewards, you'll likely get outvoted and outshouted, the bigger bullies with better weapons and resources delivering crushing defeats. Work and money and opportunities may be limited to subset economies because majority populations consciously protect their advantages in the larger economy. Majority groups rule in business, create laws and impose tariffs in congress that quash economic and social competition for resources and discourage foreign competition. The Ku Klux Klan preserved its way of segregated life and inserted its members into local government to enact laws that segregated by race, keeping racial minorities removed from the means of economic freedom. District rezoning keeps neighborhoods poor, so they receive only the levy funding that their poor districts can drum up.

Majorities looked the other way when the civil rights of racial, religious, and ethnic minorities were oppressed, and continue to look the other way, though some essayists don't agree that minority civil rights are still being abused. In an editorial, George Will asserts that the U.S. Commission on Civil Rights wouldn't be missed if it folded (*Dayton Daily News*, March 10, 2005). Will goes on to state that civil rights rhetoric from the former chairperson, Mary Frances Berry, was unsubstantiated and designated racial problems as being related to civil rights, though they weren't. "Not every need is a right, and ... not every right is a civil right–one central to participation in civic life," Will writes. The new chairperson, Gerald Reynolds, Will writes, "says that the core function of civil rights laws is to prevent discrimination, meaning 'the distribution of benefits and burdens on the basis of race.' But if so, today a ... principal discriminator is government, with racial preferences and the rest of the reparations system that flows from the assumption that disparities in social outcomes must be caused by discrimination and should be remedied by government transfers of wealth."

Whites who choose to believe that equality has been attained also believe that they will be called on less often to make concessions to minorities. The belief that racism is no longer prevalent lets some whites deny involvement, support, and continued retribution of past injustices. "Not only are working-class whites rejecting civil rights goals, but African-American youth increasingly are rejecting the idea of racial reconciliation" (Muwakkil).

Otherwise decent people, with full selfish rationality, discriminated when hiring employees as a way of reserving purchasing power and good lives for members of their own racial group. Groups often form based on racial similarity, gender, age, and common interests assumed to be shared based on these demographic criteria. Within each group, most members want limited resources for themselves and others like them, not for other groups whose numbers in our democracy are too small to beat the majority in a fair fight.

Historically, majority races continued their treachery by believing and propagandizing that minorities had all sorts of inferiorities and infirmities. Majorities have tried to deceive minorities into believing that the treatment they received was for their own good, using violence, fear, psychological belittlement, and unfair laws to maintain a lower status for minorities.

Racial discrimination has been used consistently as a rational strategy to defeat competition for jobs and society's limited resources. Trashing minority races as a survival goal secured greater freedoms for the majority and preserved a way of life.

Some social commentators advocate the voluntary relinquishment of power as a response to shame in how predecessors had acquired it: "Whites must see the problem of race as one of giving up power. They have to acknowledge that our economic, political, and cultural systems have been designed in part for the benefit of whites.... [Whites] need to acknowledge the shame they feel, rather than reflexively blaming those who cause such feelings to come to consciousness. They need to know that their feelings of shame will begin to vanish only when they begin to take part in dismantling racism and redistributing power ..." (Mura, p. 81).

Though liberal socialists rebuke capitalism as being an economic system created by whites to benefit whites, capitalism is not a weapon of race-based exclusion. Power and economic rewards are the result of successful competition. Like any system, it is people within the capitalistic system who choose to act unfairly, unethically, and illegally, to the limits of capitalism's government-regulated boundaries. Whites sacrifice their principles and dignity for the power they achieve in the system. They play the game to advance their material opportunities. The capitalistic game, with its non-color-specific rewards, must be played, and some of the rules include proper grooming, clear speech, customer-oriented social manners, and acting in a way that lets customers trust the competence of their business partners. Capitalism is a tool that can be misused by all people of all races. Those who refuse to work within the prevailing system should not logically expect others to migrate to other systems. Few whites feel shame and will not concede power based on feeling better for having performed kind acts.

People who have little real economic or social power feel that any tactic, such as denouncing capitalism, is fair. If the powerful and wealthy continue to discriminate against minorities who play by capitalism's rules, then unfair counter strategies are seen as justifiable. Many would suggest that two wrongs don't make a right, and the indiscriminate application of unfair strategies against people who have always played fair definitely does not feel right. However unfair some strategies may seem for obtaining society's rewards in the capitalistic system, they succeed because they play on emotion and a guilt-ridden sense of what is fair in general. One particular strategy, the overused charge of racial discrimination, succeeds because it throws the burden of providing proof upon those in power, thereby forcing members in power to concentrate time, energy, and money to disprove accusations.

Racial discrimination and active racism serve the self-promotional ends of human tribal systems. Humans group together based on some commonality to work as teams to acquire the limited rewards available in a society. A group based on race feels that its members better understand the people who are like them. People want people like themselves to be successful, and they have a racial agenda to hire people like themselves so they can associate with them on the job and in affiliated social groups. So, when members of a racial group get their foot in the door, they feel an obligation to help others of their race. Often these groups, which develop a secondary need to survive and thrive as a group, use repressive means to reduce the chances that other recognized groups will acquire the rewards. Societies throughout time have used class division to maintain group wealth and control of large quantities of material and power. Those in lower classes often have had little recourse but to revolt or accept the crumbs that came their way.

Worried that allowed to vote, a minority might be elected to political office and attempt to protect minority rights, majorities withheld the right of minorities to vote. The false public justification for refusing the vote was that political thugs would easily coerce minorities, forcing them to vote the way the thugs wanted them to vote.

Racial discrimination and racism are a part of white oppressive history in the United States. Originally, the belief that a single race can be intellectually, naturally, and culturally superior to all others was employed by Adolph Hitler in his quest to create a master "race," and he led a highly civilized country to support the barbarism and atrocity of the holocaust. In Germany, Hitler carefully brainwashed a population through expert use of language, propaganda, and fear mongering. In the United States, racism stemmed from a convenient belief in superiority, which allowed white slave owners to justify their dehumanizing treatment of blacks, advancing their own financial position through enslavement prior to 1865. Overtly through the mid to late 20th century, majority races protected their status and advantage by segregating social services and rights–public education, transportation, property ownership, permissible racial discrimination for business services and products–remaining physically and morally safe through segregative distancing. Attitudes ingrained by history can be seen in the continuing belief in negative racial stereotypes and in the easy false generalizing across populations from isolated negative instances. To sustain their attitudes, many whites cite minority crime, rioting, educational failure, out-of-wedlock teen births, regressive and mid-range pornographic values epitomized in rap music, unemployment, drug use, lower life expectancy, and poverty statistics.

> **Observation:** Every measure used to describe one race can be applied to any race, providing a comparative basis.

Majority racial groups suppressed competition from minorities by denying freedom through slavery, then denying civil rights, and then giving lip service to civil rights to avoid legal punishments. Slaveholders worked the system, declaring their slaves as three-fifths human, allowing whites to both declare slaves as property and as full votes when added together, gaining a potential majority in the senate to vote for sustaining the system of slavery. Selfishly restricting others' civil rights advanced and expanded the civil rights of the majority. It was hoped that the tyranny of the majority perceived by French historian Alexis de Tocqueville would be a benevolent, paternal one. Without equal power, which is arguably achieved by equal size and representation in democracies, minority groups were often unable to enforce their rights and promote their interests and entitlement to representation either equivalent to or greater than their percentage of the population. The utilitarian principle of the greatest good for the greatest number didn't automatically apply, and those in power weren't constrained by law to behave magnanimously.

People have always known that owning human slaves was immoral, even before the cotton gin made slavery uneconomical. Europeans enslaved because they were vicious, violent, greedy, and had no moral compunctions against making others do their work. Romans enslaved other Romans. Low castes in India have been enslaved. People were not enslaved because of their skin color, but because they were weak or less technologically advanced in the methods of defense and did not fight hard enough to prevent their enslavement. For two hundred years (prior to 1865 when slavery was outlawed in the United States by ratification of the 13th amendment), white American slave owners justified their immorality by subhumanizing blacks and then taking steps, such as instituting rules against learning to read, to ensure that few exceptions could counter the prevailing view and conceptions. It would be difficult to reconcile profit if slaves were shown to be educable, not property but wholly human and worthy of federalized civil rights. The signers of the Declaration of Independence knew slavery was wrong, though a few notable signers held slaves.

The racist attitudes of slaveholders, reinforced by blacks who believed their status as property, reduced competition from blacks for limited societal rewards, competition that would have impacted the immorally attained lifestyles of the whites. When slavery was outlawed, racist reliance on the idea of white supremacy allowed whites to cognitively reconcile enforced segregation, with an emphasis on relegating blacks to inferior facilities in much the same way that western settlers forced Native Americans onto less desirable territories and reservations. Blacks were excluded from civic culture–voting, owning property, using public facilities, owning businesses, testifying against a white, going to public schools, protection by civic police forces, and restriction to undesirable jobs in the military. It allowed whites to withhold equal civil rights and to hand down unjust legal decisions, many founded on Jim Crow premises that required blacks to pass literacy tests, pay poll taxes, and own property in order to be allowed to vote, qualifications that were considered facially neutral but constituted de facto racial discrimination. The pose of superiority was a sham for many whites that allowed them to hold and control wealth, property, and power. Blacks were enculturated with deference behavior and hopelessness and a sense of having a subordinate place in society.

When slavery was outlawed, many blacks left the south, suspicious that former slaveholders and southern adherents to the slavery system would never permit former slaves to exercise their recently acquired equal rights. Northerners were thought to be more accommodating of the exodus of unskilled blacks, though such trust was questionable. A stereotype was developed that painted northerners as insidious in their covert racism, while southerners didn't bother keeping their racism secret.

An earlier influx of unskilled Chinese laborers offers a parallel in the lack of full social acceptance of great numbers of people. In America's gold rush of 1849, there was a wave of immigration into America to seek fortune at Gold Mountain in Deadwood in the Black Hills area 50 miles northeast of Rapid City, South Dakota. About 66,000 Chinese immigrated to the U.S. between 1849 and 1860. Due to violence and overt racism against them in competition to find gold, most Chinese changed their plan to search for gold and worked on railroads or in service industries as cooks, merchants, and innkeepers and laundries. Chinese competitors were easily identifiable as outsiders, and pretended hatred of their foreign-ness bonded groups of other men, though members of all races who competed for gold were murdered out of greed to obtain land claims (Khatchadourian, p. 26).

For a very long time, white males controlled society's rewards. But as more and more non-whites and females gain power, white males have had to relinquish it. Some have been beaten at their own manipulative games; others have been shown, through diverse insights provided by members in other cultures, that they can benefit by playing fair; others retreat from their racist positions because of a compulsion to be humanitarian and generous, for the sake of the survival of all races and sexes as a larger group; and still others have relented else face legal repercussions.

Through the efforts of Martin Luther King Jr. in March 21, 1965, leading marchers 50 miles from Selma, Alabama to the capitol in Montgomery to protest and gain voting rights for blacks, a white public was made to realize that it was at least unwise, if not unethical, to oppress racial minorities. Prior to the Voting Rights Act of 1965, which was signed in August by President Lyndon B. Johnson to outlaw race barring in voting, blacks were restricted from voting based on lower property tax payment limits and literacy. At a time when many blacks in the deep south were sharecroppers, in debt, kept from public schools by parents who needed help in the rented household, meeting property tax and literacy conditions preempted many blacks from the voting process.

> "A key provision of the [Voting Rights Act of 1965] prevents 'packing'–placing all black voters in one district. That would probably ensure a black candidate being elected from that district but would also prevent black voters from

having a voice in other districts and thus give minorities reduced influence in relation to their numerical strength. The law also prevents spreading black voters thinly among several districts in such a way that they might have some influence but would be unlikely to elect a minority candidate" (Miller, *Dayton Daily News*).

In 1982 "additional amendments to the Voting Rights Act were passed that made it possible for blacks or other minority plaintiffs to challenge any jurisdiction for engaging in electoral discrimination if election results showed that the number of blacks, Mexican-Americans, or other minorities elected were not commensurate with the overall population proportions in a city, country, or other jurisdiction" (Fuchs, p. 426). There has been no serious defiance of the Voting Rights Act of 1965 and its amendments, and no credible evidence of blacks being kept from polling places in the late 20th century, despite urban myths to the contrary.

Equal opportunity and civil rights legislation have attempted to give minorities a fair chance to succeed, though racial majorities still rule. Policy and federal law forced publicly supported colleges to favor minority admission applicants and forced employers to hire a quota of minorities. Minority set-asides for government contracts have been structured into law. Affirmative action policy has been instituted. Meritocracy, as an ideal criterion or predictor of good and fair governance, took a backseat to racial ethnicity as an overriding criterion for society's rewards. Such reverse racism policies failed to reduce white racism, actually increasing white resentment against blacks and the government that permitted racially partial laws. Whites began to doubt the merit, integrity, and motives of people who were able to succeed by using racially discriminatory criterion.

> **Observation:** Those who say "Don't hate the playa, hate the game," deny personal responsibility for unethically exploiting loopholes in a poorly designed system for personal gain that unfairly denies others equal opportunity.

When the equal opportunity legislated through the 1964 Civil Rights Act, the Voting Rights Act of 1965, and the 1968 Open Housing Act failed to equalize socio-economic conditions between whites and blacks, America's political leaders fashioned a new "compensatory justice" social order defined by new state and federal laws and administrative guidelines and regulations. The new order mandated racial preferences for non-whites and proportional distribution of benefits among ethnic groups.

Chief among these preference systems were the affirmative action policies enacted as law in 1962. The policies forced employers to favor ethnic minorities over other qualified–and often better qualified–whites, who may never have racially discriminated against anybody, as a way to redress the grievance of past racial discrimination against others. No time cap was instituted for phasing out the policies, no standard was set for determining when past discrimination would be adequately punished and minorities fairly recompensed, and no definition was offered for what constitutes fair restitution.

Affirmative action policies were a desperate and doomed attempt to meet a perceived need to pay restitution for the years of demoralization of the black race, to make up for the past injustices and slavery, and to somehow retroactively extract punitive damages from contemporaries for the sins of those who withheld services and rewards from blacks in the past.

Systematically basing a percentage of employment on race led to resentment. Incidents "of differential treatment evoke deep feelings of disappointment, even disillusionment, and a sense of grievance at the unfairness of double standards" (Blauner, p. 74) in whites, who were excluded from benefiting from affirmative action. Though some blacks may have been happy to have the tables turned and to be considered for employment, both whites and blacks, in general, understood that qualification to fill a position should be based on skills and experience and education. However, white employers were forced to pay full salary and additional funds to train underqualified people whom they were forced to hire: "'And now competent people are having to stand on their heads trying to contain bosses who are incredibly incompetent'" (Blauner, quoting Virginia Lawrence, p. 208).

Many blacks feel that most whites are living well *because* black fathers and grandfathers were prevented by whites from getting equal opportunity to advance and get well-paying jobs. "'You can't break a man's legs and blame him for limping. You have a moral responsibility to fix it. If you've been living off it, you can't say you're not part of it, that it was done by somebody else. If you want to be fair, you can't have a head start and say, "catch up," without doing something to make up that difference'" (Terkel, quoting C.T. Vivian, p. 342).

Blacks resent that whites who have lost their jobs to affirmative action programs grouse about the unfairness of blacks getting jobs. Cases of proven discrimination can be cited, but only people indicted in those cases can be held accountable for breaking a "man's legs." As for catching up, in competition, rarely do competitors who are winning help those they're competing against; there is no moral responsibility except as it is subjectively defined by each competitor. It's unreasonable to ask all whites to reduce their standard of living and slow their success.

Others criticize that affirmative action policies didn't go far enough to correct past employment discrimination: "'[Whites] got some slots for [blacks]. And once they're filled, that's it. That's one of my criticisms of affirmative action.... that creates hostilities'" (Blauner, quoting Len Davis, p. 307).

Affirmative action policy is humiliating, according to Charles Johnson: "A person, otherwise deserving, may be perceived as something special, having gotten a degree of help he didn't need. But without affirmative action, the first step toward hiring blacks would never have been taken" (Terkel, p. 16). The stigmatism of benefiting from affirmative action policies isn't punishing enough to keep minorities from accepting these benefits from employers who were forced to enforce the policies.

Failure to abide by affirmative action policies can lead to trouble for employers. David Rubin, a professor in CSU's Department of Biology and chief negotiator of the American Association of University Professors union committee (AAUP), published a reasoned letter in a special edition of the *AAUP-CSU Newsletter* (July 15, 1992) in which he rebutted accusations that he is racist. The accusations were based on Professor Rubin's opposition to the CSU senate's willful violation of its own procedures and rules for approval of honorary degrees. The university's attorney stated that "during bargaining ... the Administration had been told that the AAUP-CSU negotiating team was being 'tough' at my direction and for racial reasons." According to Rubin, the attorney also implied that "the Biology Department faculty (including me) were not concerned with affirmative action." CSU, Rubin maintains, placed more priority on affirmative action hiring than on long-standing department policy for hiring.

> "The person whose hiring I grieved is a former student and current friend of mine. I told him, *before his hiring*, that if he were hired I would have to grieve that action because proper departmental procedure was circumvented and provisions of the Collective Bargaining Agreement were blatantly violated. Our Department Chair refused to call in two top applicants because he 'would not feel comfortable' with their hiring. Since the University's case revolved around affirmative action, it was obvious that the lack of comfort had to do with color."

Rubin asserts that his actions are not based on race, and that he makes recommendations and grievances based on standards, institution policy, and qualifying criteria. He reports that he recommended a black for emeritus status and writes many letters of recommendation for both black and white students, fought to gain tenure for black and white faculty, and in 22 years never had a race-related problem with a student.

Rubin feels that the charges of racism are being used as "a means of dividing the faculty, and then to use that division to nullify growing faculty empowerment and subsequently to eradicate AAUP-CSU." In closing, Rubins writes: "For an Administration to use claims of racism to its advantage is unconscionable at an institution such as ours. The issue of racism must be dealt with openly by this faculty if we are to function effectively as a cooperative body in teaching, research, service, and within AAUP-CSU."

To fire a minority can invite a bureaucratic and legal nightmare. The employer may be forced to consult lawyers, doctors, company benefits committees, unions, and various levels of management. If a manager's decision to fire a minority is overturned by upper management based not upon a review of the employee's performance against a performance standard for the position, but upon fear of the fuss that the employee may kick up making unfounded charges of racism, then the manager loses some credibility. The employee may continue to perform poorly, having already proven the ability to win based on an implied threat. Employees playing race cards in the corporate kitchenette are assured a continued paycheck.

Real and pervasive racism within tight-knit employment settings, such as on police forces or in fire departments, can debilitate a team. The conflict starts when minorities get positions on local safety forces as a result of lawsuits alleging discriminatory hiring practices. Discriminatory hiring practices are presumed if the percentage of a work force in a profession and locality doesn't reflect the percentage of racial composition of those who live in the locality. In a summary judgment in a case in which a fired black fireman alleged racial discrimination, Judge Pickering wrote, "The fact that a black employee is terminated doesn't automatically indicate discrimination" (Charen, quoting Pickering, p. 47). In a similar case in Dayton, Ohio, U.S. District Judge Walter H. Rice dismissed a lawsuit filed in 1989 against the city by the Dayton Association of Black Professional Firefighters for not having enough blacks in the ranks of Dayton's safety forces. In another case also brought by attorney Taylor Jones Jr., Rice determined that the Interdenominational Ministerial Alliance, in a bid to get more black police officers hired in Dayton, had failed to meet requirements to prove that some of its members had been directly affected by alleged racial discrimination (Hills, *Dayton Daily News*).

A study of Dayton, Ohio police and fire department employment statistics showed that blacks filled 18% of positions with the police and 3.3% with the fire department, while blacks constitute 43.1% of the employed residents in Dayton (Smith, July 26, 2007). Two obstacles to recruitment, according to Dayton City Commissioner Dean Lovelace are that 1) blacks who don't see blacks in police and fire departments don't see themselves in those employment positions, and 2) oral examinations for police jobs might help more black applicants pass performance standards requirements. Other strategies to recruit minorities include grouping those with test scores in a certain range and selecting a minority applicant from the group, permitting remote testing, making salaries more attractive, offering relocation assistance and mentoring, and providing training in diversity. The report suggests that the low rate of minorities in the police and fire departments is due to few minorities applying for these jobs, not few qualified minorities. However, easing the testing and application processes should not lead to conclusions that Dayton is targeting otherwise less qualified minorities; these strategies would also attract less qualified non-minorities who, it is hoped, will be given equal consideration when decisions are made regarding who will fill positions that often deal in matters of life and death.

> **Observation:** A society that assigns its resources on the basis of irrelevant race attributes rather than ability suffers. Few in society want to be treated by unqualified doctors who've been given breaks in earning their MDs primarily because they are a certain race.

Often, blacks who measure objectively better than whites cannot be found in sufficient numbers to fill the number of positions in a company to reflect the population of blacks in the community in which the company does business. To avoid charges of reverse racism from non-minorities citing lack of qualifications of minority hires, some employers used the practice of race norming. In race norming, every job applicant is given the same skills test, but failing minorities have points added to their scores equal to the difference between the average result for non-minorities and the average result for the minority group. Colleges and universities adopted race norming, whereby scores are reported only as a percentile within one's minority grouping (defined as a minority based on race, color, religion, sex, or national origin), thus allowing a hypothetical raw score of 50 to look better than one of 90. Race norming, often called dumbing-down standards, obscured the fact that qualified white students were being passed over for underqualified non-white students, thereby soothing the rancor that would have resulted had the injustice been publicized.

The Civil Rights Act of 1992 supposedly outlawed race norming by requiring the complaining party to show that a particular employment practice had a "disparate impact," as defined in the landmark Supreme Court ruling in *Griggs v. Duke Power* (1971), on blacks or others protected by the 1964 Civil Rights Act, Title VII section, which provided for "affirmative action" in some cases of discrimination. The 1964 Civil Rights Act, in conjunction with enforcement by the Civil Rights Division of the Justice Department and the Equal Employment Opportunity Commission, served as an affirmative remedy for past and present discrimination in employment, restricting hiring and promotion procedures (ability tests with potentially discriminatory impact having to meet strict business necessity standards) where blacks were concerned, and requiring consent decrees (agreements to match every white hire or promotion with a black hire or promotion) for the hiring of policemen, firemen and union craftsmen.

Legal rulings are frequently revisited, amended, and overturned.

Up until June 1978 when "the U.S. Supreme Court upheld Allan Bakke's contention that the admissions policy of the University of California at Davis had wrongly discriminated against white applicants," (Blauner, p. 247) colleges were required to file affirmative action compliance reports. These reports showed that they had not turned away a percentage of black students determined by the college's location, regardless of the black students' SAT scores, which is one example of a criteria on which many colleges base acceptance of students. "The Court held that affirmative action plans could not mandate racial quotas, as the university had when it reserved 16 percent of the places in its entering class for nonwhites" (Blauner, p. 247).

Affirmative action policies forced corporations and colleges to resort to the deception of race norming (also termed within-group scoring and within-group adjustment) simply to appease government legislators and to maintain community support. Affirmative action fosters unequal and unfair treatment based on race, a concept that minorities readily recognize and disapprove. Whites who opposed the affirmative action laws went out of their way to ensure failure rather than work toward ensuring success. A big part of the opposition resulted from objection to the flawed idea of unjust racial preference. Secondary opposition was based in the psychology of resisting any new system that forces reevaluation of beliefs anchored in current systems. When people are ordered to do something that drastically changes the ways they currently do things, they want the new system to fail as a way to show that the new way is bad and that their way was better, hoping to get the status quo reinstated. Sometimes, objection is based on the fact that the suggested change is purely wrong-headed.

Whites, in general, resent and mourn the loss of their power and material, angry that the rules of capitalism have been perverted by affirmative action and racial quota systems, no longer favoring those who work hard or take aggressive risks, regardless of their race. They fight to ensure the failure of race-based systems on principle, and are joined by blacks who advocate for hiring on merit. They feel animosity, even though only small segments of the black population may be using unfair strategies that whites can't use. This anger and frustration at being cheated by the law often manifests as racial prejudice.

Many important laws that focus on racial parity under the law involve desegregation, the premise being that non-minority neighborhoods, schools, and services offered quality that outshone the quality available in their minority counterparts. Busing white children to predominantly minority schools in poor districts and black children to non-minority schools was seen by educators; business, political, religious leaders, and community citizens as a method of reversing long-standing separate-but-equal dogma. The practice was as traumatic to white children as to black. In his Ghetto Snob tour in 1996, comedian Chris Rock described ghetto snobs as black parents who didn't think their children belonged in the ghetto and bused them to white schools outside the ghetto, where the black children ended up isolated in white classrooms.

If better education was to be achieved, forcing more children to have a mediocre education was not the answer. One hoped-for consequence of busing white children to minority schools was the spurring of concerned white parents to take initiate, donating more of their time and money to improve minority schools so that their bused children would receive as good an education as it was perceived they would get at a school in a predominantly white district. Instead, resources went to campaigns targeted to overturning the law of forced busing.

Language in the U.S. Supreme Court's 1954 decision in *Brown v. Kansas City Board of Education* was interpreted to mean that no child has a right to attend a school near his or her home, allowing local governments to enforce busing in order to fulfill a social engineering agenda to integrate schools. Clarence Thomas, in a related opinion, did not challenge the intent of the *Brown v. Board of Education* language, but rather questioned arguments that suggested that black institutions were, by their very nature, inferior. Local governments invoked the corollary of the decision's language, that parents had neither the right nor the choice to send their children to a school in their neighborhoods, and that the choice would be made by government. However, the "view that someone has a right to an integrated education comes from a misreading of the ... decision" (Watras, *Dayton Daily News*). A "poll of 500 likely voters found that more than two-thirds of those surveyed disapprove of busing children to schools to achieve racial balance. More than 81 percent of whites disapproved.... Among blacks ... 43 percent disapproved" (Fisher, *Dayton Daily News*).

Following the trend against race-based policies in public arenas, on June 28, 3007 the Supreme Court struck down plans in Seattle and Louisville public schools that consciously classified students by race and assigned them to schools to achieve or preserve integration and racial diversity. The plans use race as a tie-breaker for admission, after examining each school's proportion of minority students. For kindergarten student Joshua McDonald, a white student in Louisville, KY, this meant 90-minute bus rides past several other schools that had met their racial quotas, and his custodial parent, Crystal D. Meredith, sued the school board. Chief Justice John Roberts wrote with obvious simplicity and truth, "The way to stop discrimination on the basis of race is to stop discriminating on the basis of race." Justice Anthony Kennedy supported the decision, but depended on blatant idealism grounded in utopian society engineering: "This nation has a moral and ethical obligation to fulfill its historic commitment to creating an integrated society that ensures equal opportunity for all its children" (*Dayton Daily News*, July 8, 2007). In his partially concurring statement, Kennedy allowed school authorities to "devise race-conscious measures that address diversity in a general manner, without basing the treatment of individual students on their race" (Jeter, *The Virginian-Pilot*, June 29, 2007), creating what's termed racially conscious attendance zones as a back door to escape compliance with laws against considering race in assigning students to schools in a district.

Support for busing students for racial reasons eroded because there is no proof that a more effective education is universally achieved when children go to school outside of their neighborhoods. Solutions to busing include redistricting school districts to include higher income neighborhoods, reducing poverty in poor districts, and building better schools and hiring better teachers for all students. Busing lets children of parents who don't pay their fair share of taxes to reap the benefit of attending better funded schools paid for by those who pay higher taxes for that right.

As recently as 1986, the NAACP was filing federal lawsuits on behalf of Dayton, Ohio residents to seek court-ordered desegregation of Dayton's schools. "The NAACP produced evidence that Dayton's school board had operated a dual system for blacks and whites for decades, through manipulation of attendance zones, staff assignments and other actions, and that those actions denied black students equal opportunity to education" (Fisher, *Dayton Daily News*). Under Kennedy's lax interpretation of the Meredith v. Jefferson County Board of Education ruling, attendance zones aren't a viable answer even 20 years ago.

The Supreme Court ruled on March 31, 1992 to stop federal supervision of desegregation plans in local school districts in general and Dekalb County, GA schools in particular. The court also indicated that it is not necessarily unconstitutional if mostly black and mostly white schools exist in the same district if the same racial patterns occur in those school's neighborhoods. "Racial balance is not to be achieved for its own sake," Justice Anthony Kennedy wrote for the court. If the racial imbalances are due to demographics rather than school policies, there is no racial discrimination. If integration is a private choice, it does not have constitutional implications. "A school district is under no duty to remedy imbalance that is caused by demographic factors," the court wrote.

The ruling didn't fit well in Cincinnati, where eight public school teachers and the Cincinnati Federation of Teachers sued to overturn the race-conscious policies of the Board of Education. The Board's policies state that teachers can be transferred based on their race to help reach a racial balance of the teaching staff within the entire system.

Desegregation efforts aren't limited to grades K through 12. In response to a U.S. Supreme Court ruling that Mississippi state courts hadn't done enough to desegregate its public universities, the Mississippi state College Board considered closing Mississippi Valley State University and demoting Alcorn State University to college status. These institutions are two of the three predominantly black universities in Mississippi. The College Board hoped to force the students enrolled in the two institutions to enroll in the five predominantly white universities in Mississippi. Black politicians and university officials for the two affected institutions rebelled: "'Mississippi traditionally follows that role where you take the victims and make them victims again," said Ed Blackmon. "'[I]t's something that we as black institutions have to defend ourselves against,'" said Mississippi Valley President William Sutton. Alcorn State President Walter Washington added, "'These institutions extended a ladder to the basement and helped blacks climb out for years'" ("Mississippi Colleges," *Dayton Daily News*, October 18, 1992).

Integration was against the law in some places up to the 1940s, when there was essentially a walking around tax for blacks in the deep south and in Georgia. Churches were, by law, segregated (though not because blacks would then compete with whites for God's favored attention). By law, blacks sat on the back of buses, had separate public drinking fountains, and had to enter theaters from the side, not the front, and were forced to sit in the back rows. They had to sit in the back in eateries and not at the counter. White church pastors, social organizers, and other community service providers drummed up purportedly nonracial reasons to obtain legal injunctions against integration in churches, child camps, white country clubs, etc.

A white sitting down for a meal with a black was also illegal in certain jurisdictions. Which was why there was a culture shock on the integrated commune of Koinonia Farms in Georgia in the late 1940s when black farmers in the commune were paid the same as whites. That raised the expected asking price of blacks employed by other farm owners. Farmers were forced to raise the level of pay. Local blacks and whites were denied enrollment by the Americus High School Board of Education because their children lived at Koinonia Farms. In 1968 in Memphis, TN, there were still colored-only hospitals.

Blacks had to fight economic boycotts of black businesses and rebuild when white racist coalitions destroyed their means of business. Whites in integrated groups of boycott strikers faced retaliation by bombings, violence, and destruction of white-owned properties. Sometimes destruction of property wasn't enough to halt the advancement of minority successes; minorities were murdered. In Birmingham, Alabama in 1963, four white supremacists bombed the all-black 16th Street Baptist Church, killing four black girls who were inside; in May 2002, a man was finally convicted of the bombing. Recent fires in black churches, 64 set between 1995 and 2004, however, showed "no evidence of a white racist conspiracy" (Charen, p. 67), and only 4 of those fires were conclusively shown to be racially motivated, and set by the same group of people.

Under President Truman, the military services were commanded to be racially integrated. Institutions could be legally bound to desegregate and demonstrate their intolerance of racial separateness, but individuals within the institution could retain and promote their racist attitudes and behaviors, though personnel were censured for saying the N-word in the U.S. military services. Prior to military desegregation, blacks served in segregated platoons and on troopships in WWII, and were housed in separate barracks. According to Gates, in 2003 26 percent of the Army was black—commanders, sergeants, leadership command positions. Promotions gradually began to be based on merit and demonstrated capability, and excellence is rewarded regardless of race, color, or creed.

Americans are confronted with a long history of taking part in the undoing of racist institutions around the world. In 1986, "Duke University students protesting the investments in apartheid South Africa erected shanties in front of the university chapel" (Tifft, p. 102). Duke was whites-only until 1961, and some 250 of the campuses' buildings were codesigned by Julian Abel, a black architect in the otherwise all-white Philadelphia firm of Horace Trumbauer.

In 1962, James Meredith was the first black to enroll at the University of Mississippi, causing campus riots that resulted in 2 dead and 160 wounded. In 1966, Meredith started on a walk of 220 miles from Memphis to Jackson, Mississippi "to prove that a black man could walk free in the South. [His] ... goal was to inspire African-Americans to register and go to the polls" (Butler, p. 23). His goal was not realized: "Shotgun blasts rang out across the highway, striking Meredith in the head, neck, back and legs" (Butler, p. 24). On Highway 51 near Hernando, Mississippi, Meredith lay alone in the street in agony. "The civil rights movement had lately been strained by internal dissent, with leaders such as King calling for nonviolence and integration and others, such as [Stokely] Carmichael promoting a more radical black power stance" (Butler, p. 24). In support of Meredith's goal, King, Carmichael, and Floyd McKissick led marchers for 3 weeks, registering thousands of black voters on the way to Jackson.

In May of 1966, National Guardsmen blocked blacks from crossing the Third Street bridge in Dayton, Ohio. An annual March for Racial Harmony in Dayton commemorates the event, with the pledge to encourage racial unity and equality. Freedom Riders in 1961, largely college students of both races, defied segregation laws to ride on interstate buses across the South, encountering violent beatings by local citizens for their disobedience (Johnson, *Dayton Daily News*, January 1, 2007, p. 7).

Progress in civil rights caused violent reaction and aggressive responses by whites, who resisted and counter punched. As recently as July 8, 2003, Doug Williams, an armed white coworker with a documented history of racism, killed six blacks at Lockheed Martin Aeronautics in Meridian, Mississippi in a hate crime. Williams had made threats to kill "niggers." The massacre prompted black civil rights groups to demand that the U.S. Federal government cancel all contracts with Lockheed as punishment for Lockheed not taking greater preventive steps when it was made aware of Williams' death threats and racial slurs. As yet, there is no consensus among racial communities about how to defuse negative connotations applied to the N-word (*Dayton Daily News*, February 22, 2007), though there is agreement that when a white man speaks it, he has incendiary intent.

Siler City, North Carolina has seen racist rallies against illegal Mexican immigrants, whose numbers have increased 274% in the 1990s. The INS says 2 million people sneaked across the border in 2004.

Two important businesses that have a tremendous impact on public life are ripe for racial discrimination abuse–real estate and banking. Though laws like the Fair Housing Act (FHA) and the anti-discrimination enforcement mechanisms established in amendments to the FHA in 1988 prevent realtors and landlords from discriminating against buyers and tenants based on race, realtors and landlords may continue to discriminate based on applicants' inability to pay rent, pet ownership, poor references from former landlords, poor credit history, and unavailability of properties that fit special disability needs, etc. Realtors are prohibited from falsely declaring that the property isn't for sale, because such availability is public record and prospective buyers can sue for racial discrimination, whether or not racial discrimination is the reason behind the false declaration.

Few cases have come to light in which a realty firm's code of ethics explicitly directs its associate realtors not to sell property to minorities. Discrimination is covert. Residential and commercial property owners have been alleged to reward realtors not to show adjacent neighborhood/business park structure properties to minorities, though few cases of monetary incentive to keep areas minority-free have been proven. One prominent exception of revealed illegality is demonstrated by the case of the Rosemoor Association of businessmen in Chicago. The Association made contracts with whites that gave the organization first shot at buying the properties of whites who were relocating out of targeted neighborhoods. The purpose was to prevent the properties from going on the open market where they might be sold to blacks, integrating the neighborhood. Realtors have built-in incentives to protect the value of properties in their listings. Realtors who have several property listings in a high value white neighborhood don't want to risk depressing those values and their commissions by selling to minorities.

Neighborhoods undergoing integration frequently suffer from a phenomenon called white flight. Flight is often encouraged by realtors who practice another illegal tactic called block busting, in which realtors represent to white homeowners that all their fears of deteriorating housing prices due to integration are valid. With this fear in place, realtors are able to charge white home sellers up to 18 or more points on the transaction, or pay less than market value for the house, thus realizing greater profit by convincing more white home owners in the changing neighborhood to list and sell their properties. Block busting is prohibited under federal anti-block busting law, 42 *United States Code* §3604.

Whites fear, based on experience, that if they don't sell quickly when minorities start moving in, their homes will lose value. Lost value is based on instances of minorities allowing their properties to become shoddy and bringing teen crime and antisocial behavior, such as vandalism and intimidation, to the neighborhood. Minorities who buy upward in quality, attempting to position themselves in the middle class, may have overextended their capital ability to afford needed repairs on the property after making the mortgage down payment. The new owners may lose pride in the appearance of a declining property, thereby not performing even inexpensive maintenance and upkeep. If such minority owners also become unable to pay the monthly mortgage balance, the bank evicts them, boarding up the house or keeping it perpetually on the market, lowering its price to make it more attractive. The lowered value of one house in a neighborhood negatively affects the valuation of all of the houses in the neighborhood. The perception alone of this negative forecast, whether or not such an outcome will occur, compels white flight. Fleeing from cities like Chicago in the 1940s, affluent whites took with them the tax base that supported education systems, leaving poor country blacks behind in the inner city.

> **Premise:** Moving from a neighborhood where blacks are moving in is not necessarily a racist response.

Conversely, some minorities feel that when whites move into predominantly black middle and upper middle class neighborhoods, whites get relative bargains compared to the amount of money they would pay to live in similar white neighborhoods. As more blacks sell out to the whites, the property values raise to white demographic levels, and these new prices prohibit less highly salaried blacks from purchasing in these formerly prestigious black communities. Departing minorities often take pure profit for their property. That profit is rolled over as higher valuation of the property. Small increments in property value entice others looking for undervalued investments to pay a little more to buy a property in a neighborhood whose valuation appears to be rising. As the property prices rise, people—both black and white–who don't have enough money/credit to purchase the newly appraised property don't purchase it, assuring that new buyers are more likely to have enough capital to maintain the property to high standards set by the local housing and neighborhood associations.

To ensure that the predominantly ethnic upper middle class neighborhoods whose property value is increasing remains populated primarily by minorities, current minority owners could refuse to sell. They would still benefit from the value that comes with higher demand for their properties–better police protection, better schools, more community activism, better public facilities, more bargaining power with city councils, etc.–and they can sell at any time in the future. Offers by whites that constitute a substantial amount over what the owners originally paid for their homes are very enticing, however. A conscious decision to let greed, materialism, and a need for immediate monetary gratification raises property values for everyone, not just the members of a particular race.

Linguistic profiling stings are intended to catch unethical realtors who may be consciously committing racial discrimination. In such stings, an investigator phones a realtor and mimics either black speech patterns and dialects or white speech patterns when inquiring about the same property. The number of times a black voice inquiry versus the white voice secures a promise to view the target property, with all other key components held constant, is tallied. A preponderance of promises to show to the white applicant leads investigators to conclude that the realtor may harbor racially discriminatory tendencies.

The results of such stings, based on linguistic stereotypes, are anecdotal; the sample size is too small to show statistical or legally actionable significance; there is no study control group; there is no control over consistency in statements made over the phone; and the realtors phoned may not be able to reliably distinguish a black voice from a white voice. Any conclusion of discrimination is suspect because a great number of valid economic associations can be made based on the education levels of people who use substandard English and grammar, which is often the approach taken by people who attempt to imitate typical ethnic speech. Realtors can't be legitimately accused of discrimination if they base their decision not to show expensive property to those that they suspect don't earn enough, based on their limited language skills or verbal interaction presentation, to acquire the required loans, thereby wasting the realtor's time. However, the business practice of profiling potential buyers and leading blacks deemed to be poor earners to purchase homes in poorer, all black neighborhoods has been criticized as racist.

Financial lending practices are closely tied to property sales. The Community Reinvestment Act (CRA), passed in 1977, is a measure meant to curtail discriminatory lending practices. The CRA is imposed on lending institutions and forces them to lend in

> "all neighborhoods where they take deposits, particularly low-income communities.... Narrowly focused community activist groups and their lawyers use the regulatory process to force loan concessions from the banks. For these groups, the key to success is to keep the focus on racially disparate lending practices of banks" (*Consumer Research*, p. 21).

Activist groups use CRA as a legal weapon to leverage special concessions from banks that must specifically show compliance with the regulations to be permitted to conduct financial deals. Activist groups use the racially unbalanced CRA to unfairly leverage loans from banks that go to people and organizations that don't qualify under the banks' standard lending criteria. However, the compliance documentation clearly indicates the bank's criteria for making loans, illuminating reasons unrelated to racial discrimination that banks frequently cite to decide not to lend to applicants who have bad credit histories, bare assets, and sketchy employment experience.

Prior to CRA, federal bank

> "examiners generally looked at rejected mortgage loan applications from blacks and other minorities. If they found a reason for the rejection–such as a flawed credit history–the examiners would conclude no discrimination existed.
>
> "To see if minority applicants receive different treatment, examiners now will look at the reasons minority applicants were rejected and then look at applications from whites to see if the same problems were overlooked or waived" (*Dayton Daily News*).

Legal costs to fight unfair lending practice allegations based on CRA requirements are passed on to other banking service consumers:

> "By relying on faulty data to prove racial discrimination, the federal government and activist groups make it potentially dangerous and expensive for banks to open branches in low-income, minority neighborhoods in the first place. The potential cost of either riding out a legal challenge or making a deal to commit resources to more risky mortgage loans," is a disincentive for smaller banks to attempt serving these neighborhoods, which deprives the neighborhood residents of banking services (*Consumer Research*, p. 24).

Though the "total number of bank branches increased by almost 50% from 1970 to 1989, the percentage of poor neighborhoods containing bank branches fell" (*Consumer Research*, p. 24). Successful suits citing violation of CRA stipulations may "actually discourage minorities from taking actions to strengthen their own financial solvency and improve their credit history, since the incentive to take those actions is reduced" (*Consumer Research*, p. 24). While waiting for the windfall from CRA lawsuits, minorities might work on becoming more creditworthy by pooling their assets and developing credit histories.

In one case in which an activist group calling itself a Community Reinvestment Steering Committee threatened to file a complaint based on raw lending data that suggested discrimination, a "proposed two-year $175-million lending agreement with area financial institutions to help redevelop areas of the community with heavy concentrations of black residents ..." was made (*Consumer Research*, p. 24). The plan asked lenders to use their best efforts to lend $80 million over two years to black households and neighborhoods; increase the number of black people in upper management positions and lending institution board of directors, and consult with the Steering Committee prior to these appointments; aggressively purchase goods and services from black-owned businesses; earmark funds specifically for development of black-owned businesses; establish a $5 million loan pool for high-risk black borrowers and permit the National Business League to administer the loan pool; and set aside a $60 million economic development fund "to be used by (but not limited to) for profit and non-profit black developers to acquire, build and renovate real estate...." The loans "will be paid back if the project is economically feasible and bankable" (*Consumer Research*, p. 24).

By law, lenders must ask for racial identity information on loan forms so that minorities can be protected from racial discrimination, as indicated by the lending institutions' loan denial trends. "'It's imperative that there is parity in terms of lending,' said Eleanor Stocks, president of the Dayton Chapter of the National Business League. 'We're concerned about African-American business being undercapitalized, having just enough loans to fail'" (Beyerlein, *Dayton Daily News*, July 1992). Despite a resolution that asked lenders to reduce loan rejection rates for blacks by 50 percent within the year, George Brack, vice president of corporate compliance at Citizens Federal Bank in Dayton stated that

> "'lenders base their decisions on applicants' ability to repay and credit histories. If your credit history is not good, it's going to be hard to get the loan, no matter what color you are.' In April [1992], a *Dayton Daily News* computer analysis of Federal Reserve Board data showed that almost half of all Montgomery County blacks who applied in 1990 for home loans from the area's largest lenders were rejected. The rejection rate for blacks was 46 percent, compared with 20 percent for whites" (Beyerlein, *Dayton Daily News*, July 1992).

Rejection numbers don't describe rejection reasons, so readers of such reports are expected to conclude that because the statistics are sliced by race, then racial discrimination is strongly suggested as the reason for the rejection. However, if race weren't a demographic checkbox on the loan forms and loans were given strictly as bank loan officers say they are, then rejection would prove only that the loan applicant was, from all credit history, a bad credit risk. If rejections were based on race alone, there should be 100% rejection of black applicants and 0% rejection of whites. Amidst the statistics quoted in the news article was a curious absence of loan default statistics by either blacks or whites, paired with credit ratings of those defaulters.

Anthony W. Robinson, President of the MBELD&EF Inc. in 1992, stated that "'the banking community has displayed a consistent and pervasive attitude of hostility toward practically any circumstance involving minority business interest and the minorities in general.'" Rhonda Robinson, founder and president of the Ohio Black Expo, states that for "black-owned businesses to succeed, they must be adequately capitalized–and that's difficult because lenders often are unwilling to grant adequate loans to new minority businesses" (Beyerlein, *Dayton Daily News*, August 1992). However, a congressional inquiry in July 1992 to determine the validity of "allegations that blacks continue to be denied equal access to housing and business opportunities routinely accorded to white Americans," amounted to nothing (Beyerlein, *Dayton Daily News*, July 1992).

The poor who are considered too financially unstable to qualify for a bank loan are often the willing victims of small and unregulated mortgage companies, like the Fleet Financial Group, who charge high interest rates. Poor whites don't have the option of citing racial discrimination against mortgage companies when suing them under federal usury statutes. If blacks and other minorities are targeted by these unregulated mortgage companies, it is because these people are easier to coerce. Other associated traits make them attractive marks: inability to find money elsewhere, desperation, inability to secure legal counsel, and lack of sophistication when it comes to borrowing money.

If banks were less regulated, meaning they didn't have to comply with community reinvestment, loan disclosure, and other rules, such as those set forth in the Home Mortgage Disclosure Act (HMDA), and they didn't have to rely on CRA committees to choose feasible community redevelopment projects for them to finance, they could "make up to $30 billion in new loans" (Coorsh, p. 6).

There is a long history of minorities receiving abusive treatment from law enforcement officials, the most notable being the beat down of Rodney King. On March 3, 1991, four white Los Angeles Police Department officers clubbed, kicked, beat, and struck Rodney King 56 times, fracturing his skull in several places. The officers had converged in their cruisers on the scene after chasing King's car for several miles under the suspicion that the car's driver was under the influence of alcohol. The beating was caught on videotape by bystander George Holliday, and a selected emotionally inflammatory segment from the videotape was shown on local and national news broadcasts repeatedly over the span of a year, throughout the jury trial of the officers, who were charged for exerting excessive force to subdue King.

While King was in custody, one of the officers was overheard to refer to King as a gorilla. Many who later heard that this comment was made construed the comment as racist. The officer defended the comment as referring to King's strength and ability to take punishment, refusing to remain lying on the ground, even after being tasered at 70,000 volts. A nurse in the hospital where King was taken after being beaten testified that Officer Lawrence Powell continued to taunt King: "'We had a pretty good handball game tonight,' she heard him say. 'You lost and we won'" (Smith, *Dayton Daily News*).

During the trial, defense attorney Michael Stone told the all-white jury in the Simi Valley, Ventura County courtroom that the police officers feared for their physical well-being, and had assumed that King was under the influence of PCP, a drug that can make people dangerous and impervious to pain. It also came out at trial that the two other passengers in the car driven by King that night, who were both black, complied with police orders, and were both unharmed by the police. King's police record for armed robbery also came out at the trial, though this information wasn't available to the officers when they were arresting King. Immediately following his arrest, King was also determined to have been driving while legally drunk. Fifty-six witnesses were called during the trial, though neither the prosecutor, Deputy District Attorney Terry White, a black man, nor the defense called Rodney King to testify at the trial.

By implication, the entire LAPD, headed by L.A. Police Chief Daryl Gates, was on trial for creating a work environment that permitted and fostered brutality by L.A. police officers, in general. The videotape and trial showed L.A. police to be violent, authoritarian, and untrained in the appropriate mindset for protecting every member of its community.

The videotape of the Rodney King beating was impeachable as evidence against three of the four police officers–Theodore Briseno, Timothy Wind, and Sergeant Stacy Koon–and only officer Lawrence Powell was found guilty of one charge; this verdict was overturned when the trial was declared a mistrial. The "videotape alone could not resolve all the legal issues in the case, the critical issues of authority, participation, training, procedure, perception, and credibility. And the media was unable to communicate these issues from the courtroom to the living room, especially where the viewers clearly had preconceived notions of the facts of the case" (Rose, *Dayton Daily News*).

Following the overturned verdict for Powell, Rodney King in a televised news conference asked, "Can we all get along?"

Three days of rioting, looting, burning down of business buildings, and social disruption in South Central L.A., primarily committed by poor inner city blacks, followed the verdicts for the four police officers who beat or permitted the beating of Rodney King. President George Bush ordered federal troops to the city. At least 46 deaths and more than 2000 injuries have been connected to the violence. Other reports place the injury numbers between 700 and 1400. Various reports place the number of arrests during and after the riot between 378 and 4300. The damage to nearly 2,000 commercial and residential buildings across a largely impoverished section of Los Angeles was estimated at $550 million, maximum, and $200 million, minimum (Deans, *Dayton Daily News*). Los Angeles County coroner officials said the dead (36 in early reports, in contrast to 46 reported in later sources) were nearly all men, mostly black, and ranged in age from the late teens to nearly 50. Three whites and three Hispanics also were killed. At least 28 died of gunshot wounds, six in encounters with police. Some were armed looters caught in the act. One man died defending a store from looters. Some died in crossfires of random shooting. A pedestrian was hit by a car. Three died in fires (*Dayton Daily News*, p. 9A).

Koreans were overwhelmingly targeted by blacks, possibly because Koreans had a stronger retail presence in South Central than whites. Relations between blacks in LA and Korean shop owners had worsened in the spring of 1991 when Latasha Halins, a 15-year-old black, was shot to death by a Korean merchant in a dispute over a bottle of orange juice. Soon Ja Du, 54, received probation instead of prison, further raising the ire of the black community. Koreans interact from a different culture and speak very little English in an area that has high crime rates. Supporters of the LA rioters justified violence against the Koreans on the grounds that the Koreans' prices were too high, and that they showed disrespect for black customers.

The rioting was seen, and justified by some social commentators, as a response to outrage at the injustice of a verdict for a crime that seemed from the videotape of the King beating to be a clear cut case of racist police brutality against a black man. Blacks were angry with America for not living up to the promise to treat black citizens as equals. Defending the riots as an indirect response to slavery, Rev. William W. Hannah, pastor of Faith United Christian Church, said "'One of the real problems with America is that she has never repented for putting us into slavery'" (Lacy and Patterson, *Indianapolis Star*).

However, outrage at the verdict transcended race, gender, and politics. When placed in a nonracial context, the actions of police were less motivated by race than by overzealous performance of duty. In Simi Valley, where the community is a very strong supporter of the police, the jury may have been influenced by predicted political outcomes of failing to support the instruments of law and order in a volatile situation.

One contributing factor to the riots may have been fear that the government specifically wasn't protecting blacks. People riot out of a sense of fear, anger, lack of confidence in the administration of justice, and a sense of political impotence. The rioters were shocked, angered, resentful, hopeless, alienated, and frustrated. Perhaps to show whites how such absence of police protection felt, some blacks looted, rioted, beat and killed whites in multiple instances as retaliation, all out of proportion and incomparable to Rodney King's beating by police, which certainly did not legitimize the violence. Killing and looting are inappropriate forms of social protest, and the rioters showed a lack of social restraint.

One reporter reminds readers that "upwards of 30 million African-Americans did not take to the streets [during the 1992 riots], and those who did are clearly part of a relatively small urban underclass ..." (Morganthau, *Newsweek*, p. 28).

> **Premise:** Perceived injustice overrides perceived cushions of community and personal safety.

Many blacks may have committed illegal acts following the King verdict because they wanted to exaggerate that when blacks commit crimes, they go to jail, whereas whites, like the officers who beat King, don't. They wanted to emphasize the inherent unfairness of a "racist" justice system. However, the two situations are not comparable, one being force by officers to subdue a single suspect, while the rioting was done by many people wantonly destroying, stealing, maiming, and killing. Rational people can correctly analyze the unfair comparison and conclude that the protests are logically invalid as metaphoric propositions.

The Rodney King verdict was for some, "confirmation of the fall from grace black people have suffered in recent years. Blacks have lost the moral high ground. They are no longer the brave soldiers of conscience. In the span of a single generation, young black men like Rodney King have come to be seen as violent, predatory, out of control" (Minerbrook, p. 36).

Many looters were in the street simply for the free merchandise and lawless fun, not really caring about the injustice of the verdict.

Other rioters were more serious. White truck driver, Reginald Denny, was dragged from the cab of his truck by three black rioters, who then kicked and slammed Denny in the head with a brick. One of his attackers stood back and performed a happy dance of vindication while Denny lay beaten in the street. Later, the prosecuting attorney in the trial of the three black men charged in the televised beating of Denny exercised his right to challenge a sitting black judge. As a result, "a small group of demonstrators outside the court chanted 'No justice, no peace' and 'Burn it down.' Yolanda Madison, 21, shouted: 'We want things to change.... If [Denny's attackers] do get convicted, I suggest everyone burn the city down'" (*Dayton Daily News*, August 26, 1992). Such threats attempt to intimidate whites from applying society's laws to blacks because one member of the minority race is perceived to have gotten a raw deal with the law. It is not okay to beat any man nearly to death. Normal laws against assault and battery apply to everyone when apprehended, and such attacks are not somehow justified, nor more horrible, because they are committed out of racial anger and hatred.

Many have conjectured about the social outcomes of the acquittal of the four LAPD officers. One of the ramifications of the Rodney King incident, according to author Joseph Wambaugh, is that "'no white male currently on the [LAPD police] force is going to be named chief" (*Dayton Daily News*, February 29, 1992). The reality is that minorities generalize that all white police are racially insensitive, and to keep future peace in the populace, the police must turn over power to blacks or else appear racist.

Following the Rodney King incident, law enforcement agencies around the country became very sensitive to police violence against citizens based on the citizen's race. In the case of an off-duty Kettering, Ohio police officer Dondi Marsh shooting an armed robber, the NAACP got involved to ensure that the shooting death was not racially motivated: "Police and the local NAACP branch quickly pointed out the shooting wasn't racially motivated. They feared some people might construe it as racial in nature since Marsh works for Kettering, which is mostly white. But Marsh is one of two blacks on Kettering's force of about 80 officers. 'The officer was black, the female who was there was black and the person who was killed was black,' Dayton Police Chief James Newby said" (Dwayne Bray, *Dayton Daily News*). The first concern wasn't whether the off-duty police officer used unnecessary force against the armed robber, but whether the victim's race was a factor in the decisions the officer made, and whether the officer was black or white. Clearly, priorities were misplaced in concerns regarding the shooting.

"New police officers in Ohio will have to be trained in handling race, gender and cultural problems under a requirement announced ... by Attorney General Lee Fisher. Fisher said there is no question that racial minorities are treated differently than whites." This conclusion was supported by LeRoy Martin, a retired Chicago Police Department superintendent: "'Blacks in this country are just viewed, because of insensitivity on many people's part, as being a potential threat,' Martin said. 'No evaluation is made of the individual and the circumstances. Police do pull over and mistreat black citizens at a much higher rate than it would occur to white citizens,' he said." 24 hours of basic training is now required to cover cultural sensitivity topics (*Dayton Daily News*).

Many advocates of strong police presence, fed up with lax penalties and punishment for criminals, entrust the police to do whatever they must to protect the community, and sanction harsh restraint. People are willing to look the other way when police use excessive force because they realize police work is tough and that if police aren't supported, the community will be less well protected, since fewer people will go into police work and the current police will become lax in protecting communities for fear that they will be remonstrated for their actions.

Apologists agree that cops suffer from a siege mentality, which is set off more readily in some neighborhoods than in others. "'A large black man is viewed as much more threatening by whites who live in the suburbs than by people who live in South Central Los Angeles'" said William Mellor, president of the Institute for Justice, a conservative Washington public-interest law firm (Williams, *Dayton Daily News*).

The all-white jury in the Rodney King case was seen to typify a deep-seated racial animosity in southern California. Simi Valley suburbia "in most cases [is] physically and emotionally distant from all blacks and certainly from the black poor. It is fearful and uncomprehending, politically disdainful of black concerns and contemptuous of black leadership, and it blames the increasingly isolated blacks of urban America for the inescapable traumas of their isolation" (Teepen, *Dayton Daily News*). Had the same Simi Valley jury included blacks and come to the same conclusion, the riots may not have occurred, though it is illogical to conjecture such outcomes. Blacks may have trusted that someone of their own race had been looking out for their racial interests and had justifiably concluded from the trial evidence that the beating wasn't racially motivated. Blacks would have felt that they were part of the justice process. Of course, what-ifs and what-might-have-beens fail the reality test. Conjectures of "what-if" and "if-I'd-been-white (or not black)" also can't be reality. Things are as they are, not as they couldn't be and weren't. Speculation about impossible, hypothetical alternate treatment is pure fertilizer.

Inner-city blacks feel abandoned and alienated because the government has largely ignored high unemployment, racial injustice, inadequate education and insufficient health care. The arson, looting, and killing in Los Angeles was committed by people "who feel they have no stake in the civility of American society," Jesse Jackson said. "That is not good for democracy.... When people have been this much demeaned, when they have been deprived of their humanity, they do not act rationally." Mayor Bradley felt that the rioters "chose the opportunity to steal, loot, vandalize and, indeed, to kill." Many people felt that, because of economic inequalities, they are justified in taking back what would be theirs had they worked for it.

Kevin Phillips, a conservative political analyst, believes that the riots of the 60s were caused by rising expectations: "'Blacks wanted more things more quickly.... Now we have outbreaks in a decade of diminished expectations. This time they are frustrated that prospects for a better life are disappearing, for blacks in particular.' Increasingly [California] is populated by sharply contrasting classes of people: wealthy suburban communities growing richer but with populations shrinking as young people are driven out by the high real-estate costs; crowded cities full of poor people who strain local budgets and services; middle-income communities shaken by the job losses produced by upheavals in aerospace, real estate, banking and other once-steady growing industries" (Williams, *Dayton Daily News*).

By contrast, the Kerner Commission advanced the idea that the urban riots by blacks in the mid and late 60s "were spontaneous manifestations of discontent arising from discrimination and prejudice" (Blauner, 15).

Observation: One incident of racism does not mean that all whites are racist.

People in this country live in far worse conditions than those in L.A. in 1992 did, and these impoverished people do not tolerate an ethos of random violence and looting as L.A.'s residents did. Looting for urbanites in L.A. was an easy and illegal way to get attention and to get material goods. The King verdict was just an excuse to loosen societal inhibitions. Michael Lerner writes that "it's totally wrong to justify the rioting and looting as somehow 'appropriate' behavior. It is not a rational response to racism and it's not a smart strategy for achieving economic redistribution" (Lerner).

Laws constrain in nearly every area of commerce and social service, virtually assuring equal application of civil rights to all races. The next frontier in free speech law where race is concerned may be the full constraint of speech by whites in criticism of blacks. A reporter for *The New York Observer* quoted Senator Joe Biden, commenting on Democratic 2008 presidential candidate Barack Obama's character, calling Obama a "mainstream African-American who is articulate and bright and, and, clean and a nice-looking guy." Biden's compliments were purposefully misinterpreted as a presumption that Biden believed that blacks in general weren't articulate, the word, *articulate*, said to be a coded signifier for Biden's low opinion of blacks. It was okay for Biden to call Obama a nice-looking guy, a compliment that hasn't yet instigated the racial creativity of race baiters. The concept is that whites arrogantly exert the power to assign who is articulate and who isn't, whereas blacks making the same comment say it from a sense of pride, since so many blacks had previously been deemed inarticulate. Double standards are obvious where race is cited.

Even when a politician's speech isn't race related, such as Senator Hillary Clinton stating a fact in her 2008 campaign for president that President Johnson passed the Civil Rights Act after conferring at length with Martin Luther King, black spokesmen accused Clinton of implying that a black man needed the help of a white man to effect political change, and by extension, implying that Barack Obama would make an ineffective president by virtue of his race. Political lies are protected speech.

2

A Little Logic for the Sake of Argument

Making a choice to discriminate based on race implies a rational selection process. It's practical to survive in comfort, to want more until you feel you have enough. The concept of what's enough is subjective, based on individual value systems and what's available and one's means to attain what's available. However, the rational cost/benefit process–desire constrained by circumstance, perseverance, and talent–doesn't assure rational thinking nor logical conclusions.

To be clear, rational choices often aren't moral choices, and rationality shouldn't be paired with morality on either an individual or universal basis. Winning isn't measured in terms of rationality, and neither is the use of tactics to secure wins. Rational choices may not always be logical choices. Rational choice means only that options were weighed and reason was employed. People can't be forced to have rational beliefs when they don't understand what being rational means and when they've been misinformed about risk probabilities in the context of a decision-making opportunity. Common sense isn't common; it's based on having common interests and knowledge, and everybody sees sense differently as it affects each individually.

Most people know logic fallacies. They know that a billion things can happen that don't directly cause other things that happen later on, but a couple of things sometimes do act as a cause or can be correlated as a potential cause or condition. Those couple of causal things in combination tend to legitimize hasty false correlation.

People know that the extent of damage in a situation does not serve as proof of causation, though family survivors of horribly murdered victims still wish the harshest punishment on suspects identified by police and district attorneys as though the suspects were already proven guilty. They know that allegations of a crime aren't proof of a crime. People know that giving evidence of what *didn't* happen is not evidence of what *did* happen, and testimony doesn't dispel accusations, making character witnesses just about worthless. For instance, former child stars who testified that Michael Jackson *didn't* molest *them* is not evidence that Jacko *didn't* molest others.

People know that falsely saying a person steals and then attacking the person for theft is intended to degrade opinion about the alleged thief. They know that saying a person's breath is bad rather than dissecting the points of his argument is a tactic to divert attention and reduce general respect for the person. They know that saying abortion should be opposed *because* people oppose it is circular logic. They know that coming to conclusions that aren't supported by facts doesn't follow sense and may have personally detrimental results if practiced regularly in one's life. They know things aren't black and white, that there is a continuum of thought and opinion and action, and that there are degrees of thought within a philosophical and political position on an issue. They know that exceptions exist for every generality and that any exception invalidates a general rule.

People know that an authority in one field doesn't make him an authority in other fields. They know it's not fair to hold a criticized process to a standard by which other processes would also fail, and then omitting any reference to how those other processes also fail to measure up while promoting them.

People know that stereotypes are based on commonly repeated exaggerated character traits, that these exaggerated traits can be rare, not prevalent, and that they're loosely based on a few real instances and aren't true in every future instance, given a new set of variables. They know it's unreasonable to expect absolute elimination of all forms of racial prejudice and discrimination in all people, but they impose zero-tolerance policies which punish people for voicing any opinion about race-related realities. They know that statistics can be broken any number of ways to support any number of contentions or propositions: "… if you take any group and break it down just right, to exclude people who don't help you make your case, you can always, always find a cluster of something" (Fumento, p. 246).

People know that correlation–and there may be innumerable instances of correlation in any given comparison–doesn't mean causation, yet disproportionate underrepresentation of minorities is often cited as proof of racial discrimination. People know, but they often don't apply what they know to things they learn every day. For instance, Julian Earls, assistant deputy director of the Lewis Research Center in Cleveland, Ohio, which has lent science teachers to Wilberforce College, in Xenia, Ohio as part of science and engineering career training, stated that the "proportionately low percentage of black scientists and engineers threatens to evolve into a national crisis" (Fisher, *Dayton Daily News*). National crisis? Is the anticipated value provided by blacks in science, as opposed to other races and nationalities, so great that organizations like the National Aeronautics and Space Administration (NASA) specifically have to encourage blacks to take greater interest? In an attempt to provide federal research dollars to support historically black colleges, NASA awarded a 3-year $1.3 million grant to Wilberforce College. The money was designed to attract blacks into science and engineering careers by pumping up course offerings. The award is an example of an entitlement program. Leonard Cobbs, graduate of Howard University in Washington D.C. and the only black pilot in 1979 with NASA at the time stated that he "doesn't believe discrimination has kept black pilots out of NASA. He said most of the black pilots he knew in the Air Force chose flying for commercial airlines instead of a government career" (Harty, *Dayton Daily News*).

The argument that racial discrimination *causes* disproportionately fewer numbers of minorities to be working in a given profession or endeavor is illogical. The use of fallacious reasoning packs a greater emotional wallop for those who want others to see injustice and rally to correct it, regardless of whether injustice exists. It is unfortunate that many do not have the analytical skills to discern the fallacy of such arguments, and that those who do, actually begin believing the false arguments. The need to see villains and eradicate them is that compelling.

The worst lapse in logic, the one having the greatest detrimental impact on race relations, is generalization. People tend to generalize negative impressions based on reports about racial conflict and on a few personal experiences they've had with other races. Generalization is a psychological attempt to structure meaning in one's personal life, to reduce life's complexity by allowing people not to think in detailed, clear terms, and to form general categories based on patterns of knowledge that help them live their lives more habitually.

Typically, people become aware of only those patterns in other people's behavior that support their existing conclusions, making re-education on race issues difficult. Generalizations mean never having to question a guarded schema of beliefs so that more learning can take place regarding the wide world of diverse cultures. Rather than learn the features of peoples from a variety of geographical areas, most people prefer to identify ethnic minorities based on physical characteristics, such as degree of color, facial features, or speech. Dependence on generalizations also means never having to go out of one's way to discover experience that conflicts with negative generalizations. Just as people would rather avoid all snakes and spiders than make the effort to learn which are dangerous if they never plan to be trapped in a wilderness setting, they avoid people of different races rather than learn which on an individual basis might pose a threat.

The greater the number of reports about racial divisions, the more attuned people become to the issue, though not more informed nor more sensible. They become more wary, more circumspect, more apprehensive, and more frightened by each crime report. Prejudists fail to disassociate the negative behaviors of a few in a race from all of a race. They exaggerate the prevalence of the conflicts and consciously shape new experiences to fit into their customized belief structure. Gradually, they may decide that they live in a racist society and must always be on guard against racism. They seek instances in their lives that can be said to be the result of other people's racism, whether or not those instances can be or have been proved to be racist in intent. They attribute the motivations of other racial groups to the single cause of racism, trivializing and depersonalizing their own actions and accepting no responsibility in an interaction. Racism becomes pervasive in the person's beliefs.

When made about any group, generalizations lose sight of individual contributions and failures, encouraging blanket allegations and condemnations. Those who deserve blame aren't specifically blamed, and those who deserve praise don't receive it. Generalizations lump everybody together and obscure both the ideas that work and the actions that interfere with progress. Broad impressions are influenced by the negative behavior of members in the group, since the positive is generally expected. Generalization leads some blacks to think that all whites are racist supremacists, or could be. It leads to blacks committing violence against whites who are innocent of any crime against any black, which is what happened to Reginald Denny, the truck driver in the Los Angeles riots who was beaten by three black men who were mad that white police officers had beaten Rodney King, a black man, and that still other whites, the juries in the trials of the white officers, vindicated the police officers.

Broad generalizations lead to misconceptions or absolute ignorance about a race's culture and lifestyle, but ignorance does not presume racism. Few people specialize in comparative cultures, and lack of knowledge can lead to a xenophobic distrust of different cultures, a fear of the unfamiliar which should not be interpreted as racism. However, programs that bring people of different races together to receive first-hand experience and knowledge often fail because what one learns from a family of five or the few students sprinkled among a formerly segregated-race school cannot reliably be generalized to others in the race. The organizers of such interracial mixers often control the quality of the participants so that the exposure to other cultures is artificially contained. Also, forced integration for some magnifies the negative traits that people want to see in other races. Forcing people of different races together often shows only that each race's preconceptions about other races were right.

All blacks and whites don't speak with one racial voice, from one personal, philosophical, or political perspective, which makes judging only individual members of a race for their actions apart from their race difficult in the cacophony of voices.

Recent Gallup and Public Opinion polls provide convincing data that the vociferous views espoused by highly visible leaders of black-interest groups do not reflect the views of the black general public. Carol M. Swain compiled the results of these and other polls in an essay published following the Clarence Thomas Supreme Court confirmation hearings. According to an opinion poll conducted for the American Enterprise Institute, she found vast differences between the attitudes of the black public and black-interest-group leaders on the issue of supporting preferential treatment of minorities in employment and in college admissions:

> "77 percent of black leaders supported preferential treatment of minorities, yet only 23 percent of the black public did. The same poll revealed similar patterns in the perceptions of the black public with regard to the magnitude of job discrimination (74 percent of the black leaders believed there was substantial discrimination, but only 40 percent of the black public did). Another question of whether or not blacks were improving their economic status was another divisive issue: 39 percent of the leaders said no, while 66 percent of the black public said yes. Thus, 61 percent of the black leaders saw a deterioration in black living standards compared to only 34 percent of the black public" (Swain).

Leaders of black fund-raising and black-consciousness-raising organizations depend on the public thinking that race problems exist so that the organizations can be paid to exacerbate them. If specific race problems were *in fact* problems for everyone and recognized as such, there wouldn't be such broad opinions about their existence or the decision to label a situation as a problem. Such irresponsible leadership encourages racial/religious violence.

Emphasizing individual motivations, however, neglects the context of social forces and group relationships, and misses the bigger picture. Rather than generalize the traits of a few to the larger group, the larger group can be divided into smaller groups, not along racial or physical or demographic lines, but by the ideological values held by the disparate subgroups. Speaking of political and ideological groups within a race should minimize generalizations that encompass and condemn an entire race.

A startling example of generalizations that young blacks make is provided in Lynn Minton's 1993 interview of teenagers who were attending Eastern Senior High near Washington, D.C. Their answers, for the most part, point to all white people as conspirators in the violence in predominantly black inner cities:

> Nichole: "One cause of black-on-black crime is drugs, because people fight over drugs and turf. Black people don't make drugs, they don't run the country, and they don't control how cocaine gets into the country. White people do.... Another thing is how guns get into the country. The white man is responsible."
>
> Devin: "If you blame the white man for bringing guns and drugs in, then you have to blame him for everything that happens. If a whole lot of drugs come into my community, I'm thinking: 'I can make a million dollars off of this.' I see a lot of guns, I'm thinking: 'I'm going to shoot everybody who gets in my way.' Blame the white man.... Whites are indirectly responsible, but I don't blame them."
>
> Nichole: "... if the white people don't supply [drugs], then [blacks] won't demand it."
>
> Tiffany: "The white man's not going to stop, because he's making too much money.... I think that's what the white man wants–for us to destroy one another, so our race can just be destroyed totally. The white man is keeping the drugs in here because he knows that we're going to keep on buying, we're going to keep on selling, we're going to keep on wanting. The white man is turning black people against one another so we'll just be out of here, just erased off this earth."
>
> Amina: "Why do you think white people didn't want black people to read back in slavery times? They knew that, if we knew how to read, we'd know how to write, we'd be smarter. We'd know how to take over."
>
> Nichole: "All this violence is eliminating so many of the good people.... White people don't have to kill black people–they just give guns to black people so they can kill each other. It eliminates the competition.... I think that a lot of white people have a secret fear that their positions might be taken by a person of color. So they try to do certain things to prevent that from happening."
>
> Arnold: "The white people, they're the ones who create the movies and put it in the black man's mind to kill another black man."
>
> James: "I just think it's genocide, because, if you look, it's black people taking over everything–sports, television, this and that. And certain white people sit down and say, 'Hey, we've got to find a way to stop this.' And the best way is to divide and conquer. So they just kill us from within."

Tiffany: "The white man is on top of us, and when we take a step, he's going to take that step back from us.... But if I graduated from Howard University and was applying for a job, and you had a white female applying also—from another school that wasn't as good as Howard—that white female would get the job. Because of racism. I think the white man does not want black people to excel."

Jamila: "I do think that the white male, the white race in general, is kind of responsible for the fall of the black community because of the drugs: White people hold positions of power in this nation."

Devin: "I don't think I will ever be treated as a white man's equal. There's always going to be a color factor, wherever you go.... [Minton, p. 6].

Implicit in the generalizations about whites made by these students are generalizations about blacks. Blacks have no control, or can get no control, in government, in drug and firearm trafficking, or in personal decisions to use and sell drugs or firearms. Blacks have very low temptation thresholds. Blacks let greed force them to eliminate other blacks who have something they want, an Oakland Raider's coat, for instance. Blacks blame whites for many of the maladies that affect blacks and are unable to see that many of these maladies affect whites to an even greater extent. To these students, the motivations of blacks and whites are clearly different.

Labeling a race through generalizations provides a vague kind of perceptual handle on the world; nobody can be expected to personally experience every event that happens to others, and so people generalize to gain at least a minimal understanding. People depend on a few written or spoken re-tellings of experiences to gain a conceptual framework and knowledge, and they must form opinions based upon these reports, paired with personal experiences.

Premise: The primary causes of unintended racial prejudice are generalizing that *all* people of a race have a specific trait, or specifying that *only* people of a race have a specified trait.

Not all people of a given race have the same philosophies, religions, or politics. It is unlikely that any philosophy, religion, or political system is embraced by only one race.

One person making outrageous race-related claims does not speak for everyone in that person's race, regardless of that person's claim to be representing his or her race. People claim to represent their race, sex, or disability, but when someone claims to speak for his racial group, there is no rational basis for making sweeping generalizations about what that group should want, should think, should accomplish, should do, or should feel. Once this is understood, race can be disregarded as a component factor when making a judgment about a specific spokesperson's lack of intelligence.

Labels encompass a class of people and fail to recognize the diversity within that grouping. There's a tendency to judge people by the labels we attach rather than judge each person's unique character, which ignores the individuality of a group's members, individuality that may be expressed in ways unrelated to the group's stated missions and political direction. Some labels, such as the name of the National Association for the Advancement of Colored People (NAACP), help the group's members refer to themselves. The NAACP label identifies shared attitudes or interests that its members hold about issues concerning blacks. But the label also makes it easy for white racists to condemn the entire group, often heaping undeserved disfavor and negative attributes onto all those in the group: "damn NAACP racists." The tendency to attach pre-existing prejudices to new labels is difficult for people to avoid in their search for narrow meaning and fast rules in life. However, labels are a tool, and it is the people who use the tool who remove its neutrality when they attach negative meanings.

Negatively classifying all members in a group lets people preserve their prejudices, easily associate negative or undesirable traits to group members, or maintain conditions in which one group has a distinct advantage over others. However, classifications that ease communication may be morally acceptable and responsible. Classification permits mutual agreement about the traits of members of a class. For instance, if a girlfriend wants to warn her friend not to get involved with a certain boy, she might say, "The guy's a player. He'll treat you like dirt." If both girls know the traits of a "player," that is, if both define that person in the same way, then the concern is understood. "Player" avoids having to describe every undesirable trait the boy may have: "Boys who wear alligator flats, who have more product in their hair than in their mother's cosmetic case, comb their hair with four styling brushes, who drive a Porsche, who flatter women for practice, etc., are bad news for a nice Christian girl like you." Attributing traits to groups of people makes it easy to refer to them in a general way.

Classifications reduce life's complexity. They give people the freedom to limit the amount of individual-specific knowledge they must learn. Recognizing fewer classes lets people be indifferent about the more discrete and segmented classes of people in a society. For instance, dichotomous views of the world, while leading to over-generalization about the traits of people that make up the two classes in question, simplify social interactions. Greater numbers of smaller recognized classes allow more consideration for the individual differences and variability of people in those classes. People must make the effort to become more aware that each person in a class doesn't have all and only the general traits of the class.

Classifying people often ignores individual differences and emphasizes similarities. Prejudiced people look at superficial similarities–skin color, nose size, body weight, economic status–when they apply their prejudices. When people classify based on visually accessible traits, such as skin color, which is a nonessential criteria, such classifications are racially prejudicial, degrading, and insulting.

More than gaining understanding, generalizing negative traits based on prevailing reports lets people reduce their risk by avoiding the group of people associated with these negative traits. People generalize because it makes them feel they are actively making their lives safer. If safety is a primary motivator in a person's life, and numerous reports indicate that violent crime is more frequent in black communities than in white communities, that person will fear and avoid black communities. Other people seek danger, thrills, the unknown, the exotic, novelty, so they might welcome the chance to dispel the generalizations about dangerous black neighborhoods.

Stereotyping is an almost universal cognitive function that also helps people organize a very complex world, giving people confidence in their ability to understand a situation and respond to it quickly and appropriately. People stereotype on age, culture, education, employment status, family status, gender, national origin, physical appearance, race, regional origin, religion, sexual orientation, diet and eating habits, clothing fashion, smell, punctuality, and thinking style, among other demographic and lifestyle traits. Stereotyping is the "process in which repeated observation leads us to discern patterns and form probabilistic rules" (Seligman, *The Wall Street Journal*, November 19, 2003).

In a few instances, stereotypes based on a combination of demographic characteristics may be true. The validity of every stereotype is susceptible to any exception. Some blacks don't play basketball, don't have "natural" rhythm on the dance floor and in the bedroom, and don't love big bootie or watermelon. It takes only one exception to refute any stereotype. Any time someone says whites have no rhythm, have tight asses, and can't jump ... you get the idea. In most cases, such broad strokes are intended humorously, though humor is lost on some. You could be a racial stereotypist if you think CPT is a valid time zone in Atlanta, Georgia (CPT is Colored People Time).

Racial stereotypes originate in at least a single instance, and then are referenced, usually by the popular media, with a frequency out of all proportion with the prevalence of the belief, value, habit, or lifestyle being referenced within a racial group. Exaggerated emphasis usually serves to create and present a negative example. Serious reliance on stereotypical thinking shows an ignorance of the true ratios of habits within a race and may, in some cases, lead to racial discrimination. In the late 1800s, blacks were stereotyped as loyal Toms, carefree Sambos, faithful Mammies, grinning Coons, and wide-eyed Pickanninies. In the 1970s through the 1990s, blacks were shown to be violent pimps and crack dealers with no concern for human life, racism whiners, and African princes who wanted comforts befitting their privileged racial status. In the 21st century, blacks are portrayed as gangsta rappers, playas, and athletes (c'mon, not all stereotypes are negative). During these same periods, stereotypes of other races were as unflattering and fluid.

When encountering someone on the street who fits the stereotype of a violent personality, it's rational to depend on the stereotype and seek safety from a perceived threat, especially if there's little personal risk in avoidance. Occasionally, prejudging someone to be potentially more violent based on race may insult those who don't intend violence. Making prejudgments known to others may lead to accusations of racism, but everybody just has to deal with it.

> **Premise:** It's rational to desire personal safety, but irrational to misconceive risk based on generalized single events applied to the whole spectrum of events or possible events. Actual safety differs from safety comfort levels.

Even stereotypes of positive qualities can have negative outcomes if acted upon. Thinking a situation is safe or that a person intends no harm leads to bringing down one's guard in the presence of someone who may actually intend harm. Positive stereotyping, therefore, is also based on irrational generalization, resulting in a kind of false positive.

Some people feel that if they're going to be negatively stereotyped anyway, they might as well justify the stereotype rather than be falsely accused. In the movie, *Crash*, a white female character played by Sandra Bullock seems to be seeking protection on the arm of her husband when they approach black males on the street, though the men don't appear by their clothing or posture (both a disguise of respectability) to be a threat. The black males hypocritically and sarcastically discuss between themselves their indignation at the woman's prejudicial beliefs, though they've misinterpreted the character's motivation in getting closer to her husband, and then jack the white couple as they'd intended. To become a criminal because somebody will always believe that you are a criminal is a choice, just as doing good in the hope of dispelling negative preconceived race stereotypes is a choice.

Another area in which attempts are made to curtail critical thinking is the use of connotation to implant false impressions. In many newspaper reports, most statistical disparities, unless they favor minorities, are assumed to be the result of racial discrimination–"Disparity in cancer death rates between blacks, whites widening." Disparity is a word that obscures the true comparative significance by loading it with the value judgment that the difference is somehow unfair. The media doesn't use an emotionally neutral term, such as *difference* in place of *disparity*, because one of the media's goals is to drum up excitability and indignation in readers about implied injustice.

Citing disparity in employment, for instance, presumes that society's rewards should be apportioned according to the percentage of people who belong in each race rather than according to the skill, training, dedication to work, and the educational levels of the people who make up that percentage, that is, merit. Many in the news media comment that numerical percentage equates with employment qualifications: In 1980, "blacks were under-represented in the nation's executive ranks by 50 percent. Today, despite a near-doubling of the number of blacks in executive jobs, the study shows that there still are 40 percent fewer blacks in such positions than should be expected by their share of the work force" (*Dayton Daily News*, August 16, 1992). Many blacks and some misguided white congressional lawmakers feel that an equal percentage of a race should, in the absence of any other factors, possess all of the rewards created in society according to their percentage of the population. In fact, the percentage of the population composed of any race in a meritocracy has no relationship to the distribution of jobs, goods, or rewards. This distribution is based on many factors, a major one being free choice and the early-life choice to become prepared and qualified to compete for such rewards.

Premise: In any profession or organization, it is objectionable to racially discriminate against majorities to achieve a racial balance that reflects population percentages.

Allegations of under-representation by a minority race don't apply in professional sports, in which blacks constitute 87 percent of basketball players and 75 percent of NFL football players. In these fields, skill and talent and work ethic are recognized as contributing factors to success, regardless of race. Disproportionately high numbers of minorities comprise professional basketball and football teams, but that is no indication of discrimination against players who are not black. For whites to criticize the low percentages of whites in these sports would be committing a fallacious argument based on racial double standards. There's always ice hockey to offset the percentages.

There are few black architects, for example, but the reason may not be because architectural colleges and firms discriminate against blacks. A common factor among the population of architects is that few come from poor families. Architecture is an elite profession. It's also just possible that minorities are not interested in being architects.

Minorities experience disproportionately high hospitalizations and medical problems, but the proportion isn't proof that medical insurers racially discriminate by withholding equal quality preventive coverage to minorities or that health care providers discriminate. Minorities are less likely to seek health services for minor health aggravations than non-minorities, preventing early detection of major diseases. For instance, "African-American women with a family history of breast or ovarian cancer are 78% less likely than white women with a similar history to get genetic testing" (*Time*, April 25, 2005). A study released on June 28, 2005 "found that up to 36 percent more black men die within five years of being diagnosed with cancer than white men, and 17 percent more black women die of the disease than white women." "'The problem here,'" said Robin Hertz, "is that there's been more progress in the white community.... That's a step in the wrong direction.'" The right direction, then, would be to reduce white progress to narrow the "disparity"? No analysis into causes for the difference in death rates between the races was provided, though most "blacks aren't screened and cancer is less likely to be detected in its early stages among blacks...." (Burgin, *Dayton Daily News*, June 28, 2005). Reasons that blacks aren't screened also weren't specifically explained in the article, though readers are left to wonder whether health care providers were intentionally failing to screen blacks because health care providers are generally racist and believe that the health of blacks isn't as important to sustain as is the health of whites. The results of study conducted between October 1998 and August 2000 that surveyed 6,712 health care patients and recently published in the *New England Journal of Medicine* "suggests that Americans–rich, poor, black, white–get roughly equal treatment, but it's woefully mediocre for all" (Donn, *Dayton Daily News*, March 16, 2006), with 58% of blacks reporting that they received high quality health care versus 54% for whites.

Disproportionately high numbers of black males in prison based on the percentage of blacks in the population most likely reflects the disproportionate rate of crimes that black males commit, get apprehended for, and are publicly defended by low-paid public defenders in a due process court. Yet, many minority spokespersons question the racial bias that may be present in the process, which could mean that law enforcement officials and the criminal justice system might just be racist.

Media also deludes readers into accepting biased conclusions through statistics. A good example can be taken from an August 1992 report in *The National Law Journal* in which environmental racism, which in this example is the storage of waste in poor black communities, is illustrated:

> "penalties imposed by the Environmental Protection Agency and the speed in which the problems of hazardous wastes sites are addressed varied widely, depending on whether the communities involved were white or were inhabited by minorities.... Penalties under the hazardous waste laws were as much as 500 percent greater at sites in largely white communities than at sites in largely minority neighborhoods.... The average fine in areas with the greatest white population was $333,556 vs. $55,318 in areas with the greatest minority population.... [Fines] were on average 46 percent greater in largely white communities than in minority areas.... Under the Superfund law, hazardous waste sites in largely minority areas took 20 percent longer to be placed on a national priority action list than sites in largely white areas. The start of Superfund cleanup efforts also generally were delayed longer in minority locations.... The EPA more often chose less-preferred methods of dealing with hazardous waste sites when the sites were in minority areas. For example, the report said, the so-called 'containment' method of dealing with a hazardous waste site was used 7 percent more frequently in minority communities than in largely white communities. The 'treatment' procedure, where wastes would be eliminated, was used 22 percent more often in sites in white communities."

The report implies that the EPA is a racist government regulatory body. The following pertinent facts about waste disposal, storage, and containment were omitted from *The National Law Journal* report:

- The speed in which problems at hazardous waste dump sites are addressed depends on the type of hazardous waste, how people are exposed to the waste, and the number of people threatened by potential exposure. Smaller communities, regardless of racial composition, mean that fewer people are impacted or expected to be threatened by the waste, a major factor in determining the priority of attention, cleanup, and placement on national action priority lists.
- "Largely minority neighborhoods" and "inhabited by minorities" are living conditions that include non-minorities, so the reporter used these phrases hoping to covertly fool readers into seeing a racial injustice.
- The location of dump sites is often determined based on environmental amenability of properties to waste storage; other factors aside from white racial

composition in white communities near hazardous waste dumping may contribute to the larger fines and faster investigation of the problems.

- No information is provided about whether communities near disposal sites were built before or after the property was zoned and was being used as a dump. If dumps were known to pre-exist when residents purchased homes, risks were known and home purchasing decisions were made based on personal economics rather than buyer race.

- No comparison was made regarding the property damage dollar figures from potential hazardous waste leakage in minority and non-minority communities.

- Penalties depend on the extent of waste contamination, the type of hazardous waste, and the method used in depositing the hazardous waste, factors that weren't examined in the statistics presented in the report.

- Delays in clean up can be attributed to the lack of strong objection that would force the Superfund's action sooner.

- Selection of methods to deal with hazardous wastes—either containment or treatment—depends on the number of people who are exposed to the waste and the type of waste, and the volatility and dangerousness of disinterring waste, not on the racial composition of those who would be potentially exposed.

The percentage of all whites living in toxic-waste neighborhoods compared to the percentage of all blacks hides the raw numbers of both whites and blacks affected. Waste disposal companies select sites based on cost to option the site, the proposed site's proximity to cities that generate the wastes, and suitability of the geology for waste storage. Landfills tend to cluster because the viability of a site for one landfill makes it attractive to other landfill concerns. James R. Logsdon, a vice president of Waste Management Inc., states that complaints of environmental racism by blacks living in southwest Dayton where a new landfill was being planned were baseless, that the area was used for waste disposal before people began moving there. "'Our opponents moved out there and built those homes after these facilities were in existence,' he said. 'They're still building them. They're building new ones every day'" (Brinckman, *Dayton Daily News*, p. 1B).

Readers are advised to research the full story behind statistics of interest.

Analogies are used to compare a complex problem with a more simplistic problem that is similar in a few respects and with which one's audience may have more experience and background knowledge. The hope is that people will gain a deeper understanding of the more complex concepts through the analogy. The rhetorical technique of analogy is a breeding ground for deception. A black firefighter, defending government-mandated consent decrees (agreements to match every white hire or promotion with a black hire or promotion), makes liberal use of false analogy:

> "In 1983 James Hanson, a white fireman, and Carl Cook, a black fireman, both took the Birmingham Fire Department test for lieutenant. Both passed, but Henson ranked sixth among all who took the test, with a score of 192, while Cook ranked eighty-fifth, with a score of 122. Under the consent decree Cook was promoted to lieutenant and Henson was not.
>
> Henson became part of a group of whites attempting to challenge the consent degree. He argued, 'I can understand that blacks had been historically discriminated against. I can also understand why people would want to be punitive in correcting it. Somebody needs to pay for this. But they want me to pay for it, and I didn't have anything to do with it. I was a kid when all this went on.'
>
> Cook countered, 'Say your father robs a bank, takes the money and buys his daughter a Mercedes, and then buys his son a Porsche and his wife a home in the high-rent district. Then they discover he has embezzled the money. He has to give the cars and house back. And the family starts to cry: "We didn't do anything." The same thing applies to what the whites have to say. The fact is, sometimes you have to pay up. If a wrong has been committed, you have to right that wrong'" (Edsall and Edsall).

Cook's analogy is false because he compares a very dissimilar scenario in which even his conclusions are unsound; the scenario is completely unrelated and irrelevant to the original situation because:

1. The bank embezzler committed an illegal act that was illegal when he committed it.
2. A specific person–the embezzler–was found guilty of a specific crime.
3. The repayment is the actual material that the embezzler was shown to have gained with the specific illegally acquired funds.
4. The person who actually stole the funds, and only that person responsible for the theft, was forced to make repayment.
5. Everyone in the community, indiscriminately and based on race, was not asked to pay for acts for which they weren't responsible.
6. It is not a fact that people in general have to pay up for other people's crimes.
7. It is not true that people in general are legally obligated to right a wrong.

Knowing rules of logic doesn't prevent people from continuing to think illogically about race issues, intentionally making illogical statements when it serves to fool others, and making exceptions so that they can believe in emotionally satisfying conditions they know to be false. People believe flawed information because it makes their thinking and their lives easier, more efficient. And their thinking gets lazy, flaccid.

> **Premise:** Irrational people can realize their life goals, and be high functional, contributing members of society.

Irrational thinking, whether intentional or psychologically reinforced, works for many people, but so can rational thinking. Rationality can't dispel valid fear, and shouldn't when fear is a rational response based on known crime statistics in a geographic area by a specific minority. It also can't override reality. Rationalism is a method of dealing with problems and generating solutions, a tool. It offers a less emotionally charged view of facts and events. It has no race nor national pride; no agenda, no job to protect, no history to avenge; no culture-specific tradition; and no unequal opportunity. Paired with accurate information, a rational, situation-centric approach can improve poor race relations.

Many current policies, laws, and practices aren't working, such as hate crime legislation, forced integration, demands for slavery apologies, jury nullification, riots, reparations and restitution, sloganeering like "no child left behind," preferential hiring and affirmative action job quotas, hyphenated reference to race that emphasizes separateness, political race baiting to win elections, and differential sentencing for poor-man versions of the same illicit drugs. Bridging cultural gaps between races and forcing people of different races together socially, geographically, and educationally often don't resolve erroneous and illogical thinking about race issues. People will always have some kind of prejudice, what Fumento defines as "an inclination to think and act in a certain way without having all the facts in," (Fumento, p. 274) because it's in their best interest in a dangerous, competitive world.

The problem is that people in power who want to right past wrongs accept the flawed rhetoric of minorities and find ways to unfairly transfer resources from everyone to minorities through government decree, laws, prohibitions, and forced taxation. A large-scale example of such government-supported theft and redistribution of wealth is the reversal of apartheid systems in South Africa in which the South African government decreed that most of the property owned legitimately by white farmsteaders be given to black farmers without recompense to the whites.

Premise: Laws applied across entire populations that incidentally disproportionately affect the poor may not be intentionally discriminatory against a specific race.

The racial fairness of state voting laws requiring state-issued picture IDs at
registration stations intended to combat voter fraud has been questioned. Poor
blacks are thought not to have the proper paperwork to apply for state IDs.
Since poor people of every race or those who have chosen to remove themselves from the social identification process have the same problem, the new
requirements aren't racist.

Race is just a convenient way to set the sights for resentment. Tax dollars go
into a welfare system to support a disproportionate percentage of poor unem-
ployed/underemployed/illegally employed minorities in the population, or those
earning untaxed money who don't pay into the social support system, and people
forget that the sheer quantity of freeloaders aren't minorities. The unemployed
poor pay nothing for medical, roadway maintenance, and social human services.
Employers don't want the government removing the choice of who they can hire.
In the absence of other financial factors, white employers should be eager to
employ a minority simply to reduce and disperse the tax burden. But there are
always other factors.

3

Minority Tactics, Major Results

Minority populations (Scientologists, homosexuals, blacks, honest attorneys) can sometimes feel outnumbered and against overwhelming odds. It's rational to scramble for power by any means necessary, but some unethical tactics to gain footing against other races backfire, such as subversive and unfounded allegations of racism. Extremist and irrational accusations by racial minority spokespersons create negative race impressions; listeners will generalize–it's what listeners do– and associate the vocal minority's entire race with the outrageous and indefensible statements.

Minorities are left with weaker tools, none as powerfully immoral as the slave auction block, lynching, social exclusion, and not-so-covert legal subjugation. Instead, many minorities make transparently false and insupportable allegations of racism, expecting the majority to disprove the claims as a way to failsafe systems against racism. Minority spokespeople assert that urban violence committed by impoverished black male teens is a result of systemic social and economic inequality perpetrated and supported by the majority, who should, in all fairness, correct these conditions. They ask suspected (white) descendants of racists to feel guilt and pay for past injustice through limitless, government-sponsored entitlement programs. Some minorities and their non-minority Liberal counterparts attempt to invalidate standards of merit in favor of racially preferential rewards (workforce racial quota requirements, for instance) as a way to offset past injustice; through unfair minority advantages, many minorities hope to excel despite having substandard education and qualifications. Since past government officials can be shown to have indulged in conspiracies to oppress minority groups, programs that exclusively benefit minorities are demanded as a way for government to disprove the continuing existence of insidious race-targeted conspiracies.

> **Observation:** Conspiracy theories obscure factual details with speculation, instill a sense of hopelessness and frustration and anger, and maintain ignorance about issues. Conspiracy theorists rely on the perverse attraction of

secrets. Conspiracies show the ingenuity and creativity of mankind, the admirable quality of group cohesion and the power of human components working together, the possibilities of detailed planning to achieve goals, and the secrecy that lets the imagination run wild.

FEMA's sluggishness and ineptness in providing relief to hurricane Katrina victims in 2005, for example, wasn't a racist conspiracy simply because the majority of New Orleans' residents were minorities.

"A survey of black Americans showed that nearly half believed that AIDS was created by the U.S. Government, and that a very sizable percentage believe that it was part of a plot by the CIA to kill minorities in this country as a form of genocide." Sandra L. Thurman on the Tucker Carlson show responded: "There's been such denial that AIDS was in the black community, in particular, based on a lot of homophobia, racism.... We've got to explain to people that this is a disease that only mother nature could have created."

Whites have conspiracy theories, too, and just as implausible. AIDS may have been introduced on probes from alien abductors, an assertion that is harder to disprove than the assertion that the CIA had a hand in spreading AIDS–aliens are widely known not to keep a paper trail.

Appealing to white liberal guilt is a popular and successful tactic, since feelings of guilt can bloom even when removed from the soil of actual personal responsibility, having no basis in a cause and effect relationship. A sense of fair play makes a fertile ground for brainwashing. Historian Daniel Boorstin recognizes the guilt: "'I think Americans continue to have a deep sense of guilt over the inheritance of the institution of slavery.... But that guilt should not be embodied in our current institutions. We must give everybody a fresh start and not try to compensate for past injustices by creating present injustices'" (Szulc).

Tied to establishing guilt in gullible majorities is establishing a price tag for retribution. The cost of past discrimination cannot be estimated. Direct correlation between past wrongs and impact on current descendants cannot be determined. All, including minorities, are forced to pay for the sins of forefathers, and all are innocent. It can be no other way because the slaveholders and government officials who permitted slavery are no longer around to punish or take responsibility.

Some minorities feel comfortable playing up the victim angle, though it damages them psychologically if they begin thinking that the role of victim is their only and life-long reality. Victims see whites as social oppressors and cite the plight of impoverished blacks in housing projects and inner cities who choose to resort to crime to survive. The economic disparities force the poor into substandard schools and hospitals. They're stigmatized by standing in welfare lines because they've been shut out of jobs by white employers. As a subset of charges of racism, victimization is more general.

Can the majority blame the minority for wanting to level the playing field (a misnomer since nobody's playing here and the field wouldn't stay level long enough to cut a ribbon commemorating it)? The following tactics raise a lot of resentment and border on bad sportsmanship:

- Intimidation and violence
- Calls for broader, discriminatory interpretations of existing laws and creation of new laws targeted to benefit only minorities
- Lobbying for public funding that will benefit only minorities
- To gain attention for racially discriminatory and unfair consideration, boycotts, sitins, demonstrations, marches, symposiums, all visibility tactics, street renamings, and holidays in honor of individual minorities
- Media coverage to spout rhetoric that is so outside rational discourse that interest is incurred by the sheer perversity of an extremist's earnest posturing
- Reverse discrimination and segregation.

Whites have used similar tactics to oppress minorities and to gain even more awareness and bigger advantages. More wrongs won't solve racial strife and do little more than raise resentment over the use of unfair tactics.

Allegations of Racism

Falsely charging racism can gain big concessions from whites. Feeling a warped sense of karmic and poetic fairness, some whites fearfully examine their motives, whether the charges are blatantly false or require further serious investigation.

In Dayton, Ohio on February 21 of 2005 the burning of a cross on the face of a church was initially attributed to racial hate crime. It was later found to be from an electrical short in the backlighting. Charges of racism have become so commonplace, that even electricity is suspected of harboring racial hatred. (The possibility of a thought crime by electricity is offered under the principle that if you don't laugh, you'll cry.)

In another case in Troy, Ohio, about 20 miles north of Dayton, the NAACP became involved when high school basketball coach James H. Clay, who'd been fired from Troy Christian School for allegedly making inappropriate comments to staff members and was currently being charged with a felony count of sexual battery against a 15-year-old Piqua, Ohio girl. The coach's house was fire bombed, and his car was spray painted with the words guilty and leave. Because the coach was black, and despite the firing and alleged sex crime known to the community, both potentially motivating factors, local NAACP president Derrick L. Foward declared the crimes against Clay to be racially motivated hate crimes meriting FBI involvement. "Forward said the fire was reminiscent of the fire bombings of black homes in the South during the 1950s and 1960s" (DeBrosse, *Dayton Daily News* December 23, 2007). The method of protest does not necessarily equate with race, just as a noose for hanging people doesn't equate only with the lynching of blacks; horse thieves and criminals of every race have been hanged throughout history—a noose is emblematic of death, not racism.

In response to allegations by civil service employees of racism in job promotion practices at Ohio's Wright-Patterson Air Force Base (WPAFB) in June of 2005, a Southern Christian Leadership Conference (SCLC) spokesman responded, "Wright-Patt is the last great slave plantation." On July 7, 2007, the SCLC held a "prayer action rally" to raise awareness about alleged racial discrimination at WPAFB, with a national march on the base planned for the Fall of 2007 that "will make Selma to Montgomery look like a Sunday School picnic," said SCLC executive assistant Bishop Richard Cox (Magan, July 8, 2007). One on-base employee claimed that "nearly 100 workers at the base are treated unfairly and denied promotions because of their race."

In Government institutions, there is always the assurance that slave plantations will die out under the crushing weight of paperwork and regulation. Comparing a military base to a slave plantation adds only clutter to investigations into allegations of racially discriminatory hiring and promotion practices. Similar allegations had also been addressed in 1992 when commanders at WPAFB explained that blacks are in less valuable positions, have low rank, and get unusually low performance ratings, making them prime targets during layoff actions. Recently hired employees, whether they are white or black, are also candidates for reduction in force (Clark and Gaffney, "AF cuts concern NAACP," *Dayton Daily News*).

Less inflammatory, but equally extremist, are doomsday opinions made by Theodore Shaw, president of the NAACP Legal Defense Fund, in response to the impact of the Supreme Court ruling involving school districts in Louisville, Kentucky, and Seattle, Washington against allowing race-based criteria in proposed diversity plans: "we've reached an Orwellian state" (*NewsHour*, PBS broadcast June 28, 2007). We're "going to see is a continued re-segregation of many of our nation's public schools," Shaw continues. "[W]hat they're trying to justify is integrated education," Shaw accuses the Supreme Court justices who voted against race-based student assignment. A decision striking down the programs "'will be a reversal of historic proportions" that could "send this country backward'" (Crawford-Greenburg and Rosenberg, ABCNews, June 28, 2007).

> "Diversity is a fact of life in this country. To suggest that, in the 21st century, we should allow ourselves to slip back to a kind of 19th- or 20th-century racial isolation and segregation in a global economy is suicide for all of our children and all of our citizens" (*NewsHour*, PBS broadcast June 28, 2007).

Roger Clegg, president of the Center for Equal Opportunity, arguing in the televised interview as an advocate of the Supreme Court's decision, wisely stayed on message, repeating the rationale that racial discrimination for most purposes is wrong:

> "There's nothing wrong with diversity, but if the only way that a school can achieve this politically correct racial and ethnic mix is by telling school children that whether you can come to this school depends on what skin color you are, that's too high a price to pay for that kind of diversity."

A later response by Shaw, "Mr. Clegg and his colleagues suggest that we ought to gouge out our eyes and pretend that race doesn't matter anymore." Continuing on point, Roger Clegg summarizes,

> "But the best way to fight discrimination is not by piling more discrimination on top of it, not by creating new victims of racial discrimination. The best way to fight discrimination is by enforcing the laws that we have on the books against discrimination and by helping impoverished people, who come in all colors, but regardless of their skin color.
>
> If there are poor kids or kids who are not getting a good education, help them improve their schools, but it should be done for all of them, regardless of their skin color, whether they're white or black or brown or yellow" (*NewsHour*, PBS broadcast June 28, 2007).

False charges of racism, as those implied by NAACP Legal Counsel Fund President Shaw, work because too many addle-brained liberal Americans

- Won't sue for libel and slander
- Care more about the reputations of their slandered businesses than they do holding accusers responsible to provide proof supporting their allegations

- Feel that even if the allegations are false, blacks have been treated so unfairly historically, that they deserve whatever they can extort (give'em an "A" for boldness)
- Don't want to chance that the charges are false, extending the benefit of a doubt (a variation of the rationale for objecting to the much more permanent circumstance of a successful capital punishment)
- Feel that blacks are presumed to be more attuned to subtle racism and, therefore, better able to detect it than whites
- Accept that the (usually) wealthy among the accused have funds enough to disprove a negative–which is, that they *didn't* commit racial discrimination–and that the accuser has too little money to prove baseless allegations.

Let's be honest. But people aren't. They don't confront people who obviously play for a race team. They don't demand impartial examination of individual issues. They don't confront people who use deceptive and deflective arguments based on racial irrelevancy: "It's because I'm black, isn't it?" They don't voice their objections to deceptive, race-based campaigns because they might be falsely accused of racism, which may negatively impact the opinion of those in business and society who matter. Though they resent that they must study, pay for college education, and gain experience to qualify for jobs that many blacks can get simply by making the employer fear allegations of racism, a number of non-minorities often don't rock the boat.

People are overwrought with the possibility of racism, viewing racism as a given when people of different races in America get together. Minorities condition the mindsets of other minorities and anyone who wants to be part of a cause, to see racism as a major factor in every innocent transaction. Emphasis on conflict between the races, for some, makes racism a latent factor in the everyday actions and assumptions of mainstream American life, giving allegations of racism far greater credibility than they deserve. The felony indictments of four adults for arson and ethnic intimidation for burning a cross on a black family's lawn in Middletown, Ohio, also lend credence to suspicions of racism in cases like the electrical short in the light behind the church cross in Dayton. Unsubstantiated and premature blame for a hate crime indicates that people are thinking in ways that are constrained by a need to see racial controversy where it doesn't likely exist.

Increasingly, the term racism is being misapplied to perceived racial injustices that don't merit the charge. Charging racism as a means of rebuking people who exhibit garden-variety prejudice was an initially successful technique for eliciting compassion and condemning whites, who felt an urgency to address the alleged racist action. Racial etiquette, according to columnist Walter Williams, "requires that whites not openly criticize blacks, ask embarrassing questions, or hold blacks and whites to the same conduct and performance standards" (Williams).

Playing the race card, a term popularized in nominee Clarence Thomas' confirmation hearing and during the O.J. Simpson murder trial, has an insidious impact on race relations. According to Blauner, the "tendency to cite racism as a blanket explanation for all manifestations" of failure erodes "the black community's belief in its own autonomy and capacity for self-determination and to minimize the value of individual responsibility" (Blauner, pp. 318–319).

In contrast to racial discrimination, racism isn't illegal. Illegal actions, and sometimes intentions, gain the attention of investigatory, law enforcement, and prosecutory authorities. However, those who cite racism as a way to gain attention and perhaps preferential treatment rely on emotionally explosive rather than rational reactions to false charges. A rational reaction would be to force frauds to prove that the accused has, beyond having a politically incorrect attitude, committed an actual crime, and then prove damages. The burden of proof should be the accuser's.

However, charges of racism must be answered, especially now since proven racist attitudes as motivation in the commission of a crime translate to longer prison sentencing through hate crime legislation. It's no longer just a dubious honor just to be called a racist in a press release by small but powerful and volatile minority groups known for directing their appeals to the emotions.

Racial discrimination *is* illegal and, in theory, must be proven by the accuser. Equal employment laws (set by the Equal Employment Opportunity Commission (EEOC)) state that people can't be discriminated against in their bid for employment based on their race, creed, religion, sex, and age. Job applicants who suspect that the hiring and promotion practices of a company are racially discriminatory must provide proof that racial considerations motivated those with the power to hire and fire. Until "you have established that an evil act has been committed, it is utterly worthless to proceed on the basis of motive" (Fumento, pp. 139–140). Suspicions, denouncements, and condemnations based on nothing more than a feeling and the ultimate failure to land a job are insupportable in court. As with any psychological and emotional state of mind, until the racist translates his feelings into written, verbal, and physical action, those feelings are difficult for external observers to prove, making allegations of racism impossible to prove. They're also impossible to reliably disprove, which makes them easy to assert.

Allegations of racial discrimination burst onto the front pages of newspapers and quietly disappear from public view on the back pages, whether or not the accuser's story bore out as true. Most news reports sway the public to root for the underdog, and purport that the onus of proving a negative (that discrimination didn't occur) in a no-win confrontation is on the accused employer or service provider. Did the accused actually participate in an egregious racial injustice against a minority? Maybe the case was settled in arbitration out of court else risk attracting more bad publicity if the accused does nothing, receiving no follow-up publicity. Maybe the accuser cut bait and left the inhospitable corporate pond. Maybe the corporate victims capitulated, caught in a coercive double-bind of having to deny the unprovable, making them appear unconvincing and slightly ridiculous. Corporate victims can pay off their accusers and ask them to retract their statements and go away. Alternately, they can hire the demonstrably unqualified and deceitful accuser, planning to find some duty in the company that the accuser may be competent to execute, or planning to phase out the job and the employee in the near future. In government civil service positions, office managers often have a six-month employee probationary period in which to develop viable grounds to fire employees who don't fit race preferences but who were able to pass the competency test. Few whites hired in, and then summarily fired from, predominantly black city government offices lodge complaints of racial discrimination, happy to learn a life lesson on par with "lending a friend $20 and never seeing him again is worth it."

Witnesses are usually in the break room when an employer or organization states, "Because you are black, I'm not giving you this job or the chance to participate." The absence of witnesses, failure to prove a history of racially discriminatory practices within a company, and inability to demonstrate that an action was racially motivated make proving a case difficult for people outside of a company or organization. Laws that require businesses to post documents regarding their conformance to racial equality in the workplace, and employer sponsoring of in-house sensitivity training regarding race issues have further insulated companies against charges of racial discrimination.

Many falsely accused victims surrender because they can't afford the time and energy and money required to prove that a person's race, religious background, ethnic affiliation, or physical handicap were not factors in a corporate decision to withhold perceived rewards or opportunities. Employers will often grant rewards rather than attempt to prove conformance to equal employment laws. In either possible response–attempting to disprove the allegation or surrendering in the interest of saving energy, time, and money–the use of the racism charge as a tactic is validated.

> **Premise:** The tactic of charging racism strengthens with every success, gaining attention and forcing reaction with little honest effort by accusers.

Those who understand the difficulty of proving illegal racial discrimination are sympathetic when they hear of alleged incidents; it feels unreasonable to expect financially strapped minorities who may have little access to good counsel to build a case under the legal tenets that everyone else is expected to use. It doesn't seem fair that people who cite racism are increasingly assumed to be crying over sour grapes for failures that may be caused by other factors. It doesn't seem fair that those in power aren't legally bound to take some responsibility to prove their integrity, to allay the doubts evoked by those who charge racial discrimination. The American public unrealistically views an instance of alleged racial discrimination as an unconscionable affront against an entire race rather than against a single job applicant.

Business can be viewed as either a scapegoat example of hard-hearted business interests, developing a bad reputation for squashing the powerless, disadvantaged minority, or a compassionate and racially sensitive model, a laudable representative of employers and service providers everywhere. In fact, businesses fall along a continuum of ethics, not all lily white, not all cowardly wimps, and not all interested in being culturally diverse.

Corporations can repudiate accusations, maintaining that they encourage a multicultural work place. Employers who discriminate find ways to get around laws, such as preferring to hire from within the organization, though laws require public advertisement of open positions. Corporations are now diverting efforts into exercising additional care to avoid accusations, often sacrificing profits to generate the perception that they are attuned to the problems of minorities, that they are politically correct. They submit out of fear that their community image will be tarnished, spending to improve their public image because a good image is good business sense.

The accused rarely acts from a sense of guilt to immolate the accuser, but more from a sense of potential loss of respect in the eyes of people whose opinion means something more substantial. They surrender because they fear repercussive financial damage, not through reprisals from accusers or their friends, but from potential boycott reprisals by others who blindly accept the veracity of unfounded accusations. The buying public often fails to analyze the evidence underlying accusations; fails to question the motivations of accusers; fails to consider that for every minority who didn't get the job, ten whites also didn't get the job; and fallaciously equates disparity in racial representation in any profession with racially discriminatory hiring practices rather than the absence of qualified or interested minority job candidates.

Corporations are forced to counter-manipulate public perceptions and hope that, through their conscientious cultural diversity programs, they can prove that they are racially neutral when their human resources personnel decide that a minority applicant isn't qualified to perform an advertised job. They learn to fight manufactured perceptions with manufactured perceptions, and the touchy area of racially discriminatory practices is circumvented, at a great cost to corporations, a cost that they often decide to pass along to customers.

Where gains have traditionally been obtained through hard work, political debate, persuasive rhetoric, and threats of violence and actual violence, now it can be obtained through the hint that someone or some company is racist. Nonminority corporate insiders need not worry; they may still make plausible allegations of sexual harassment to achieve similar promotion gains.

> **Premise:** The racism routine is successful because it affects perceptions, which affect profit margins. The routine diverts attention from the more likely reasons for an individual's failure.

Corporations and distributors can also appease accusers by expanding marketing efforts to include the interests of non-target ethnic markets. It isn't profitable to design a limited line of specialty products and address those products to a small percentage of the population by race, the members of which may have relatively little purchasing power in contrast to majority populations. The fishing gear retailer in a predominantly white community may surrender precious shelf space to stock Jheri curl hair products targeted to blacks just to avoid being accused of discriminating against black consumers who might stop in with the unrealistic expectation of finding anything but fishing poles and lures. Cable network providers sacrifice profits to broadcast programs in areas with low demand and for which advertisers can't be found so that the provider can show circumstantial proof of its multiculturalism.

> **Premise:** False charges of racial discrimination divert attention from actions for which legal remedies *are* available. This diversion of resources is termed opportunity cost.

When denouncing false allegations of racial discrimination, corporate spokes-people and politicians face attacks by special interest groups who jump on any statement that underplays discrimination as a reason for anemic success by minorities. The goal of the outcry is to compel institutions to restore dignity by censuring those who voice rational dissent and stepping up plans to give minorities more opportunities in the institutions. These opportunities are available as affirmative action and quota programs and costly education programs/grants for the minority group.

Sometimes, small businesses can't win no matter what they do. Take the case of Mike Welbel, the owner of the Daniel Lamp Company in Chicago. Local government stated that the region in which he ran his business would dictate that he hire 8.45 black employees. He had hired only 5.0, unable to find less than a whole person in the job market if he tried. He also employed 21 Hispanics, since his business was located in a largely Hispanic community. A black female applicant for a position Welbel advertised who was denied employment cried racism and the federal investigation got underway. Based on the regulations drawn up by the EEOC, Welbel was asked to spend $10,000 for newspaper ads seeking blacks who had applied but had not been hired by his company, and then another $123,991 to pay them for not working for him. After 18 months of negotiations, Welbel whittled the total amount to $25,000, $5,000 going to the lady who accused him of not hiring her because of her race, and the rest being paid in installments to the EEOC. In this case, the store owner's inability to disprove the accuser's allegations cost him dearly, and cost the accuser nothing.

Failure to sign or re-award contracts with minority suppliers of industry manufacturing components has led to charges of racial discrimination. If a manufacturer is cutting the ranks of its suppliers and one supplier happens to be minority owned, that supplier often voices concern that the cut was motivated by race, failing to consider that if race were a concern, the company wouldn't have signed the supplier's contract in the first place.

> **Premise:** The option of minorities to threaten charges of racial discrimination holds corporations hostage, giving those minorities who are unscrupulous the option to become incompetent in their jobs, unprofessional, and belligerent, until such documented behavior may be cited by extorted businesses as reason for dismissal.

Attempting to disprove any racial discrimination charge lends assumed validity to even the most spurious claims. If all cases were to go to court, the judicial process would sink in the bogs of circumstantial and hearsay evidence. People who falsely charge racial discrimination know this. They also know that discrimination is usually committed by those in positions of power. Since powerful figures also have more money, they're more often targets for low-rate accusers looking for a quick extortion. Americans feel obligated to ensure that discrimination doesn't occur, that weaker minority members are not victimized. We want to err on the side of humanity and safety, on the side of those who can most afford to pay for the benefit of a doubt. Common opinion makes the "haves" feel obligated to disprove allegations of racial discrimination by the "have-nots," thereby partially dignifying the allegations and increasing their credibility.

False charges of racial discrimination capitalize on the desire of Americans to appear politically correct, to right wrongs, to take responsibility for the misfortunes of others, regardless of how those misfortunes were induced. The method is easy to use, quick, dirty, achieves instant parity through fear, and relies on a double standard: minorities can use it with greater credibility than whites. It bypasses accepted channels for advancement and material gain, making the avenue to success much shorter for minorities. No other single method gets such quick results, not education, not hard work, not respect for others and earning respect from others, and not using the system of rewards for performance and withheld rewards for failure.

Distrust of those who allege racial discrimination without hard evidence, whether honestly or dishonestly, is making discrimination even more difficult to prove. Racists destroy evidence, and most evidence is often intangible or easily refutable. Accusers can't afford the time to get evidence, time best used to be making other unsubstantiated allegations. Many poor don't have the kind of resources and connections to see allegations through the court's due process. Suspicion that someone has actually deprived a black because of race is increasingly making claims less plausible. Denouncement of a person's actions as racist is not proof.

Charges of racism give politicians looking for black votes additional opportunities to make even more promises they can't keep. In classic race baiting to stoke the fires of racial animus, white politicians pretend that they side with black resentment. They want to please minorities, invoking guilt in white voters who would ignore race issues, scrambling through black townships in their avarice for votes, or aping the idiocies of fringe black spokespersons, careless about the social and economic repercussions if momentarily championed policies were ever enacted, exacerbating racial tension and black voter indecision. Political lobbyists, coordinators of political campaign contributions, PACs, and special interest groups who exclusively benefit from gifts that attest to a politician's power might disagree that discriminatory application of laws serves only the collective interests of minorities, but these myopic advocates are paid not to extend their efforts in the interests of the general populace.

Black politicians follow suit: Sharp James, black, mayor of Newark, N.J. since 1986, racialized the 2002 mayoral race, calling his Democrat opponent a white Republican to divert attention from the issues. Politicians mirror the argument that not enough blacks are in political office jobs, and if elected, they promise to ensure appointments. In clever insinuations, they accuse opponents of being racist. Racism becomes just another campaign strategy. Politicians may lie to block judge nominations to the Supreme Court and to portray Clarence Thomas as a racial traitor (Charen, p. 46). The charges give reporters opportunities to criticize, to indignantly condemn, to demonstrate their social consciousness, and to persuade the public to be altruistic and less egocentric. But mostly, the media uses the charges to fill their drab front pages and foment generalized anger against heartless, monolithic political campaigns—a convenient enemy when no corporations have been accused recently.

Most people who charge racial discrimination intend to defraud and deceive for anticipated profits, not because they actually have been slighted based on their race. Racial profiteers are rewarded with media and peer attention, government policy changes to provide unfair and preferential treatment to populations based on their race, or payoffs (legal settlements by the falsely, and sometimes legitimately, accused employers). To repair a history of disenfranchisement, government bodies pass discriminatory laws that support unequal and favorable treatment based on minority race. These laws include affirmative action policies, hiring quota algorithms, subsidies for black business enterprises, public assistance, and social programs for the poor, a greater percentage by population of whom are minorities.

Charging racial discrimination as a first resort does not mean that racial discrimination doesn't exist or doesn't exist in the alleged instance. Instances of proven racial discrimination give even greater credibility than unproven charges to all charges of racial discrimination, so accusations of racial discrimination ought to be individually and scrupulously tested. Many instances of adverse, unequal treatment of minorities have been legally decided. A Denny's restaurant in San Francisco forced groups of 10 or more blacks to prepay or pay cover charges after 10 p.m., denied them free birthday meals, subjected them to racially hostile comments or asked them to leave the restaurant. In a suit filed against Denny's, co-counsel Patricia Price for the defendants said that the policy requiring groups of 10 or more to prepay after 10 p.m. applied without regard for race.

Free birthday meals were denied when applicants couldn't produce documents certifying that their birth dates coincided with their patronage on a given day. Subsequent allegations followed, most notably by a group of black Secret Service agents visiting Denny's as bodyguards for President Clinton, who was scheduled to visit the restaurant. It should be emphasized that Denny's wasn't charged with racially discriminatory hiring practices, but with being rude to black customers.

Racism isn't charged only against businesses, which have deep pockets and frightened public relations attorneys who advise payoffs. Evidence of the divisiveness of unsupported charges of racism can also be found at universities. Indiana University basketball coach Bobby Knight felt the heat of charges of racism when he posed over one of his players with a leather bullwhip given to him by his players. Knight said his players were spoofing his image as a taskmaster when they gave him the whip and that he was using it as a motivational tool. The NAACP was flooded with calls that Knight should be fired for his "racist" behavior. Frivolous character assassination based on false charges of racism can ruin a person's life, career, family, and chances of ever re-gaining respect in his or her field of expertise.

Jermaine O'Neal, in an amazing twist of logic, linked racism to the NBA's desire to put a minimum age limit on professional basketball players being drafted into the league: "As a black guy, you kind of think that's the reason why it's coming up. You don't hear about it in baseball or hockey. To say you have to be 20, 21 to get in the league, it's unconstitutional. If I can go to the U.S. Army and fight the war at 18, why can't you play basketball for 48 minutes?" (FOX-Sports.com, April 12, 2005). The racism connection that O'Neal is implying is that black athletes don't have many options for earning money during high school and soon after graduating high school; since sports is one way out of poverty for many black males, increasing the age limit postpones primarily black athletes from earning their fortunes. There was no concern that white athletes would use the years up to the new age limit to become better b-ballers and possibly take a black athlete's spot based on merit. O'Neal had no evidence that Commissioner David Stern and the collective bargaining committee used age limits as an insidious means of effectively practicing an indirect, less identifiable brand of covert racism. The more probable reason for raising the draft age limit is to allow athletes the option of attending college after high school, allowing them to gain both an education and the discipline imposed by college basketball programs. More mature basketball players often have more court experience, are closer to being worth what owners pay them, and have a better idea how to handle the riches.

People have lost their jobs after being charged with racism. James Parry, an administrator at Wright State University in Fairborn, Ohio, was fired after Karen Townsend, a colleague and coordinator of WSU's Minority Scholars Access and Achievement Program, accused him of racism when he said that he would not be comfortable with a minority political member serving as chairperson of the committee. Parry is white; Townsend, who was in line to become chairperson, is black. Parry filed a counter federal lawsuit, denying any racist intent in his language, and asserting that his constitutional rights of due process and free speech were violated when he was dismissed.

Spike Lee, producer and director of the film *Malcolm X* is notorious for his high-visibility charges of racism. He charged that the film industry was racist when it placed a funding cap on *Malcolm X.* He accused Warner Brothers of skimping on financing, saying that the studio had thrown away much more money on bad movies by white directors. Lee did not produce statistics for the number of films whose financing Warner had capped for going $5 million over budget, nor did he describe how such excess placed *Malcolm X* under the control of a completion bond company. He also failed to note that the white directors he used in his argument of racial favoritism had a history of making films that raked in money at the box offices in the past, a track record that makes studios more willing to take risks with them.

Spike has stated that he prefers to be interviewed by black journalists. Warner Brothers "insisted that [Lee] had not set down a rigid rule barring whites from interviewing him." "'What I'm doing is using whatever clout I have to get qualified African-Americans assignments. The real crime is white publications don't have black writers, that's the crime.' Lee said black journalists would be more responsive and sympathetic to the events of *Malcolm X.* 'If newspapers or magazines can't find a black writer to write about Malcolm X, then what's the point?'" (Weinraub).

If Spike were interested in getting black writers assignments, why wouldn't he try to get them assignments in general, not just for himself, and for other predominantly white publications, interviewing white celebrities, too? There is no evidence that same-race interviewer and subject make for more interesting biographical articles, though Lee was probably hoping he'd get more sympathy play from a black writer than from a white one, under the fatuous principle that only another brother would understand what a brother goes through in a racist society. And the presence of few blacks on magazine writing staffs isn't evidence of a crime, as Lee asserts.

In other Warner Brothers news, anticipated charges of racism led Warner Brothers brass to change a scripted version of Tom Wolfe's The Bonfire of the Vanities: "the most sympathetic character was a white Jewish judge who has no problem putting a pack of opportunists–most of them black–in their place." The book from which the script for the film was adapted depicted a Jew dominating blacks, so Warner Brothers cast a black actor, Morgan Freeman, in the judge's role (Arar, *Dayton Daily News*) to avert race controversy. Warner Brothers knew that double standards allowed blacks to berate other blacks and still be viewed as a racially traitorous demanding father figure, but that a white in the same position would kick up charges of Jewish racism.

Cities are not immune. Xenia, Ohio, is often accused of being a racist town by black students from Wilberforce and Central State University, two predominantly black institutions that are less than two miles from Xenia. The support for these accusations is that businesses in Xenia do not hire Wilberforce and CSU students. Managers of these businesses also watch the students very closely when they come into stores, implying that because the students are black, the merchants feel they will steal. The fact is that any group of transient young students wouldn't be trusted and make unlikely candidates for hiring. Students at a commuter college are rowdy, have little money, and often have not learned the value of good work ethic, such as being at work on time. Also, since most of the students have commuted from inner cities where crime is more prevalent, they bring with them a reputation, a belief which was enforced in those businesses that did take chances hiring and allowing students to roam through stores unsupervised. The students were undependable employees, were late, stole merchandise from businesses, stole merchandise as customers, and helped their friends steal merchandise. It is not true that merchants in Xenia do not hire blacks. They hire adult blacks who live in Xenia; they just don't hire visiting students.

Communities generally respond to charges of racism by launching corrective campaigns against social injustice and by compensating victims. Cities attempt to attract developers and convince expanding companies to locate new plants and offices into areas where blacks live to ensure a predominantly black work force, thereby avoiding charges of endemic government racism.

Lending institutions are also accused of conspiring to keep black communities from flourishing. When minorities do receive financial backing, the amount of the loaned capital is frequently reported to be not enough to give the new business a solid start. When granted, the loans are reported to be for amounts less than similarly qualified whites receive. And when loans are made, such as for car purchases, the interest for blacks averages 7 percent versus 5 percent for whites as of May 2007 in Dayton, Ohio. The way the statistic is phrased screams that race is the reason for the disparity.

Blacks, resentful of what they are asked to believe are denied loans and higher repayment interest levels for blacks because of their race, then claim that they receive less money in loans because they're black, and because whites want all the power with none of the black competition. Bankers, white and black, care less about how minority-owned businesses stack up in competition with mainstream businesses than about getting their money back, with contractual interest. The details not revealed in charges of racism against banks is the poor performance rating a loan officer receives for every defaulted loan he makes, and how poor performance reviews make him cautious. Rates of loan defaults and statistics on business failings tell lenders that black borrowers are more likely to default. What does "similarly qualified" mean when applied to whites by minorities denied loans? Does it mean that both applicants walked into the bank? The area in which the minority businessman plans to do business may show higher fail rates than businesses in a similar, integrated, geographic area. The criteria–credit histories, applicant assets, strength of a business plan, and employment experience–for making loans and how minorities don't meet the criteria is a more probable reason for racial disparity in bank lending practices.

A case of high rates of black loan applicant rejection by banks in Georgia generated "widespread attention partly because it illustrates the sharply limited options minorities confront when they must borrow money. Federal and private studies show, for example, that banks reject black applicants for mortgages at more than twice the rate of white applicants."

Changing the word "race" to "unqualified applicants" or "qualified applicants" on bank loan applications would remove the racial connection, and the focus of the news story would have to change from an implied accusation that race was a primary causal factor to poor qualifications to obtain bank loans.

Sometimes, when minorities run afoul of the law, their defense is to charge racism. Dayton, Ohio funeral director Wayne Wheat blamed racism when the State Board of Embalmers and Funeral Directors fined him $20,000 for allegedly mishandling a body: "'That's only because I'm a black man,' Wheat said. 'I'm merely a victim of a racist system. All these boards you have to go in front of do not understand black-on-black business'" (Bray, *Dayton Daily News*, January 30, 1992). The mishandled body was that of a black woman whose family could not pay for Wheat's burial services. The following year Wheat was under investigation for running a crack cocaine distribution center out of his funeral establishments.

An especially questionable use of the racism charge was made by Melvin Girton, a black reverend who asserted that Mike Tyson, the former heavyweight boxer, would not get a fair trial for raping an 18-year-old Miss Black America beauty pageant contestant on July 19, 1991 unless three blacks, rather than two, sat on the jury. During the trial in Indianapolis, Girton said that Indianapolis "'is a known racist, conservative town.... They thought they got the toughest woman … who has been tough on black men,' he said. 'The two black men on the jury can decide in Tyson's favor, guaranteeing him at least a hung jury'" (Simms). During the trial, exhibit posters on which was written "Justice and Fairness for Mike Tyson. The World is Watching Indianapolis" were stapled to trees and sides of buildings. The implication of the language was that if Mike Tyson were convicted, he would be convicted because of his race, which would make it unjust and unfair. Girton used implicit racial discrimination charges in an attempt to sway public opinion and failed to recognize that his solution, three blacks in the jury, presumes that all blacks are prejudiced in favor of other blacks, in much the same way that a black interviewer is presumed to be partial to a black celebrity and won't report the celebrity's negative news. Girton's misguided presumption that blacks must sit on the jury in a trial with a black defendant insults whites, insinuating that whites can't be objective, are racist, or can't understand or unfairly discount the mitigating factor of race to the commission of the crime.

The two black men on the jury did *not* decide in Tyson's favor.

When a large proportion of urban black high school students fails to meet standards of achievement, black organizations often cite racial reasons for the failure, whether the reasons are that blacks have always been discriminated against, or because the testing procedures are biased and unfair. George L. Forbes, an official with the NAACP, using circular logic, charged that the "statewide proficiency tests which [Ohio] high school students must pass to graduate are unfair to minorities because they have been victims of discrimination" (*Dayton Daily News*). According to the newspaper report, the racial fairness of the test was less an issue in the failing of 1600 Cleveland high school juniors than how failure would affect the chances of the students to get well-paying jobs without diplomas.

In an attempt to reduce racist attitudes, some blame racism for contributing to an overall poor economy in the hopes that people will focus on the imperative task of improving the economy while forgetting to question whether there is a significant connection between racism and the economy. Stuart Butler, an economist at the conservative Heritage Foundation, stated that the imprisonment of 25 percent of black men and teenagers exacted an annual price tag in 1990 of about

$7 billion. His blanket conclusion was that "Racism always leads to a reduction in the GNP in any country" (*Dayton Daily News*, August 1992).

Perceptions of race and what constitutes racism are most clear in unguarded commentaries by regular folk. In his book of interviews on race issues, Studs Terkel got a variety of viewpoints about race: "'To be a racist, you have to be able to oppress another race. To do that, you have to have economic and political power'" (Terkel, quoting Kelly, p. 205). Every employer, manager, court judge, teacher, and prison guard is a potential racist by this definition. Every minority in these positions could be a racist. It's unclear what constitutes oppression. Anyone can be called a racist for denying either power or privilege to one or more members of another race for any reason. According to this view, anyone who has the component requirement of being *able to* exercise the power to oppress anyone, regardless of anyone's race, can be a racist.

Other comments to Terkel illustrate white frustration, fatigue, and resentment: "'I'm tired of caring. I don't feel guilty anymore. They [the blacks] can just look after themselves. I keep wondering what kind of message young blacks have been getting these past fifteen years from society at large. Perhaps they've been encouraged to think of themselves as victims and that the system is stacked against them. The message would be: "You're bound to fail and it's okay to fail. It's not your fault." That must surely inculcate fatalism'" (Terkel quoting Rian Malan, p. 328). Such comments reflect that the public in general, including blacks, is tired of black excuses—racial discrimination—for failure.

Charges of racism have been leveled by respected and powerful black citizens for failures of blacks to fairly compete against other qualified candidates for jobs. Discrepancies in the quality of housing between white and black neighborhoods have been blamed on racist realty practices, while real factors for the discrepancies, and thus real solutions, were left unexamined. Locating landfills and waste dumps in predominantly poor communities is often blamed on racist policy rather than interest in the geological qualities that make an area viable as a dump site or of precedent in an area for the creation of future dumps; some of the poor can't afford to live in more attractive areas that don't have landfills that depress the property values. Racism is often cited as the cause of harsh police action against minorities. Some accuse urban police forces of racism for not being more diligent in stopping opposing black gang members from killing one another. Some minorities, with straight faces, have cited racial discrimination because they haven't been given *preferential* treatment over whites. Some have accused the U.S. Government of racism for not going to war to protect Tutsis who were slaughtered in Rwanda by the Hutus, though the U.S. had no business interests nor security threats in Rwanda.

Of course, charging racism for the exclusion of a black-oriented cable channel trivializes and dilutes the impact of the method. Charging racism in the midst of other horrendous offenses to humankind also trivializes it. A black minister, asked to comment about Jeffrey Dahmer's inhuman crimes, in a blatant move to gain attention for the issue of racism, cited racism as Dahmer's major offense. The minister's observation asserts that racism is more horrendous than cannibalism, murder, necrophilia, homosexual rape, and sociopathic psychosis.

In the hearings to confirm Clarence Thomas as a Supreme Court judge, Clarence Thomas blamed the subjection of his moral goodness to public scrutiny as a racist conspiracy to make him appear unworthy. At the time, so much was written about how his nomination was based on his race, it seemed a natural conclusion that the accusations of Anita Hill were also based on Thomas' race, as well. Clarence Thomas' mother, after her son was elected to the Supreme Court, told television reporters, "I pray for those who didn't vote for my son," insinuating that they were racists, and racists go to hell.

The excessiveness of charges of racism and demands for political correctness are subject to endless lampooning. In a *Saturday Night Live* skit, two white men attempt to rob a bank whose customers are predominantly black. Black customers in the bank accuse the robbers of racism because they selected the black man's bank to rob. One of the robbers attempts to explain that they selected the bank based on their analysis of its weak security system. During the apologetic explanation, the police arrive and the robbers flee without the money. After they'd gone, a black bank teller complains that had the bank's customers been white, the robbers would have taken hostages, implying that racial parity means demanding that blacks not be deprived of even the pain and suffering normally reserved for whites.

The skit demonstrates how ridiculous some accusations of racism are, but more importantly, it shows how these accusations lead to desired results: one of the white robbers, feeling slightly guilty, fearing that they weren't being politically correct or sensitive to black concerns, wastes time consoling their accusers, giving the police time to arrive. The skit also demonstrates that the reasons behind actions—such as robbing the bank—may have no racial motivation.

There's a lot in the charges of racism that defies logic: robbers hypothetically taking hostages if the SNL's skit bank customers had been white, for instance. People wonder if outcomes would differ if the races of the participants were changed out. "Had I been white, things would be different," or "if I hadn't been black" are examples of veiled, insulting, and ridiculous charges of racism. At the moment an undesired action occurs, no one can ever know that a different action would have resulted had the color of the person's skin been different. It is unreasonable to ask others to believe that if eventualities could be proven, then blacks would be able to demonstrate discrimination. Even if racial discrimination is disproved, the accusation can still be made that the investigations that provided the proof, or the criteria on which the proof is based, is biased, which asks those in charge of disproving a negative to further examine their methodology.

Completely unprovable, some statements project into the future had something in the past not happened: "Blacks would not have made their current advances had it not been for the efforts of specific past black leaders." The future can't be reliably predicted from hypothetical changes in the past of someone's race. No one can say whether other black leaders wouldn't have emerged with the same ideas and better communication methods if not for the leader who had actually garnered all of the attention. Every preceding generation lays the groundwork, or destroys the ground, for the next generation, regardless of race, and often without an intention to lay groundwork. Sometimes, people simply live their lives and allow their children to live their lives.

Quaint, metaphorical slogans also defy logic to the point of being downright lies. The assertion that denied equality for one is equality denied for all is a false metaphor based on the incorrect premise that all humans have the same degree of social connection to all other humans, based on a single factor, such as a miscarriage of justice. All blacks don't belong to a symbolic family, and improving the circumstances of one doesn't directly affect the circumstances of another. Altruist, socialist, liberal assertions of connectedness and assumed responsibility for others' lives in the community based on similar race, age, and goals are complete socialistic ... idealism. One person's hardships or hardships endured by any person of the same racial composition, do not excuse or justify criminal, unethical, immoral behavior. Many blacks irrationally believe that blacks are more connected based on race than whites are. Sometimes, black victims have to be mugged several times by a socially affable and friendly fellow black to disabuse them of this faulty feeling.

Anyone who states that all whites today have some kind of diluted personal responsibility for slavery that morally obligates them to make reparation is either lying or rote regurgitating the lies of others. People who make such allegations turn a white's personal sense of honor against him, likely place little value on the concept of true personal responsibility, possibly live their lives shunning their own personal responsibilities, and publicly impugn their own integrity by uttering the allegation. It's sad that so many whites, seeking racial redemption, surrender to such lies.

Another shot at parodying allegations of racism was taken by Garry Trudeau in his "Doonesbury" comic strip. In the story line, a university professor is flabbergasted and incredulous that impartially applied standards for achieving quantifiable grades on math tests can be questioned on grounds of racism and nationalism ... by a white student in a Greek fraternity. The student accuses the teacher of being racist and the proofs in math to be "absolutist, Eurocentric ...," defending his incorrect answers to a math problem as arguably correct from a cultural perspective and demanding entitlements based on the professor's low expectations of frat brothers. The math professor's participation in an illogical argument with the student lands the school in a $5 million lawsuit for stigmatizing and stereotyping the Greek culture.

The health care industry frequently comes under attack for perceived slights based on patient race. It is true that most of the blacks on the waiting list for organ transplants are near the bottom of the list. So are poor whites who also can't afford to bribe doctors, whose bodies are also distressed by poverty, and who waited too long lacking health care insurance to get preventive checkups, making them poor candidates for organ transplants. Since about a third of the black race is disproportionately represented in the roles of the poor, blacks are also disproportionately represented for services that being poor has made them ill-prepared to receive.

Unequal health care is the stated reason that blacks don't live as long as whites: "Middle-age black men are dying at nearly twice the rate of white men of a similar age, reflecting lower incomes and poorer access to health care" (*Dayton Daily News*, p. A5). The journal *Health Affairs* devoted most of its March/April 2005 issue to the topic of health care discrepancies between races. Relatively "low incomes of black men compared with whites, a rise in gun-related deaths among blacks, their disproportionately high death rate from AIDS, and higher rates of heart disease and diabetes" are a few of the factors in the discrepancies. In a story a year later, Jeff Donn reported that a study by the Rand Health research institute showed that "... once in treatment, minorities' overall care appears similar to that of whites" (Donn, *Dayton Daily News*, March 16, 2007).

Terje Anderson, director of the National Association of People With AIDS comments on reports of findings of the 12th Annual Retrovirus Conference held in Boston: "We just have a burgeoning epidemic in the African American community that is not being dealt with effectively.... Researchers and AIDS prevention advocates attribute the high rate among blacks to such factors as drug addiction, poverty and poor access to health care." The rise in the prevalence of the AIDS virus is from 1 percent to 2 percent of blacks. White rates held steady at 0.2 percent. Though blacks make up only 12 percent of the population in the U.S., 68 percent of all new HIV cases in 2004 were in the black population, with fully 50 percent in black women between the ages of 24 and 45. Blacks are 13 times more likely to die of HIV than whites with HIV. 500,000 blacks in the U.S. are infected with HIV, according to 2005 CDC statistics, a little fewer than half of all cases of people with HIV. In prison, the rates of HIV among black males is 5 times higher than in the general population, with 40 percent of men of all races in prison admitting to having sex with other male inmates during their incarceration. The high rates of AIDS deaths in and imprisonment of black males explains the diminishing ratio of black males to black females outside of prison, currently averaging 85 males to every 100 females of marriageable age, giving black males, even with HIV, more heterosexual mating options with black females desperate for partnerships and families, though those very same options often compel horny, savvy, infected black males to play the field of desperate black females.

Minorities in South Central L.A. blamed white racist culture and jury verdicts in the Rodney King case to excuse their rioting, which was carried out primarily by black male looters and vandals who destroyed and pillaged black and Korean-owned businesses. Given free rein while remaining anonymous in the face and force of mobs of indignation, the rioters destroyed and stole from businesses owned by their own race, so their response to "racist" verdicts was simply an opportunity to steal and destroy with the imprimatur of racism's blank check. In a creative attempt to include whites as greedy recipients of the spoils of racism charges in Nashville, North Carolina, "Four young whites shot a black man and set fires in hopes of starting a race riot so they could loot stores. The four also were charged with painting racial slurs on school property"(*Dayton Daily News*, November 18, 1992).

Racism should not be used as "a legitimizing rationale for violence, crime or the endemic problems of the urban poor" (Morganthau, p. 28). Colin Ferguson, the Jamaican gunman on the Long Island Railroad commuter train who killed 5 white passengers and wounded 20 more, blamed "Adelphi University racism, EEOC racism, Workmen's Compensation Board. Racism of Gov. Cuomo's staff.... Additional reasons for this: Caucasian racism and Uncle Tom Negroes" (*Dayton Daily News*, December 9, 1993, p. A1).

Premise: There are extremists on all sides of race issues.

Black activists frequently target the criminal justice system and the dispropor-tionately large number of imprisoned blacks as evidence of a racist system. Inves-tigations were conducted to discover possible racial disparity in the stiffer prison sentences in Minnesota for crack cocaine possession than for powdered cocaine. Crack cocaine is used and sold almost exclusively by inner-city blacks, whereas more affluent whites use powdered cocaine. The disparate sentencing was thought to be racist because, under federal sentencing guidelines, a gram of crack calls for the same sentence as received for possession of 100 grams of powdered cocaine. However, Congress reasoned that crack is easier to transport and can be more addictive. Its relative affordability makes it easier for children to obtain. Also, one gram of powdered cocaine costs about $100 and that amount can pro-duce 10 doses of crack costing $20 to $25 each.

Those in lower economic strata often use charges of racism to position them-selves as superior to newcomers. This brand of racism allows existing community members to gain a sense of cohesion because they are fighting the same, easily identifiable encroacher. It allows them to beat another race out of jobs or out of town by making them feel unwelcome, inferior, and powerless. They want to hog resources and use racism to keep another group from getting or successfully com-peting for them.

Some leaders in the black community are launching a massive public relations campaign to trick apathetic whites into thinking that what's good for black soci-ety is good for whites, too. This rising-tide/rising-all theory persuades whites to help blacks. This is in contrast to attempting to gain the support of whites through browbeating, crying racism, inducing guilt complexes for victimization, etc. Another method is to accuse whites of not knowing they are actually racist. Some blacks feel that whites who think they're not racist are even more racist than those who admit it, since they're denying and hiding their racism. Even if racism is not demonstrable through behavior, it is assumed to exist in the subcon-scious. This belief shifts the burden of proof to whites who are asked to quantifi-ably prove their lack of racism by performing acts that directly benefit only blacks or that curtail anti-black sentiments, like protesting KKK marches. Another Freudian re-invention is the use of denial to prove racism. In Freudian psycho-therapy, when patients disagree with their therapists, the theory of denial auto-matically blames the patient, just as some blacks automatically blame racist attitudes if whites disagree that they are racist.

Non-racist whites are in no way obligated to prove they aren't racist by actively showing their disagreement with racist whites. People may disagree with a lot of the propaganda posited by a lot of groups–abortion rights groups, animal rights groups, feminist groups–but not making a visible show of opposition does not indicate that they agree with the tenets espoused by these groups. More often it indicates that the opponents to these groups have a life and don't want to spend their free time participating in opposition groups to prove to those in the opposition groups where their loyalty lay. Many racist groups have zero power and influence, and actively protesting them serves only to give these fringe groups them more visibility, making them more newsworthy, thereby bestowing on them more power simply through greater awareness. Protest is more detrimental to one's own cause than ignoring the small pockets of zealots.

The unforgivable number of flagrantly unsupportable charges of racial discrimination have made the public increasingly immune to their appeal. The middle and lower classes no longer automatically assume that the holders of society's rewards are obligated to disprove the charges, and the tactic is experiencing a backlash brought on by its saturation. Its practitioners are shown to be crying wolf too often, so often, in fact, that blacks can now receive respect and admiration for not charging racism and for accepting responsibility for adversity. Hershel Walker garnered respect when, in good sportsmanship, team spirit, and grace he commented that he understood that he was an inexperienced bobsled team member when he was dismissed from the bobsled team in the 1992 Winter Olympics and couldn't help the team as much as the team's former member could.

The burden of proof is shifting to those making the charges, a relationship usually demanded in legal cases. With the shift to more traditional legal tenets, the fear associated with bad publicity and legal penalties that arises from racial discrimination charges is somewhat abated. One negative effect of this shift is the increasingly probable condition of powerful members of society relaxing their diligence in exercising equality measures. At the other extreme, employers who feel they might be accused of racial discrimination if they don't hire a black may more willfully discriminate, feeling they might as well commit the crime if they're going to be accused of it anyway. Publicized high rates of reckless racial discrimination charges may lead to a self-fulfilling prophecy. Whites are resentful of blacks who change the rules about how to obtain jobs so that blacks have better leverage based not on qualifications, but on employer fear of reprisal.

Gradually, people accused of racism began to lose their fear of being perceived as racists, and rather than buckle immediately, began to challenge their accusers to use the legal system to prove the charges. "The word 'racism' was so recklessly applied in so many different contexts against so many people that it lost any real impact or meaning ..." (Katz, p. 34). The charge became so commonplace that blacks would get loud in traditionally white establishments and dare whites who feared charges of racism to tell groups of loud blacks to keep the noise down. Blacks in race discussions look for opportunities to be offended, and uneasy whites are so careful not to offend, that effective open discussion is sidetracked in favor of not hurting feelings. Race issue discussions become emotionalized and irrational, the debaters quick to believe racist motives in others. Some people will always be offended. That's a personality issue.

The effects that unsupported charges of racial discrimination in implausible contexts can have on the psyche of blacks erodes "the black community's belief in its own autonomy and capacity for self-determination" (Blauner, pp. 318–319). Blauner goes on to assert that externalizing the causes of failure minimizes the "value of individual responsibility" (Blauner, p. 319). Because of psychological partial reinforcement and imperfect conferral of historical knowledge, false, unsupported charges of racism persist.

Though it's suspected that black leaders say unsupportable, racist things just to stir up controversy, apologists defend the numerous demonstrably false or gray-area charges of racism because the charges keep society on its toes. Constant vigilance and alerts for racism ensure that there is no backsliding on civil rights advances.

With the erosion of public support, so erodes the method's efficacy. Though charges of racism bring awareness of a very real, though probably limited, problem to the minds of many people, they must be used judiciously and responsibly. Racial discrimination must be plausibly valid in situations in which it is cited to maximize support for such an accusation. Otherwise, the method's effectiveness as a way to gain action and respect deteriorates, and factual charges may go uninvestigated and then prematurely dismissed as fallacious. Those making the charges are taken less seriously, and they're forced to prove them or else be censured for making false and frivolous, possibly libelous allegations. It is ironic that in the face of government laws that give minorities preferential treatment over whites, minorities still feel they have a legitimate right to falsely charge racism for every perceived slight.

On a personal level, falsely charging racism as an automatic reaction to failure degrades the accuser's mental ability. If enough people believe that the way to succeed is to charge racism, fewer people will bother to learn how to analyze factors that may have really caused a failure, thereby preventing any chance that those factors can be addressed. Also, whites who generalize from specific cases and from their knowledge of psychological principles may diminish their respect for the analytic skills of blacks in general, reversing advances.

Calling acts racist when they aren't is unfortunate because the real issues of race become obscured behind emotionally explosive rhetoric. Those falsely accused will put up a wall, leaving little chance of reaching amicable solutions in debates about race problems. Besides, you can't reason with most true, died-in-the-wool racists, so those who truly believe that others at the table are racist might as well leave rather than attempt to discuss racial issues.

With frequent use of the racism charge may come gradual belief by those making the charge that society is racist. People who lie often enough can come to believe the lie, make the lie part of their identity and memory of their pasts, and interact with others as if the lie were truth. Believing that many failures are attributed to one's race can no doubt lead to a grinding bitterness against other races, and this can lead to racist attitudes. In addition, it must be personally very painful to believe that obstacles are put in the path of minorities because of their race, since people can't change their race or the statistically recorded behaviors of members of one's race that predispose other people to generalize. For those who believe that racism holds them back, the immutable condition of race leads to despair and hopelessness, to self-defeating decisions to fail through inaction since they believe to excel is impossible for most blacks. Blacks who use the excuse of racism don't care about the negative long-term psychological and cultural effects. Using the racism excuse reduces their work load and permits attainment of short-term goals, so they use it to excuse their own personal failure not to acquire skills required to get desirable, high-paying jobs.

Possibly more damaging than the bruised esteem of members of the black community is the failure of the community to believe charges of real racism in the flood of false charges. Some believe that most members of another race are racist, but that's only evidence of fuzzy thinking and lack of clarity. There are race discrimination and prejudice conspiracies, but until they can be proved, baseless allegations serve only to inflame the race debate. Their purpose is to gain the attention and indignation of gullible liberals.

> **Premise:** Allegations of racism aren't evidence of racism, and most allegations are untrue.
> **Premise Corollary:** Racism isn't as rampant as exceptional case histories would mislead people to believe. Racism as an oppressive force today in the United States is a myth.

Ultimately, skeptical of the waves of blatantly unfounded charges of racism, even liberals come down with a case of compassion fatigue. Liberals now blame themselves because they wrongly hyped cultural relativism and trashed performance standards to give the appearance of equal performance by minorities, and many in minority communities simply abused the reconfigurations by failing to meet even the reduced expectations. People begin to ignore charges, fail to reward them, give the accused the benefit of a doubt, and seek alternate explanations for conditions described by the accuser. The backlash of antagonism and resentment sets in, causing everyone to doubt the truthfulness of allegations.

Demands for White Guilt, Black Guilt, Reparation, Apologies, and Entitlements

Justice for past wrongs is better late than never. But whether justice takes an easy path, such as apologizing and allowing bygones to be bygones, or a rough path in which numerous and unreasonable acts of restitution must be performed for unspecified periods of time, true justice can be exacted only on those who committed the offense. Whether the pleas for reparation are plaintive and earnest or harsh and threatening, targeting the wrong people, people who had no hand in constructing or perpetuating offenses against a race of people, simply compounds the injustice. Many who use these tactics realize this, yet continue to profess phony indignation, agreeing to settle for monetary rewards if legal justice must necessarily elude them.

Rational people cringe when they see the horrors of the past exploited for profit. They resent restitution and reparation demands, knowing that a biological connection does not make people responsible for the acts of one's ancestry or others of the same race. Race is one such tenuous connection that doesn't make people responsible for economic conditions of other races.

But we live in a time in which flimsy connections constitute, for many in government, indirect responsibility, a time in which parents can be held responsible for the autonomous bad acts of their children, when bartenders are jailed for serving a customer too many drinks, when stupid people can hold corporations responsible for not imagining all of the stupid things people could do with their products. Whites are tired of hearing that black failure is due to racism and have become suspicious that some blacks call whites racists almost to justify their own racist hatred toward whites, to feel guiltless themselves for continuing to use racially based extortion methods to illegitimately access privileges and benefits in society that are traditionally acquired through honest hard work. Attempts to invoke white guilt are also losing efficacy as more and more whites refuse to take responsibility for the actions of their ancestors, or refuse to believe that there can be a bargaining standard for restituting enslavement.

Premise: Unless one's paid duty demands action, knowledge alone of an injustice does not legally obligate anyone to correct a bad condition. In a rational world, in a society in which whether to accept civic responsibility is still a personal, free choice to make, knowledge of a bad condition presents only the opportunity to consult one's personal credo when deciding whether to act. Awareness of past inhumanity does not morally obligate anyone to retroactively pay damages on behalf of those who committed it.

Humans are interconnected only as much as they each choose to be. People base the degree of their interconnections on economics, law, commonality of interests, family and tribe, and a need for association. Race may be a distinguishing commonality, but it is by choice that members of any race choose to feel inextricably interconnected with others of their race or with those of another race. Choice determines the degree to which someone becomes involved in solving problems that may be more pronounced in another race. Choice contradicts the credibility of black activists who state that any white who isn't part of a race solution is part of the problem. The statement, "if anyone is discriminated against, we're all discriminated against," is a slogan and attempts to solicit help by making others think that racial discrimination is their problem, too, though they may be untouched by, unaffected by, and unaccountable for its practice. The slogan on the 1992 annual Race Unity Day in Dayton, Ohio was "that people in Dayton don't have to learn to live with racism. What they have to do is learn to live without it," which presumes systemic, pervading societal racism.

Such guilt-inducing sloganeering assumes absolute social connections, which are only as real and compelling as audiences believe them to be. A common response to such views follows: "I did not cause the problem. I am not responsible for the problem. I don't have a desire to correct the problem. I may not define your situation as a problem. The problem does not concern me, and if you commit crime to try to make it concern me, I have paid a police force to punish you for criminal acts you commit. People who have been elected to be responsible for the problem are responsible for correcting or minimizing the problem. Charitable people who want to solve the problem may attempt to, but their desire to help does not and should not legally obligate me to help. I have a right to ignore all speeches about the problem. I don't care if you think I'm racist. Think whatever you like. I'm not here to disprove what you think about me."

Physical separation from the problem of race is accomplished by suburbs:

"The accelerated growth of the suburbs has made it possible for many Americans to pursue certain civic ideals (involvement in schools, cooperation in community endeavors, a willingness to support and to pay for public services) within a smaller universe, separate and apart from the consuming failure (crime, welfarism, decay) of the older cities.

"If a part of the solution to the devastating problems of the underclass involves investment in public services, particularly in the public school systems of the nation's major cities, the growing division between city and suburb lessens white self-interest in making such an investment [in city revitalization efforts]" (Edsall and Edsall).

Guilt does not propel most whites to become part of the solution; a great middle ground exists between causing a problem and actively working on a solution, and many whites who hear or read that their passivity or apathy contributes to the problem refuse to accept responsibility for correcting problems they haven't directly caused.

The degree of interconnectivity of the races is defined subjectively, at a personal and individual level. To induce a feeling of greater personal guilt in others, some people assert that all people are connected by virtue of belonging to the community of man, that the action of one person is the action of every person, that the responsibility for the fallout is presumed to be shared by all, and that all share the burden of solving a problem. This method is an attempt to disassociate real responsibility from those in whom it resides. It is a large-scale blame game in disguise. We may all breathe the same air in a community, but that fact isn't significant unless others have polluted their share and expect everyone else to keep quiet about their responsibility while we breathe their pollution. Dispersal of guilt dispels accountability and shelters those who are truly accountable, but perhaps cannot be prosecuted.

> **Domino Effect Premise:** Acceptance of guilt at any level develops a pattern that guilters may exploit as an example of your bad character, demanding that you admit guilt again and again to atone.

When people choose to personalize guilt through remote human connections, they feel that they are indirectly harming themselves if they don't act, which motivates them to action more than any feeling of guilt for harming others could. Ploys that emphasize interconnection of the races to encourage shifting money from one race to another are like criminals blaming upstanding citizens for causing them to commit their criminal behavior. Criminal behavior by blacks affects the direct victims of the crimes, and society in general, but society's failure to actively seek solutions to the problems of black crime isn't a "white" shortcoming. Members of all races commit crime. The criminal is the problem, not the environment, an environment in which many don't commit crime. Commission of crime is an individual choice. Hardship does not justify crime.

Black youths, distancing themselves from the concept of personal responsibility for their actions, blame violence by black youths on parents, council members, mayors, and the President of the United States, accusing these people of not trying hard enough to stop black youths from committing violent crimes (*Dayton Daily News*, September 26, 1992). No race of people is responsible for the black dilemma of high joblessness, high crime, high drug use, high poverty rates, bad health, bad creditworthiness, out-of-wedlock births and fractured families, and low test scores. It is easier to view adverse conditions as a conspiracy than to take responsibility for the conditions. Placing the blame on others, however, does not bind others to accept blame or react in a way to correct the condition. If others refuse to take blame, their refusal is not an indication that they are racist. No race is responsible for any individual's illegal actions in a bad situation, and no legal system in a civilized society will sanction crime.

Respected black spokespersons like Bill Cosby and Attallah Shabazz are refuting the concept of dispersed responsibility. Attallah Shabazz, daughter of civil rights activist Malcolm X, in a conversation with about 1200 Central State University students at CSU's Winter Quarter Convocation Series, told the students that it was "self-defeating to blame their failures on their skin color. Rather, she said, 'You are responsible for everything you do.... Perfect yourself'" (Haidet, *Dayton Daily News*). Shabazz also said that blacks have "no one but themselves to blame." People are responsible for their poverty, their problems, their choices, their children's interest in educational achievement and their own.

> **Premise:** Others' problems don't become everyone's problems. Others' needs do not legally or morally obligate anyone to take action to meet those needs. Taking action is a matter of personal choice.

White Guilt

To feel true guilt, you must take personal responsibility for taking unfair advantage, committing crime, or for any action you take or thought you think. Shared race, which is incidental, circumstantial, arbitrary, and irrelevant as a conceptual connection to strangers from the past, and even one generation removed, does not constitute personal responsibility for causing or influencing the actions of strangers from an earlier time. Whites recognize that whites enslaved blacks in America, and quite a few moralistically denounce slavers out of a sense of humanity rather than a sense of guilt. Excluding Native Americans, whom whites dispatched relatively quickly, and Mexican illegal immigrants, who sneak in quietly and take vacant crap jobs, blacks and whites have the most long-lived contentiousness in the U.S., commonly perpetrating the greatest deceits in the name of winning the civil rights pissing contest. Southern white slave owners asserted that blacks were inherently inferior, couldn't be educated, and were criminal, lazy, immoral, and sexually animalistic. Many black activists claim that the slave owner mentality persists today in whites, despite civil rights protections.

But whites today weren't born in the 17th or 18th or 19th centuries. They couldn't have influenced the decision of 12,000 slave owners in the United States, or of slaveholders of any race in Africa or any other nation to enslave people, and they couldn't have participated in the keeping of slaves. If they had been born during a period in America in which slavery was legal, which is a hypothetical that really shouldn't be brought up in an argument based on rationality, there's no evidence—hypothetical or otherwise—that they would have enslaved blacks. Even if a white individual benefits in some quantifiable way from the actions of those in the past, it isn't guilt they should feel for such benefit, but acceptance. Individuals who didn't vote for the representatives holding government offices during slavery, and who had no political sway or voice, can't be held responsible for the laws and acts that government officials passed in the 1600s. They can still feel appalled and horrified by enslavement carried out by other humans.

Whites backpedal, maybe look for their checkbooks, when a black asserts that white success can be traced to the practice by their forebears, or by their neighbor's forebears, of enslaving blacks. Though the genetic trail may be as diluted as homeopathic scorpion venom, if a white man has possessions, he's made to feel obligated to turn them over simply for being white. Making concessions can be construed as admission of genetic guilt. Alternately, gifts might be construed by some people as a sign of benevolent paternalism, which only proves to some the charges that whites hold too much power. A better case of circular logic in a lose/lose scenario would be hard to find. But put two people together, and different viewpoints are assured. Conflict is the result of having many people expecting a lot of different things from many others who have differing opinions.

To take personal responsibility for the actions of others, including others who are long dead, is a mental disorder that some in the minority community encourage. It is also a choice available to every free individual. Some blacks hope white guilt comes with a reparations offer, gratuities, and entitlements. They'll settle for hopelessly psychotic feelings of guilt in whites, feelings that aren't rationally justifiable but which can be evoked by exploiting the emotional instability. The waged campaign reminds whites that they should feel some kind of universal guilt based on their race, and that alleviating this guilt will transform them from historical victimizers to patronizers, an ironic outcome that keeps blacks dependent on the charity of whites. To many, it is more profitable and acceptable to be patronized than to be victimized, these options, declared by dishonest race exploiters, being the only ones available to blacks.

> **Premise:** Guilt and compassion are private emotions. Attempting to escalate either to extort money or concessions leads to resentment. Extortion of gratuities is the primary reason why blacks want to make whites feel guilty for past mistreatment.

Providing any reward based on an artificially heightened sense of guilt serves only to reinforce in the black culture an ingrained sense of dependence and victimization, which can lead blacks to both feel unrealistically entitled to rewards and worth only as much as the next hand-out. To "be vulnerable is to be invincible. Complaint gives you power–even when it's only the power of emotional bribery, of creating previously unnoticed levels of social guilt" (Hughes, p. 30). One's self-esteem should not be tied to the success of dependency on the base emotion of guilt in others.

Liberal white guilt stems from historical mistreatment and victimization blacks have endured, a tragedy, as was society's contemporary economic acceptance of slavery. Of all political and philosophical groups, liberals are the most likely to organize black awareness walks to soothe their consciences for other humans who mistreat humans (though liberals are less likely to give money to charities, believing usurping of charity across all of society to be a government function). A CNN/USA Today/Gallup poll of 1,001 adults–820 of them white and 146 black–in February 2002 showed that nine out of 10 white Americans believed that the government should not make cash reparations payments, while half of black respondents said it should. Sixty-two percent of white respondents also believed that the government should not apologize to blacks for legally permitting slavery, while 68 percent of blacks said it should (Viles, March 27, 2002).

Few whites feel personally responsible for oppressing blacks or causing the poor economic conditions faced by inner-city blacks, who make up about a third of the black population. No matter how often a black person resorts to trying to make a white feel guilty for everything from slavery to creating a racist economy, most whites feel only sorrow about past mistreatment of blacks. They know some whites continue to discriminate against blacks, but they do not accept the responsibility for other humans' acts simply because they are also white.

Successful white businessmen are especially harangued by women, blacks, and the poor to feel guilty, shameful, remorseful, and self-loathing for their success. Success can't be reasonably maligned based on its exclusivity to successful people. Few people would reject the education, hard work, and sacrifices that go into achieving success based only on the paleness by comparison of those in special interest groups composed of less financially successful people. Few would reject success in the hopes of raising the esteem of the unsuccessful. So, asking successful white businessmen to feel guilty for their hard work is slightly irrational and seen for what it is, envy disguised in excuses.

Poor white trash are exempt from the campaigns by blacks to invoke guilt, since it is assumed that poor people have not benefited from slavery or oppressed civil rights (though the plantations of a few slaveowners failed, plunging them into poverty). Or poor whites have chosen to decline the privileges of their race, boycotting success from a sense of moral outrage and indignation (insert snarky smiley face here). Or been too stupid to make money, since they had opportunities based on their whiteness, having doors open to them in the capitalist society that is seen to award people through racial nepotism. Poor whites owe everybody. They're innocent. Besides, the poor have no money to extort.

Broken out by race, a far greater number of whites live in poverty than blacks. This data of sheer numbers disputes the myth that whites are privileged. Some reporters and blacks who wish to invoke guilt or pity for their race, and thereby extract aid, cook the data to maintain the myth. They do this by transforming the data to percentages, since a higher numerical value can then be assigned to deceive about the apparent number of blacks living in poverty. Translating actual numbers to percentages and acting upon the percentages has a terrible impact when diverting food relief, for instance. Resources that go to groups based on race percentages leads to less efficient assignment of resources and failure to feed sheer numbers of starving people. Basing distribution on percentages would be missing an opportunity to provide the greatest good to the greatest number by giving more aid to fewer numbers of starving people in a particular racial group. The utilitarian principle of social distribution of goods should prevail. If unwise action is taken based on percentages, then percentages are not useful in describing circumstances in real terms.

These tactics–personalizing guilt, playing on the human desire to believe we are connected in a broader sense to others, recurrent assertions of connectedness by race, demands for evidence of non-racism, and assertions that successful people should compromise their success–combine to increase the effectiveness of guilting.

People also invoke guilt and shame in others as a form of revenge, to reduce others' self-esteem for malicious purposes, not to directly induce the relinquishment of valued items or services as appeasement. In a few instances, guilt is used to educate others, to make others aware that their behaviors are hurtful. Those made to feel guilty for their behaviors rarely feel positive about the people who intentionally invoke guilt in them. They may actively attempt to rebuke attacks on their self-image by finding escape clauses that allow them to diminish in their own minds the degree of hurtfulness that their behaviors may have caused in others. Victims of guilting may also refuse to feel guilt because they suspect the motives of those who try to invoke it in them. They may also not care enough about those who are hurt by their behaviors to feel compelled to make amends. Natural human tendencies to reduce guilt, and the negative publicity associated with overuse of the racial guilting tactic, damage the efforts of blacks who use guilting as a method in a strategy to gain either equal or preferential treatment.

Those who refuse to feel bad about themselves, who search for ways to reduce dissonance in their self-images, also refuse to accept accountability for the conditions of the poor, easily dismissing accusations by examining true underlying causes–the persistent and regressive cultural values of the poor that perpetuate poverty. Comparative studies are available that document those exceptional people within both black and white races who struggled and rose from poverty to attain middle-class incomes, people who exhibited respect for the values of hard work, professionalism, and honesty.

Improvement in any poor person's situation is proof that improvement is possible. Statistics of poor people under the same economic pressures show that many survive within lawful boundaries, while others commit violent crimes. Poor and wealthy alike make the choice to commit crime as one means of enriching themselves. Accounts of the poor from other cultures who migrate to the U.S. and become successful offer further proof that continuing poverty isn't inevitable. Many become successful, despite language and communication difficulties, through diligence and willingness to work hard in jobs matched to their limited skills. Opportunities for social, political, professional, educational, and economic advancement in the United States are abundant, while other nations are bereft of opportunity and repress personal incentives. Comparatively, the failure of large numbers of minorities born in the U.S. to succeed in business in the midst of the advantages of a democratic, lawful, rich, social welfare environment is obscene.

Guilting gave America Martin Luther King Day, streets named for black leaders, and more than 90 years of Black History Month, which critics charge "is merely an annual vehicle for appeasing white guilt and is a means to exploit blacks" (Shine, February 16, 1992). Many whites accurately reason that guilting is a way to make whites feel bad about their own race and uncertain as to whether they might indeed be accountable for mistreatment in the longitudinal/interconnective world view. Enjoying ill-gotten advantages from the general oppression of others often elicits guilt. Blauner has a point when he states that whites don't "want to face the possibility that their social position, even in part, might be the product of racial privilege" (Blauner, pp. 16–17). Many whites may have enjoyed middle-class upbringing because their fathers and grandfathers prevented other black fathers and grandfathers from working.

This argument is compelling and may elicit feelings of guilt. The problem is that it cannot be generalized or assumed that all white ancestors had the power to racially discriminate in the job market, or that those who had the power actively discriminated against blacks, or even played the system of white nepotism by accepting jobs they knew would only be offered to whites. Aside from this mitigating release from obligation through guilt, descendants cannot be prosecuted for an ancestor's racially oppressive ways. Suggesting that white privilege, rather than hard work, is the primary factor in success is antagonistic in the same way that many blacks feel insulted to have their success attributed to affirmative action policy. Only people convicted in racial discrimination cases can be held accountable for withholding jobs from blacks and other minorities. Competitors capitalize on the weaknesses of others to get even further ahead, and one weakness is the trait of not actually working but demanding undeserved rewards. Regardless of whether one wants to acknowledge the possibility of his guilt, one cannot feel guilty for being white or being born into a race that has a history of aggressively pursing its privilege.

The news media thrives on the controversy that special interest groups fabricate, and even encourage it. Covering racially tense issues is easy and allows reporters to put in short hours to pound out what amounts to editorials; deep research into serious issues takes energy and diverts attention from controversial issues that sell newspapers. In the case of Marge Schott, former owner of the Cincinnati Reds, the media collaborated with the NAACP to construct a media event to fill the gap between the 1992 presidential election and the inauguration. Allegedly, all black baseball players became victims of Schott's "racially charged" remark about a white man.

Ultimately, people can only be ashamed of themselves for their own morally and intellectually repugnant actions. They will not serve as racial tokens and develop racial self-hatred to assume onto themselves the shame and guilt of others in their race.

Black Guilt

Even successful blacks are being guilted by spokespersons like Bill Campbell, with Atlanta's 100 Black Men, Inc.: "The black middle class and black professionals have to assume a tremendous obligation" to give back to the black community. The goal is to guilt successful blacks into being generous and charitable to less fortunate blacks. If they don't, they're seen as traitors to their race, sellouts, and puppets of the white capitalist system. Middle class blacks can presumably disprove these denunciations by donating to and generating business opportunities for inner-city blacks. Or, they can ignore attempts to manipulate them through guilt, forsake the fight to bring all blacks of lower socio-economic classes up to a higher standard of living, and choose not to fight for political power and additional civil rights.

"There is an extraordinary move now to try to rebuild the bridges between the black middle class and the black poor. Because we [?] realize that the role models have been taken out of the neighborhoods" (Atkins, interviewing Marian Wright Edelman, p. 130). "We" are blacks and the black middle class who weren't really "taken" out of ghettos, but left voluntarily. One attempt to build bridges was an essay contest promoted by BET in which contestants were to write why black business leaders had an obligation to return to inner cities and help out other blacks.

Successful people spread their wealth within the economy and through their purchases, indirectly support those who provide products and services. Unemployed people who create no products and offer no services cannot realize this support. Successful people generally offer valuable services and products to society, regardless of their poor upbringings, race, or restricted opportunities, so they aren't "taking" from their communities. Since more numbers of whites pay into the welfare system than blacks, all blacks on welfare depend in part on white wealth. Successful blacks in legitimate enterprises also give back in the form of welfare and social programs funded by their tax dollars. By not being a welfare burden, successful minorities have met all reasonable social burdens and obligations.

To be a traitor to your race, you have to accept the terms of what it means to betray a race. You must identify with the category based only on the single criteria of race, and you must believe that the concept of community and connected-ness based on race is attained only by abiding by a prevalent separatist ideology about maintaining racial unity. Successful blacks feel guilty about severing racial ties to their former lives only because those in the city and culture that they've left behind try to make them feel guilty and ashamed of their success in the capitalis-tic, pluralistic, integrated "white" society. Successful minorities are accused of considering themselves and their biological families as more important than maintaining the broader racial heritage and returning to segregated communities. Racial heritage doesn't pay the bills or supply for material needs, and segregated community businesses often offer lower wages than integrated businesses. You're black and successful and speak English well, so some unsuccessful blacks say you sold your culture to take the white man's wealth. Don't buy the bull.

People who succeed and escape poor neighborhoods and poor educational backgrounds often don't return, regardless of their race, to give back to areas from which they've escaped: "'If you're successful, you're not going to identify yourself with failures'" (Terkel quoting Dr. Kenneth B. Clark, p. 337). Gener-ally, people "'take intense vicarious pleasure in the success of somebody else if they're not competing with that person,'" (Kahneman, *Psychology Today*, Febru-ary 2005) but such pleasure isn't enough for those who envy success and desire more concrete participation in it. Those minorities who escape poverty know how their own mentality differs from the mentality of those who don't escape, and they fear reversion or their inability to contain their revulsion in the presence of the people they chose to leave behind. They may also feel very little hope of converting the mentality of those they've left behind. Having seen so much nega-tive, counterproductive mentality, and having experienced very little encourage-ment from their peers in a segregated community for having a differing cultural/business attitude, the amount of effort required to free others from the bonds of negative mentality is daunting.

Many in America no longer consider American society to be altruistic and feel that if one person can find the breaks to becoming successful, then so can others. The premium that society places on the individual to succeed has led many to expect that all individuals should be able to succeed without requiring continuing assistance. If programs must be put in place, let them be to aid all poor, not just the minority poor, to benefit all college applicants, not just minority applicants, and all employees, not just minority employees.

Less-educated blacks attack college-educated blacks for betraying their race, education and integration being seen as a white cultural value. Because college-educated blacks had greater exposure to issues outside of race, they may no longer emphasize race as a way to antagonize whites with whom they work and socialize. Suspicion results from a perception that whites valued education for blacks as a means of forcing blacks to become more white, not from the perception that whites felt that education would make anyone more competitive intellectually for society's rewards, or that the infusion of knowledge is a reward in its own sake. Generally, it is expected that education is a tool that people can use to better their station in life, though this betterment did not materialize for as many blacks as hoped. Those blacks who did not choose higher education compare their lack of success to the success of educated counterparts and justify their choices in life by smugly retaining traditional black values, not selling out, not buying into the white man's lies: "'[Whites] say get an education, clean up, straighten up. We done all these things. And still we're not accepted'" (Blauner, quoting Howard Spence, 37).

Walter Williams, a professor of economics at George Mason University in Fairfax, VA, questions the language of some blacks who try to browbeat successful blacks into turning over their rewards to the general black community:

> "'Those who've been blessed ought to give something back.' That's emotionally appealing but deceitful. For the most part, people with high incomes have produced valuable services for their fellow man.... Incomes earned by these men stand as unambiguous proof that they served their fellow man. As such they've met their social obligations. So have grocery clerks, mechanics and pharmacists in varying degrees" (Williams, *Dayton Daily News*).

Apologies

Apologies are symbolic, but offering apologies implies, or admits, direct culpability, thereby compelling either retributive recompense for the victims, or punishment of the offenders, who are dead. Apologies may also be a first step in politics to construction of bills that redirect money to reparation funds and trusts for historical mistreatment of blacks. Ohio representative Tony Hall in June 2000 made a public request that whites make amends and apologize. Alabama's Governor Bob Riley signed a resolution on May 31, 2007 that expressed "'profound regret' for Alabama's role in slavery and apologizing for slavery's wrongs and lingering effects" (*Dayton Daily News*, June 1, 2007, p. A10). No reparation was offered, and Alabama became the fourth southern state to legislatively pass an apology resolution. Reparation activists view apologies by corporations for connections to the slave trade as possible preludes to reparation payments, and maybe even as evidence of culpability.

Government doesn't feel the punishing effect of being apologists. The taxed populace does. By redistributing their tax dollars to the construction of memorials to black leaders, city museums of black history and culture, and social programs specifically directed toward blacks, it is falsely assumed that all those who pay taxes believe, as their government representatives do, in the concept of expensive symbolic apology. But the U.S. system of government isn't a democracy; it's a representational republic beholden to the their most vocal constituents. A more direct amends might be extracted from actual slaveholders and traders, with taxes being used to track down the gravesites and garnish the wages of worker bees that pollinate the dandelions growing there.

Healing is another term assigned to how apologies help. Apologies are a first step in the healing process for racial wounds, for instance. Healing is a vague term, but in the context of apologies, the first step began with emancipation a couple of centuries ago.

One argument compares apologies for the military internment of Japanese during World War II who were suspected of collaboration with U.S. enemies with an apology to blacks for an inhumane but formerly legal system of slavery. Japanese internment by the U.S. government is not like the immoral behavior of private citizens who chose to enslave innocent Africans indefinitely to satisfy an economic incentive. So, apologies to American ancestors of detained Japanese is not a good basis to justify apologizing to the nation's current blacks population for slavery. The argument is irrational because it is a false analogy.

Acknowledgement implies sympathy. Barring any substantive subsequent show of fairly obtained and apportioned amends, apologies by themselves won't mean much to anyone. Hugs all around.

Reparations

Slavery is said to have a devastating social impact on generations of blacks following its abolishment. Reparationist blacks like Conrad Worrill, Henry Louis "Skip" Gates, attorney Deadria Farmer-Paellmann, and political activist Dorothy Tillman seek reparation payments to repair black communities damaged by white racism and racial discrimination. They demand voluntary corporate involvement in humanitarian efforts for blacks, commerce, jobs creation, housing, community building, and partnerships with black businesses. According to Worrill, "It's almost impossible for any multi-billion-dollar corporate entity in the United States not to have ties to slavery" (Cottman, June 14, 2005).

When reparationists generalize the acts of whites in the past as the responsibility of current-generation whites and companies owned by whites to make right, and demand retribution, they alienate whites from the cause of blacks. People do not feel accountable for the crimes of others they didn't know, crimes which they themselves could not have prevented, or crimes they may even have condoned within the contemporary culture. It's hard not to be resentful "'when you see people getting something for nothing and expecting it,'" states Jennifer Kasko. "'I am tired of people telling me that I owe them for something I haven't even done. I haven't gotten anything free in my life. I've worked hard for everything I have'" (Terkel, p. 211).

Though few recent reparations lawsuits are successful, with notable exceptions such as the lawsuit against the city of Rosewood, Florida for the killing of 26 blacks in 1923, most fail because slavery wasn't illegal when it was practiced (and slavery has been practiced at one time or another in most countries throughout history), and no living person today can prove that they were directly wronged by slavery.

Though there'll never be a fatal blow to the concept of reparations to blacks for slavery, a recent court decision handed down by Judge Charles R. Norgle reiterates the primary argument against reparations: "plaintiffs have failed to show a link between themselves and the 17 corporations named as defendants, and that the statute of limitations rules out damages for wrongs committed before slavery was abolished in 1868" (Robinson, July 7, 2005). The seventeen corporations, including J.P. Morgan Chase, R.J. Reynolds Tobacco, and Loews, were charged in the suit for having reaped the benefits of slave labor during the pre- and post-Civil War era (Korecki and Spielman, July 7, 2005).

Judge Norgle further states in his opinion, "'present day Americans are not morally or legally liable for historical injustices, that the debt to African Americans has already been paid, and that reparations talk is divisive, immersing African Americans in a culture of victimhood." Additionally, Norgle writes, "'Claims asserting harms against groups of long-dead victims, perpetrated by groups of long-dead wrongdoers, are particularly difficult to bring in modern American courts of law." "Norgle said the plaintiffs failed to show that they had experienced any 'concrete and particular' suffering that wasn't true of African Americans in general" (Korecki and Spielman, July 7, 2005).

An outspoken spokesman, Conrad Worrill, chairman of the National Black United Front and director of Inner City Studies for the Jacob Carruthers Center for Inner City Studies at Northeastern Illinois University, then accused the judge of having racist eyes (Korecki and Spielman, July 7, 2005). Benjamin Obi Nwoye, one of the plaintiffs' attorneys, felt sad that more and "'more corporations are admitting their direct dealings with slaves, and yet the judge will look at it and say we cannot prove the case against these corporations. It doesn't make sense.'" Sadly (for the plaintiff), Nwoye doesn't realize that the case wasn't about proving past affiliation, but proving current legal obligation to repay. He also forgets that corporations legally are being forced by the local governments in some cities in which they do business to admit distant affiliation to slavery as a condition of being allowed to do business in the city, though the affiliation may only have been through old defunct companies that the current businesses long ago purchased.

The first focus on black slavery reparations came in 1943 by The National Coalition of Blacks for Reparations in America, or N'COBRA, which was "formed a year after the United States acknowledged wrongdoing and paid reparations to Japanese Americans" (Kinsolving, July 5, 2005). Another group, the Reparations Coordinating Committee composed primarily of attorneys, including the late Johnnie Cochran, constructs federal lawsuits to force federal government payment into funds that are to be used exclusively to correct problems in the black community, and to pay themselves.

In 2003, Charles Ogletree Jr., founder of the Reparations Coordinating Committee, filed a lawsuit in a Tulsa, Oklahoma federal court to obtain reparations for hundreds of blacks killed during the Tulsa Race Riots and their descendants. In 2004, "an appeals court ruled that it was too late for survivors of the riots to sue the state, and last month the U.S. Supreme Court declined to hear the case" (Cottman, June 14, 2005).

The "U.S. government has never apologized or paid reparations to the descendants of slaves" (Kinsolving, July 5, 2005), but though the federal government may have closed its wallet to reparations, that still leaves Corporate America, apparently an okay institution to beat up. Even silly suits against cigarette companies and companies who don't warn that their coffee is hot have been successful for law firms.

The banking firm, Wachovia Corporation, recently declared that two banks it had acquired in the past (Bank of Charleston, SC and the Georgia Railroad and Banking Co.) had a history of owning slaves and accepting slaves as collateral on mortgaged properties or loans, acquiring the slaves in defaulted loan payments. Reparations activist Deadria Farmer-Paellmann in 2002 discovered that 16 short-term life insurance policies written by Aetna through the mid-1800s insured slave owners against the deaths or escape of slaves (Fears, June 20, 2005). In a class action complaint filed by her and her attorneys in Brooklyn, New York in March 2002 against FleetBoston Financial Corporation, Aetna, Inc., and CSX, Farmer-Paellman built a case that the companies enjoyed prosperity in the amount of

$1.4 trillion in current dollars through the labor of slaves, and emphatically declares that the defendants conspired with slave traders.

She sought "accounting, constructive trust, restitution, disgorgement, and compensatory and punitive damages" (FindLaw.com, March 2002) for the human rights violation, with 100 other defendants to be named at a later date. Following Farmer-Paellman's lead, in September of 2002, Timothy Hurdle and Chester A. Hurdle, biological sons of a former slave, filed a $1.4 trillion reparations lawsuit in San Francisco Superior Court naming corporations FleetBoston Financial Corporation, Aetna Inc., Lloyd's of London, New York Life Insurance Company, Westpoint Stevens, R. J. Reynolds Tobacco Company, Brown and Williamson Tobacco Corporation, and Loews Corporation, among others, "seeking restitution from corporations that helped to finance the domestic and transatlantic slave trade or used labor of enslaved Africans" (Muhammad, September 24, 2002). The suit was filed on behalf

> "of their enslaved father, formerly enslaved Africans, descendants of enslaved Africans and the general public. They allege that the defendants engaged in unfair competition through the commission of unlawful, unfair, and fraudulent business acts by financing and exploiting the enslavement of Africans, and by deceiving the public about their slave related pasts" (Muhammad, September 24, 2002).

Withheld wages for slave labor and unfair competition for those not hired to perform such labor is termed unjust enrichment. Farmer-Paellmann explains, "These are corporations that benefited from stealing people, from stealing labor, from forced breeding, from torture, from committing numerous horrendous acts, and there's no reason why they should be able to hold onto assets they acquired through such horrendous acts" (Viles, March 27, 2002).

Though a few of the companies named in the suits deny current support for past corporate presidents, "FleetBoston publicly denied a connection to their predecessor bank, the Providence Bank of Rhode Island, which allegedly helped finance the enslavement of about 41,369 Africans between 1791 and 1808, in violation of Rhode Island and federal slave trade prohibitions" (Muhammad, September 24, 2002). "Aetna Chairman John W. Rowe responded in April 2000. 'The fact that Aetna had written policies on slaves more than 140 years ago was brought to the attention of Aetna's management. They were deeply disappointed and embarrassed'" (Fears, June 20, 2005). In a statement, Wachovia Chairman and CEO Ken Thompson offered his apology: "On behalf on Wachovia Corporation, I apologize to all Americans, and especially to African-Americans and people of African descent.… We know that we cannot change the past, and we can't make up for the wrongs of slavery … but we can learn from our past and begin a stronger dialogue about slavery and the experience of African-Americans in our country …" (Anderson, June 30, 2005). Wachovia spokesman Scott Silvestri said the company is talking to the NAACP, the Urban League, and other civil rights groups about how to proceed. "'We didn't want to have a donation or gift right out of a gate,'" he said. "'We wanted to think about what's the best way to address that'" (Fears, June 20, 2005). Wachovia is following up by offering to help educate people about black history. J.P. Morgan Chase and Company, accused of profiting from slavery in Louisiana by accepting more than 1,000 collateral slaves when their owners defaulted on loans, has agreed to establish a $5 million college scholarship program called Smart Louisiana.

> **Premise:** Demanding unreasonably high punitive damages and awards and being willing to accept lower payouts is a psychological ploy that makes the mark in this con game feel as though he's getting a relative bargain, making him more likely to pay something to be rid of his accusers and the nagging sense of guilt they've planted in him.

Some cities have enacted ordinances requiring all local businesses that want to do business in the city to disclose all past ties to slavery. Chicago's 2003 Slavery Era Disclosure Ordinance, sponsored by Chicago City Councilmember Dorothy Tillman, for instance, though not intended to target businesses for boycott or closure, may be used to hold them accountable in future reparations lawsuits (Anderson, June 30, 2005).

At an individual level, "many whites believed that King's dream of a racially just society had already come to pass, while blacks were adamant that relatively little progress had been made" (Blauner, p. 3). Blauner accuses whites of believing that equality had been attained, which meant that they would be called upon less often to make concessions to blacks. He attributes their belief that racism no longer existed to their denial of involvement, support, and continued retribution of past injustices. It is the expectation that whites must make concessions to blacks, regardless of their personal justifications for denying that expectation, that corrodes race relations.

As with guilting, what qualifies for reparations is subjective. Whites, sarcastically or earnestly, can claim that since the slavery system also fueled Americans' dependence on cheap labor, a craving that partially explains why so many of our manufacturing jobs are emigrating to Mexico and Malaysia, maybe the descendents of *slave owners* should be demanding an apology for the tragic mindset they inherited. Who else deserves a piece of the slavery reparation pot?

Does the trend for corporate disclosure and lawsuits for slavery reparation mean that reparation campaigns are successful? Yes, to a degree, though they are not yet successful in the courts. Though past wrongs can't be undone, and the repayment cost cannot be estimated, only the more recent mistakes and social injustice can be corrected.

Asking for indiscriminate retribution from all whites for the racist behavior of a few in the past is racially discriminatory because it generalizes the behavior of a few based on race to all within the race. When racism is used as a method of retaliation, is there any way to negotiate with racists? Can you reason with a racist? Racist calls for reparation perpetuate racist attitudes in many whites who are tired of hearing that black failure is due to racist attitudes by whites, who resent being accused of causing all the blacks' problems, and who are told that they owe blacks a living typified by a distasteful attitude in the following statement: "My daddy suffered enough and took my share. So, I want whites to give me everything my daddy would've earned had he been white or had he been given a good job he was qualified to learn instead of polishing boots." Whites are resentful that members of a race expect back pay from someone else's labor, the antithesis of the capitalistic convention of personally earned rewards.

Restitution, or reparations, policy is based solely on race. In September of 2006, "lawyers for slave descendants asked a federal appeals court ... to revive a landmark reparations case that demands 17 of the nation's insurers and banks publicize and pay for their roles in the country's slave trade" (Heher, *Dayton Daily News*). Records show that up to 600,000 African slaves were imported to North America. The rest were offspring. "Ten million or more slaves were shipped by Europeans to North America, South America and the Caribbean in the 15–19 centuries, and the vast majority of them came from West Africa" (Reynolds). 12 million Africans were exported as slaves to the Caribbean and South America.

The more social welfare programs in effect and the fewer minorities working, the more minorities are repaid. In some, the perceived duty of others to repay ancestors of slaves becomes a lifelong pension plan.

A few in the black community resent that so many whites are uninvolved in the cause of minorities gaining equal footing with whites. They feel that whites cannot be conscientiously neutral to the plight of blacks, and that no white is neutral because all whites must atone for white historical discrimination.

News headlines and articles describe race relations as a battle, often emphasizing the use of economics as a hammer to force whites to recognize the power that minorities wield: "Black organizations given short shrift when their conventions come to town are demanding–and getting–retribution" (*Atlanta Journal*, October 1992). The battle metaphor for retribution as a race extortion strategy heightens fear levels. With retribution, demands for rewards go beyond tarnished reputation, lost respect as others question an accused's racial animosity, and courtrooms. With retribution, advances are gained through fear of financial reprisal, loss of business, physical or property harm, and payback for the harm committed by others of one's race. Minorities seem to want more than just an unequal share of power, verging on domination of whites. Threats to commit violence and actual violence by minorities against whites forces whites to prejudge blacks just to avoid risk of danger. Indiscriminate retribution is a terrorist tactic.

Militant blacks "'challenged the privileged status of whites in American society'" (Blauner, quoting William Singer, p. 101). "'If you have a predominantly Negro society, then they're gonna make the rules and say what can be done and … I think perhaps [white minorities in this society are] afraid that the Negro will want to get <u>even</u> with … what has happened to them in the past'" (Blauner, quoting Maude Wiley, p. 91).

Militant blacks may want to make whites fear and respect them, and generally find it easier to instill fear. Threats appear to be backed by the conviction of vengeance and the righteous turning of race tables. Whites fear that minorities may group together to take over power positions and oppress whites, as happened in South Africa when white farm owners had their lands legally taken as pay back for apartheid and redistributed to the majority black population.

Those in a social setting who are outnumbered based on racial composition will feel more threatened than they would in a same race group (racial minorities might respond, "welcome to my world"). Though the group makes no overt threat, their hatred may be assumed based on substantiated high rates of violence reported in the news and frequent calls for violence to be committed against whites, making the white minority believe that others might be more likely to inflict physical harm. Rapper Sister Souljah was quoted in the *Washington Post* as saying that "if black people kill black people every day, why not have a week and kill white people? … So if you're a gang member and you would normally be killing somebody, why not kill a white person? Do you think that somebody thinks that white people are better, or above dying …?" The false assumption is that blacks kill blacks simply because of their color. Sister Souljah suggests killing whites because of their color, which incites racial-based violence and promotes the continuance of racist attitudes in both blacks who believe she has a point and in whites who reject the notion of racially motivated violence.

"'A large black man is viewed as much more threatening by whites who live in the suburbs than by people who live in South Central Los Angeles'" said William Mellor, president of the Institute for Justice, a conservative Washington public-interest law firm (Juan Williams, *Dayton Daily News*, May 5, 1992).

> **Premise:** We fear what we don't understand, what is different, yet we take few steps to understand and few pains to see similarities. We *also* fear some of the things we *do* understand.

Black slaves who were mistreated are unable to obtain retribution, so self-appointed proxies argue on behalf of the dead.

Entitlements

Being entitled is having an earned claim to a right or privilege. Many who feel entitled aren't entitled by most definitions of the term, *earn*. Feeling entitled isn't a racial characteristic, though many government entitlement programs base claims to goods and services on race. One "earns" entitlement to government social welfare programs by virtue of being a racial minority or being poor. Therefore, whites who aren't poor cannot join the group and cannot participate. For racially discriminatory programs, no whites can receive the retroactive and unequal rewards and privileges that blacks and other minorities as a group receive from a government that is elected to represent all citizens equally, regardless of race, gender, age, or creed.

Criteria for awarding entitlements relies on past inequalities that were not retroactively corrected with the passage of civil rights legislation. These entitlements can be viewed, therefore, as restitution of the inequalities suffered by ancestors, or deserved special compensation for historical mistreatment. Frequently, entitlements must offer preferred rewards for the disadvantaged group members over the rights of other group's members. This prejudicial partiality is seen as a necessity to overcome the disadvantages instituted by past prejudicial treatment.

There is nothing in a capitalist economy that justifies racial entitlements. Those who do not work and contribute positive, tangible value, do not deserve entitlements. They are free to beg for them, petition for them, make people feel guilty or fearful for not providing entitlements, but there is no capitalistic tenet that states that people who do nothing and who can't show personal injury or damage are entitled to free awards. Socialist economies are different, though socialist precepts are being selectively invoked by a small group of people who wish to receive gratuities, leaving all other capitalistic expectations for other segments of society intact. The U.S. Government supports many socialist programs, so its support of entitlement programs isn't so hard to believe.

Sister Soulja states in a *Rolling Stone* interview: "But when it comes to power, it's different. If you have to personally sacrifice something, then it's another issue, and that's where the majority of whites fall short" (*Rolling Stone*, Issue 636, p. 72). Nobody, whether black or white, wants to give up power with little hope of recompense and motivating factors like beneficence, fear, or guilt. People with power should be willing to negotiate how others are to earn and use power. Nobody is just going to give power, power being a general concept whose particulars must be defined for each situation. Power in politics is earned in one way and earned another in business, but it is seldom given away, and when it is, the gift causes dissension among all those who are working within the system to earn the power who feel cheated that someone else has received it because they met a race criteria.

White employees who work for a discriminatory employer will not surrender a lucrative job on principle, as a symbolic act of reparation for slavery, or in protest for past injustices against blacks because another man claims to be more entitled to the job based on race. The principled, though misguided white employee might gain a moment of praise for his integrity and commitment to the black cause, but he won't be reimbursed for lost wages while standing in the unemployment line, and the act of stubbornly fighting Corporate America makes him less attractive to other firms.

Minorities pressure politicians to draft laws meant to end discrimination, but these laws generally favor minorities, so the laws, in effect, uphold the concept of racially discriminatory practices. Whites see these laws as discriminatory and rather than report their displeasure to the people who gave in to demands and drafted the bad laws, they indirectly hate the minorities who pushed for the laws. Pleasing a minority, which is something that many politicians and lawmakers strive to do, regardless of the social and economic repercussions, exacerbates racial tension.

Welfare benefits and other social entitlements were established to be civil human rights, leading to expectation and resentment when those entitlements are curtailed or taken away completely. If people never had entitlements, they'd never miss them and never feel entitled to them. Unfortunately, liberals have convinced blacks and the poor that entitlements are their right (or was it the other way around?). The expectation of retribution and entitlement is not misplaced, because a liberal can be found who will sacrifice your money to reinforce those expectations.

Some blacks feel entitled not to be depicted negatively in news, movies, and in history. Media is asked to protect the image of blacks because by reporting negative news and history, audiences will unfairly generalize the facts as character flaws in blacks in general. Officials at the Smithsonian Institution removed part of a museum exhibit on supernatural influence on African cultures because of complaints about the placard description associated with a photograph of two costumed tribesmen. The placard stated that "Members ... chant, dance and participate in secret rites such as orgies, cannibalism and the eating of exhumed corpses–all to acquire supernatural powers." The news story did not state that protection of the black image was the reason the museum removed the exhibit. The news story also did not say whether the description in the placard was true. Also, references to tribal atrocities and the holding of slaves in Africa were removed.

Whites resent that blacks blame bad publicity on the media's desire to portray that negative conditions are caused by blacks, when in most cases, bad publicity is simply the result of reporting actual conditions. This is another instance in which blacks want whites to censor any news that harms the black objective to appear virtuous and ideal. "Tanya Gibson, public relations office for the Wilberforce student government, criticized the news media for emphasizing negative events at [Wilberforce and Central State universities]. Gibson urged students not to give bad news a chance. 'If you don't give them a bad story, you won't have to worry about negativity in the news in terms of black campuses,' she said" (Gaffney, *Dayton Daily News*). Pretty obvious statement, but apply it to anything, any campus.

A sense of entitlement is why people don't apply for lower prestige jobs for which they are qualified rather than jobs requiring greater demonstrated skill and education. Some institutions favor black entitlements over development of opportunities for blacks to earn success, since asking blacks to earn success has been discouraged by minority spokespeople as heaping injury upon insult when the endured past hardships of innocent blacks are considered. Simply offering rights and educational, economic, and political opportunities doesn't seem enough of a repayment.

America has become a collection of "'discretely defined and entitled groups, interests and heritages'" (Fuchs, quoting John Higham, p. xvii). Entitlements create entitlement whores. Minority entitlement whores expect

- that history should be revised to emphasize black accomplishments
- special consideration based on race in gaining employment and within jobs
- the Government to cure the ills of the black society by drafting laws that favor minorities and are founded on the precept that black crime is based on race-related poverty and white racism
- double standards:
  - racially segregated black groups (Black Coaches Association, for instance) but not white groups in the same professions
  - less stringent educational standards in order to advance
  - Black History Month and Miss Black America but not White History Month or Miss White America (the implication being that every other month and all beauty pageants are somehow white)
  - the right to say nigger and not be chastised, but be offended if a white says nigger
  - the right to say a black speaker sounds black, meaning use of idiomatic street jargon typical of blacks in a subculture, but pretend offense when a similar opinion is offered by a white
  - claim racism for educational failure but precluding whites from the racism excuse, forcing whites to attribute failure to lack of interest in the subject matter, laziness, ADHD, lack of focus, bad teaching or parenting, stupidity, etc.
  - freer speech, even though that speech may be intended to incite racial violence in whites
  - use of all of the tactics of racism to advance socially, financially, educationally, and in the power structure, while denying use of race tactics by whites
  - different standards of business when dealing with other blacks (it's a "black" thing)
  - right to blame black violence against whites as a retribution for racism (gunman who shoots up a Long Island Railroad commuter train), while decrying racism as a defense for whites (gunman who kills co-workers in a Meridian, Mississippi aeronautics company elicited demands that government cease all contracts to the company)
  - right to parody whites and stereotypical large black women in movies, on stage, and on television while disallowing white males, such as Chuck Knipp, to put on blackface and portray a poor black woman named Shirley Q. Liquor
- to live in prosperity as a right
- jobs they're not qualified for

- employment positions based on percentage of blacks in population rather than qualifications
- right to rudely disrupt others as long as they have paid for a social service or product
- education in racially segregated schools while retaining the right to sue integrated schools for not letting them in
- special loans that downplay normal loan requirements
- legal representation by blacks and all black jurors
- rights of free food, housing, and medical care
- heightened sensitivity for their needs
- economic sacrifices by others to accommodate their needs
- whites to be unable to adopt black children
- more publicity for the more rare white-on-black crimes
- greater protections prior to being fired by an employer.

No one in a true capitalist society is entitled to free health care, jobs, or other people's tax money, except by government decree. There is no constitutional right not to be poor, not to have a decent house, not to receive the best medical services, and not to pay for food. In Peter Ueberroth's report on "California's Jobs and Future," he states that getting "a job is a necessity, but it is not a right" (Ueberroth). The government does not guarantee jobs. Walter Williams writes:

> "A right is something that exists simultaneously among people. My right to speech, religion and to move about freely imposes no positive obligation on you. My exercising these rights in no way diminishes your rights to the same. You have the 'negative' obligation of non-interference.... In order to deliver on a 'right' to food, housing and medical care, government must burden others with the obligation to provide the same. As a consequence, those burdened are forced to have less food, housing and medical care. If this lame notion of rights were applied to free speech, freedom of religion and movement, you'd be obliged to provide me with an auditorium, church and plane fare. (Williams, "Corruption of language cause of national decline," *Dayton Daily News*).

Demands for entitlements based on race are illegitimate. So are demands based on need, gender, age, special interest grouping, etc.

Justice for the Victim

Statistics and anecdotal reports paint minorities as victims—victims of poverty, racism, racial discrimination, prejudice, the depersonalization of stereotyping, violence, drug abuse, fractured and displaced families, conspiracies, stolen self-esteem, exploitation, humiliation and degradation as a people, less than diligent police protection and public services, profiling, earnings disparity, poor medical treatment, poor educational opportunities, poor portrayals in entertainment, lowered expectations, negative images of welfare hogs, oppression, emasculation through social aid handouts, and hopelessness and despair. Of course, the same could be said of trailer trash non-minorities.

It is in the financial, if not psychological, interest of blacks who would stoop to humiliating themselves in a display of powerlessness, that the American public be fed a steady stream of white villains, giving blacks the option to present themselves to the world as victims. Blacks have traditionally distrusted whites because of their dependent relationship with whites, giving whites the option to exercise cruelty. Victims suffer from powerlessness against the system, for trusting others who've made failed promises. As victims, blacks are eligible for preferential treatment in recompense for their victimization. A few try to cash in on this option, yet are finding that there are no trade standards. What are two hundred years of slavery worth in terms of compensation? One job for one man or two bill amendments? And when does payment stop? There's no way to know how much money it'll take to pay off such a debt of human bondage and suffering. Is interest on the bill perpetual?

> "We have become a nation full of victims, always in need of something we can't supply.... [T]he proliferation of support groups brings a sense of entitlement about victimization. That's an understandable consequence of a country whose principles include protection of the individual and that has a hair-trigger focus about being stepped on by a majority. But the trouble is we're so sensitized, we tend to victimize people just to protect their rights. The unfortunate consequence is that it disempowers people and they really do become victims" (Barber, p. 50).

As victims of conspiracies perpetrated by whites, blacks who cite conspiracy theories blame all whites for taking part, whether overtly or in their hearts, and ask whites to disprove their involvement by doing everything to stop others from committing racist acts. However, there are no conspiracies, so there can be no conspiracy victims. Whites are insulted that some blacks hold their intelligence in such low regard that they think whites can be coerced by threats that outspoken black victims of generalized racial hatred will make them look like meanies.

Pretending to be a victim is a self-fulfilling prophecy, and those who use this tactic must forsake any attempt at self-improvement so that they can justify the image. To nurture the image, victims must refuse education, jobs, and programs intended to upgrade housing or provide child care. And victims must learn to complain that education doesn't guarantee a good job (though having no education does often guarantee *not* landing a good job), that the only jobs available degrade their esteem, and that accepting social welfare from whites damages their pride. They must also complain about crime: one in five black men in his twenties is in prison, on probation, or on parole. There is invariably a component of causation and culpability for victimization that can be traced to devious, racist whites.

Making the white population aware of the victimized status of blacks extracts a certain amount of compassion, though it is usually a safe bet to assume that a person who shows compassion or sympathy for members of a victimized class embody some of the same traits of that class. Advocates very often rise from the class whose interests they advocate. For instance, blacks stick together to fight racial discrimination of blacks but not racial discrimination of whites, and black women actively defend other black women and are advocates in issues concerning black women. Compassion prompts people to give more of themselves and to be more tolerant of situations they might not otherwise excuse. Like the strategy of unfounded charges of racial discrimination, in which an appeal to a race's victimized status is implied, too much awareness leads to compassion fatigue, a recognized condition whereby people become bereft of compassion, as though there is a limit to it for any single grievous condition before skepticism sets in.

Until fatigue sets in, though, many whites will submit special compensations, entitlements, and reparations to alleviate the perception that black Americans haven't been adequately repaid for historical mistreatment. Rewards based on an artificially heightened sense of guilt for being connected by race to black victimization ingrains a culture of victimization, making blacks feel as though they're worth only as much as the next hand-out. Self-esteem is irrevocably knotted to dependency on the base emotion of guilt.

People have a tendency to make victims responsible for their own victimization. In the rape trial of boxer Mike Tyson, for instance, Desiree Washington was assumed to be responsible for being raped by Tyson because she knew the boxer's history of violence and made the decision to visit his hotel room at 2 AM. By casting doubt on the victim's complicity, those who have ambivalence about the degree of their responsibility in the victimization can disassociate themselves from it. Blaming the victims, however, is an ineffective method for rejecting personal responsibility because it enrages those who already feel victimized. Victims of conditions often do not appropriately target their anger, but they refuse to accept, just as those being blamed illegitimately refuse to accept, the lion's share of responsibility for their victimization. People who feel they are being blamed for someone else's victimization can simply examine the extent of their individual responsibility for the victimization and dismiss the charges.

Refusing to accept responsibility that doesn't fit isn't an example of blaming victims, contrary to what many social commentators have suggested. Blauner suspects that the backlash of whites abandoning the ideals of civil rights due to urban riots and Black Power militancy wasn't so much an honest fear reaction as "simply a more respectable cover for an old fashioned racism with a dangerous new twist, one that shifted responsibility for the racial crisis from the prejudices of the majority to the behavior of the minority" (Blauner, 93).

An enhanced sense of victimization leads to a sense of lack of control over one's life. Placing blame on others asks others to react in a way to correct the condition. If others refuse to take reactive responsibility, those using the victimization charge may attribute racism as the true, though unproven, reason for such refusal. Making the easy charge precludes reasoned analysis of the underlying realities and factors in situations. It leads to the perception that blacks in general feel that racial considerations lend the most weight to the actions of non-minorities, which isn't the case in most situations. Though this perception will lead whites who don't want to be accused of being racist to choose their words carefully, it may also lead whites to diminish their respect for the analytic skills of blacks in general, further reinforcing negative generalizations about the intelligence of many blacks. Dependence on the victimization may also reduce responses to other, more probable causes for failure, such as the need to acquire skills required to get desirable, high-paying jobs and other social rewards.

Victims of economic disparity receive welfare. There is no racial inequality in poverty. Urban squalor makes victims of all those who walk through it.

Hard-working folks resent paying for other folks who flunked their education and refuse to take menial jobs that would only put them below the poverty level, making too little to pay for their children. "The food-stamp program, in turn, was a vehicle to let 'some young fellow ahead of you buy T-bone steak' while 'you were standing in a checkout line with your package of hamburger'" (Edsall and Edsall).

Welfare is a redistributive giveaway program for the social and economic underclasses. The bottom third of black communities is in this socially dysfunctional underclass, which absorbs taxes sacrificed mainly by working blacks and whites and lower-middle classes who shoulder the middle-class tax burden. The underclass is seen to have criminally aberrant values. They are too poor to afford the luxury they see around them and have come to expect in a wealthy society, and they become frustrated that they cannot purchase it. They feel like victims and use their frustration to legitimize obtaining the luxuries illegally.

Welfare makes it easy for poor people not to have a job and legitimately claim their victim status. Welfare requires only that unemployed people show proof that they applied for a certain number of jobs each week, regardless of how remote the chance is of getting the job. Welfare makes it tempting to take something for nothing, which leads to welfare dependency. Some have said that welfare is a bribe so blacks won't fuss over the possibility that whites aren't offering them jobs. The Aid to Dependent Children Program (ADC) has been accused of influencing single black mothers to have multiple births to take advantage of additional government funding. Similarly, Lyndon Johnson's $4.2 billion Poverty Cure program in 1965 had the unintended consequence of discouraging women from getting married because they could lose a welfare check if their husbands made money. Aid was conditional on being a single parent, which persuaded many in the poor community to relax the stigma against having children out of wedlock. Currently, 70 percent of black children are born to single moms (Mona, p. 101).

Welfare and ADC and housing subsidies enable and ease decisions to remain poor and have multiple births (baby factories become economically practical). "A system of benefits that asked no questions and demanded no accountability from recipients," (Mona, p. 103) invites abuse. Behaviorists and philosopher essayists such as Ayn Rand argue that rewarding people unconditionally for their refusal to work ensures the continued attitude in those people that there's no reason for them to work. Again, though the evidence from behavioral reinforcement research is born out for a certain category of people, not all people are that way. Not everyone fits the behaviorist's mold.

The welfare system is rampant with fraud because its administration is underfunded and understaffed. No system is perfect. But it is wasteful to scrap a system with flaws when no alternate system can be put into its place to aid the people who truly need the system, despite its flaws. However, a system that is so vulnerable to abuse is a bad system, and very costly:

> "Public policies backed by liberals … busing, affirmative action, and much of the rights revolution in behalf of … welfare recipients, and a host of other previously marginalized groups have, for many voters, converted the government from ally to adversary. The simultaneous increase, over the past … decades, in crime, welfare dependency, illegitimacy, and educational failure have estab-

lished in the minds of many voters a numbing array of 'costs'–perceived and real–of liberalism" (Edsall and Edsall, p. 53).

Misused votes can be evaluated only after well-intentioned policies backfire in their implementation or structure. So, it's a fallacy to say that those who don't vote have no legitimate right to complain about politicians holding office. The act of voting also does not bestow an ability to analyze the quality of service provided by a politician. Freedom of speech provides the legitimacy to complain about any topic, and the truth in the critical statements made is the basis of legitimacy.

In 1992, before welfare reform measures were passed, blacks totaled about 12.1 percent of America's population, but constituted about one-third of the recipients of welfare, health care, and unemployment benefits combined and were four and a half times more likely than whites to be on public assistance (Tidwell, *Dayton Daily News*). Some statistics placed the percentage of blacks receiving welfare at 40 percent. Tax-supported local housing authorities that pay for the rent of welfare recipients. Economically displaced inner-city residents were able to survive on welfare alone, so monetary incentives to seek employment were removed.

Everyone should have the right to choose the charities they support. Liberals rarely differentiate the deserving from the undeserving poor. According to most conservatives, the deserving poor have the following characteristics: tragedy befell them through no fault of their own; there is evidence of honesty and honest attempts to be independent; they follow religious morality; they have no children born out of wedlock; they are unselfish; they care for their children; they properly use charity funds for food/shelter; they have true gratitude; they experience a temporary acute need; and they have no record of criminality. For the undeserving, liberals have a sacred esteem for quotas for blacks, welfare, and job and education preferences.

If victims don't participate in their own emancipation from poverty, welfare preserves their victimhood. They never gain the means or the influence with powerful groups to gain support for something other than another poorly designed, unfair, costly system that disproportionately lays the funding burden on middle-class tax payers. Those coughing up funding have the right to ask, "How did they get poor?" Is it because they refuse to work? Is it because they are too lazy to apply themselves to gain an education that would allow them to get a good job? Is it because they are idealistic and refuse to risk defeat in the competitive game of capitalism, preferring to forfeit the game rather than play? Do they have serious moral qualms with the capitalistic system? Do they want to remain poor because being poor means getting welfare and handouts from people who try to raise the quality of their lives on their behalf? Withholding all aid to poor people because of the few who may be freeloaders would be a failure to help those who don't abuse the system, but use it as a stop gap measure to survive. But how can the system determine those who deserve, and who has the right to say others have a responsibility to help people who have less? It is an individual's choice to help. Those who want to help, may, and those who don't should have the choice not to.

Unfortunately, not many welfare recipients fall into the neat little category of being lazy. Some are single mothers with children to care for. Some are the children. Some are mentally or medically disabled. Some have no saleable skills and have never absorbed the education provided in sub-standard school systems. Some have difficulty getting to work or conforming to the demands of the workplace (that is, they're physically handicapped). Some embody multiple characteristics–mentally and physically handicapped single mothers with little education and saleable skills who can't afford transportation and childcare while at work. All of these people will suffer without help, and many of them may have no other support net. The premise that removing government support will force the "lazy bastards" to get a job doesn't hold up for the people who don't fit the laziness paradigm.

In general, people should be accountable for their own poor judgments and decisions in life that make them unemployable. Accepting that people possess varying levels of intelligence and that the public school system is not without flaws, society, to remain fair and civilized, should make monumental efforts to determine those who legitimately cannot help themselves. No one wants to work 8 to 12 hours a day, while the welfare families they support sit around all day doing nothing but watch TV.

Government policies, such as affirmative action, community reinvestment regulations, and federally mandated division of educational funds to programs aimed at minority groups, taint the achievements of blacks with the suspicion that the success was unearned, encourage distrust of public institutions like the judicial system, and foster conspiracy theories, such as the introduction of drugs by whites to inner-city blacks as a deliberate policy of genocide. Poor policies intended to level the playing field for minorities alienate middle-class whites whose support must be enlisted if racial harmony is to be realized.

American government had been bordering on socialism for so long, that people came to expect handouts. Then the government program to subsidize dairy farmers was quashed, and farmers were made to sell milk at market prices, and the warehouses of government cheese were fully depleted, and people stopped getting free cheese. Then the welfare reform programs started kicking deadbeats off the welfare roles. There is hope that sensible programs will hold sway.

4

Integrated Viewpoints, Separatist Counterpoints

The 1964 Civil Rights Act prohibited barring people based on their race from the right to purchase products and services, attend public schools of one's choice, congregate in all public arenas, and use all public facilities. Desegregation removed barriers to access. Integrationists touted the benefits of better education, better job opportunity, better purchasing selections, and better representation in political organizations for blacks. Integration promised the opportunity for segregated minorities to practice dealing with people in the mainstream culture, expanding perceptions to encompass national rather than racially indigenous reality (opinions about race are not likely to be changed within a racially isolated community). Ideally, personally knowing minorities would etch away at broadly applied bigotry, dispel racism by providing opportunities for positive interactions, and ethnic minorities would be accepted in white communities as morally strong and good at work, which is what the capitalistic system demands. Martin Luther King advocated integration to gain the benefits offered in public competition, though Malcolm X opposed integration, persuading blacks not to wholeheartedly embrace the mores of the American mainstream culture; wearers of caps embroidered with the 'X' make a statement about their opposition against mainstream culture.

Bringing people of many races together increases opportunities to learn things specific to other groups, such as a different race's historical solutions to problems, divergent mental processes and approaches to life, cultural interests. Hypothetically, integration gains potential contributions for the betterment of all groups. Integration lets people know people of other races and ethnic backgrounds, and lets them talk candidly about racial fears, stereotypes and ways to get along.

Legally enforced desegregation, however, didn't fundamentally change American society. For instance, a *USA Today* study in 1991 showed that the "Dayton-

Springfield area is the nation's 20th most racially segregated metropolitan area, and the fourth most segregated community in Ohio" (Haidet, *Dayton Daily News*). Civil rights laws could not mandate social attitude change in either blacks or whites. No one could have anticipated the degree of disagreement several decades later within black communities about the value of desegregation, or that such dissent wasn't traceable to white resistance to and recrimination about opening their racially closed worlds, though such resistance was strong and remains strong in some white communities.

Bob Woodson, a black conservative and former NAACP organizer, said, "I never marched to be next to white people. I marched so I could have a choice."

Integration was a legal imperative, pressing blacks to adapt, though not sacrifice, their culture and their group cohesion to assimilate into mainstream culture, risking the weakening of black ethnicity. The patchwork quilt metaphor, in which each ethnic group is separate with clearly defined boundaries, won the coined terminology contest to describe the phenomenon of self-segregation.

Blacks choose black role models and heroes (the usual suspects being Martin Luther King, Nelson Mandela, Malcolm X, and Mom [Allen, February 19, 2005]), whites pick whites, Chinese pick Chinese, etc. We learn about our own people in segregated families and communities. When we consider group dynamics and cohesiveness, we want people around us who are like us, who share our set of cultural values, religious beliefs, political positions, and habits. Our race, our FUBUism. We see to it that us and ours come first when rewards are shared.

> **Premise:** Voluntary self-segregation, or de facto segregation, does not demonstrate racism. It is not enforced by violence or threat of violence. It is segregation based primarily on common lifestyle and views, segregation in which people feel connected by their shared culture. People, in general, prefer to deal with others who are like themselves and who hold their values, common goals, political positions, and religious beliefs. Self-segregation doesn't break any laws and doesn't infringe on any civil rights. In addition to gravitating to others like themselves, many blacks self-segregate to avoid conflict and competition in a mainstream society that is felt to be racist and ruled by Eurocentric legal principles and economics, while many whites self-segregate because they fear for their safety in multiracial communities.

Some blacks feel that they lost their culture to integration, or at the very least subjected it to ideological contamination from other cultures. All that whites had to lose was their attitude of racial intolerance and their right to exclude other races from their workplaces and neighborhoods. In return, whites appropriated the most profitable components of black culture, such as rap music street culture, and clothing style. In integrated businesses, white employers still have the right to tell blacks what to do and how to do it.

If blacks and whites don't get together, they can't know one another, and must form generalized conceptions about race, and the result of ignorance leads to racial prejudice and stereotypes. Some integrationists feel that if you know people and their culture, you don't fear either, and you don't hate. Such conclusions require several implausible leaps of logic and facile sloganeering considering the many reasons people can count for hating other people. No longer fearing the unknown of black culture does little to reduce racist attitudes and stereotypes. Whites, receptive to the idea of learning about other cultures, may or may not progress to hatred from such a learning experience; other emotional options are available–excitement about the novelty of exploring racial differences, enthusiasm, adventure, eagerness for new possibilities, gladness for another chance to learn, and the same kind of uncertainty and anxiety that accompanies not knowing who's going to win a baseball game.

Some whites feel that the integration efforts applied in only one direction. Minorities exclude whites from black-only organizations and establishments, creating a double standard that allowed minorities to maintain their culture while also reaping the benefits of success in the business world, which was dominated by whites, and disallowing whites-only organizations. Blacks defend the double standard. Minorities must be given the opportunity to experience success in their own culture, using standards that differ from those used to measure success in integrated businesses. Otherwise, blacks would be overwhelmed by white success and would never know what it feels like to experience pride and accomplishment in business. Similar reasons are offered for the racially discriminatory Miss Black American Pageant; black women must feel successful, and gaining success in a field traditionally dominated by whites is difficult.

There is no racial discrimination, blacks claim, in having exclusively black organizations, though excluded races and nationalities would disagree. The double standard doesn't apply for whites who would develop an organization called The National Organization of White People (which already exists as Aryan Nation, KKK, and redneck trailer trash). Blacks would consider a White Miss America pageant to be racist. If self-segregation is defined for blacks as allowing freedom of congregational and exclusionary choice, the same definition should apply for all races that wish to self-segregate. Exclusive women's and men's groups, groups based on religious beliefs, height, baldness, psychological dysfunction, and addiction, for instance, don't discriminate by race but by other criteria that all members have in common. Nonracial groupings focus on commonality, not on differences, and it is assumed that more widely based groupings accommodate people of all races.

All organizations that have the words black or African-American or colored or Negro as part of their names emphasize the fact of segregation, though many actual African-Americans can also be Caucasian. The Ohio Commission on Socially Disadvantaged Black Males, formed in 1989 by former Governor Richard Celeste, hosted the first Ohio African American Male Youth Leadership Conference on June 26, 1992. The commission created the Black Male Leadership Development Institute. There are too many specialized, separatist groups to include here.

The title, *For Black Women Only: A Complete Guide to a Successful Life-Style Change Health, Wealth, Love and Happiness,* by Ingrid D. Hicks, promotes the perception that blacks and whites experience life characteristics differently than both white women and all men, compounding the insult of separatism with sexism. Nelson George, author of *Elevating the Game ... Black Men and Basketball,* states in his introduction that the book "is not balanced. The focus is on African-American history and African-American men. I consider certain European-Americans only as they relate to the African-American experience." Stress management can also take an Afrocentric spin: Giovanni Bonds sponsors a retreat named "Stressed Out Sisters." The retreat, which encourages attendance only by black women, focuses on Afrocentric approaches of rejuvenating the spirits of black women, exclusively. Bonds states that black women have always survived by relating to other black women. "'This weekend is about women leaning on each other, building on the strengths of black women as sisters for each other.'" Bonds states that she wants retreat participants to feel "'that freedom you can get while you're around your own people" (Clark, p. 2C). Other, black-only organizations, such as the African American Women's Agenda, attempt to get "blacks at the planning nucleus of the power system so their message won't get lost in any emotional reaction" (Clark).

Many books propagate hatred against the white race. For instance, Paul Hill, Jr. in *Coming of Age: The African American Male Rites-Of-Passage* advocates institutionalizing African rites-of-passage acts "as part of the socialization process for rearing male children in a society hostile to their presence and committed to their destruction." Books like *Countering the Conspiracy to Destroy Black Boys, Volumes I, II, & III* promote fear and the feeling that blacks cannot trust whites. *Motivating and Preparing Black Youth to Work* assumes that the traditional motivators to work, to support family, to experience pride in one's work, to earn enough money to purchase luxury items, to compete with one's neighbor in terms of material possession, are somehow different for black youth.

Black business organizers also buy into the concept that blacks are more comfortable buying from black-oriented businesses: "'You want to see black faces, black salespeople. They want to see blacks at the hotels–not just working behind the counter as visible tokens.' Black meeting planners also want to know about a city's minority hiring practices and to see brochures promoting black achievements and attracts" (*Atlanta Journal*). Blacks are shown to wield enough economic force to persuade hotels to consider blacks as viable customers. Apologies by hotel management who don't treat black organizations with sensitivity "illustrate the growing recognition of the economic clout of black organizations," the article's author speculates. One questions whether businesses are apologizing to blacks or only for the money they bring, or might be apologizing from a common courtesy that is extended to all customers who complain, regardless of race.

It is assumed that those most familiar with the culture of their business' customers are more able to serve those customers, anticipate their needs, better understand their nonverbal cues. For instance, black NFL coaches are argued to be better equipped to deal with black players. They more highly value, and can build, team cohesion based on race and assumed cultural similarity. Black coaches are presumed to know more about black culture than whites and can use cultural cues to more greatly motivate black players. Cultural knowledge is wrongly assumed based on the thinking that all black athletes have the same single culture. All coaches might be better served by emphasizing the common threat of the opposing team as the bond that will bring the multiple races on a team together as a cohesive unit.

Hoping to achieve racial diversity in their business organizations and educational institutions and customer bases, public relations officials also market to finely delineated, race-based interests, promoting the racial benefits of doing business with white-owned establishments to attract blacks and their checkbooks.

Self-stratification based on group commonality, such as race, yields undeniable benefits. However, a downside exists, primarily as a result of race exclusivity and insulated perspectives, both concepts that have split minority camps philosophically for decades. Race-exclusive groups highlight the apparently hostile "us versus them" ideology and discourage sympathy about black issues among the barred race. Race jingoism creates, rather than closes, the chasm between races and cultures.

Separatist and insulated groups also maintain and propagate bigoted perspectives, rather than expanding perspectives. To achieve full cultural diversity, the voices of all races should be heard, and learning to make one's voice heard in a diverse rather than a respectful racial grouping will have greater value in life.

The "need" for race-exclusive organizations may also be seen as evidence of inadequacy or emotional weakness. Certain standards of excellence and integrity must be met as a requirement of transitioning to integration, or at least the sincere desire to diligently learn how to meet such standards. Rather than learn, however, many blacks want to be appraised by a different set of standards that acknowledge that they have had fewer job opportunities and less educational encouragement as excuses for failing to meet general standards of performance. If self-esteem, for example, relies upon achievements that are realized only among those of similar ability, without the added distraction of real-world performance and competition, then self-esteem may be shattered when those outside the minority scoff at the insignificance of these achievements.

Success doesn't only depend on the less demanding framework within an artificial representation of a broader business area. Many ethnic teachers believe that quality is improved for minority students who are taught by other minorities. They cite motivation, role models, and assumed similarity of interests/historical background. Minority teachers feel that they have more empathy for minority students than non-minority teachers, because of the assumed similarity of the minority teacher's hardships and the hardships faced by minority students and their families. Such commonality is said to increase the minority students' interest in learning and in the fields of study presented.

> **Premise**: There is no proof that similarity between teachers and students generally improves test scores or intelligence levels.

Blacks have their own religious customs and educational goals which predominantly white schools don't observe. Integrated schools seldom specifically teach blacks how to succeed in white culture by white rules, so blacks must increasingly impose black culture in integrated educational settings so that black students will not feel frustration when encountering a setting that fails to acknowledge black customs. Exceptions to this strategy include Duke University, in which blacks enforce segregated communities, and Oberlin College, in which separate buses carry students to school. Many colleges have separate parties by race and separate eating areas by race. To impose black culture within predominantly white institutions, multicultural diversity awareness programs are emphasized and whites resistant to the hypothetical value of diversity are accused of damaging the self-esteem of black children. Many whites resent the movement to bring more black culture training into the educational curriculum because they associate black values and culture with negative conditions: low I.Q., high crime, poverty, violence, and animalism.

The alleged necessity for segregated black groups and double standards further drives a wedge between people. Mainstream America will not fully modify its behavior to meet the needs of a minority, and concessions by race are hard to come by. Businesses and social organizations ask if it's wrong that blacks and whites don't understand each other and don't care to. What is wrong with living separately though having the option not to? If the personal choice of both parties is to remain separate, why should anyone force people to come together when they don't want to? Does being apart cause economic and social deterioration of either separate area, or do other factors determine more adverse conditions in the black neighborhoods? Is there anything wrong with entrenched housing patterns that cultivate insulated lives?

Many minorities attempt to economically, politically, and culturally sustain separate minority communities. They participate in and abide by general capitalistic rules and definitions of mobility and success only when such participation in mainstream functions is necessary to ensure the receipt of basic social benefits. Riches can be obtained and held by many people in multiple separate, local regional, and autonomous communities by offering specialized services and products to racial groups, such as self-segregated predominantly black resorts. However, many in the black community are divided about whether to embrace either the integrationist or the cultural separatism philosophy, unable to discern their personal and political priorities, and unable to reconcile their cultural and philosophical diversity with the ideas of integrated American economic systems. Many try to remain separate, yet demand special treatment within the integrated system.

Business is in business for profit, a truism of the capitalist system that defies attempts to link business with supporting racially separate communities, or as a means to contribute to the black cause, to the improvement of black life. Businesses in integrated communities threaten such race-specific support, such as Koreans did in South Central L.A. when they opened businesses that successfully competed with black-owned businesses. Prejudices and stereotypes against Koreans were inflamed when Korean retailers underpriced area black businesses, attracting black customers who disloyally abandoned black-owned stores for better bargains. Exclusively black businesses and social establishments lost membership to better-equipped integrated facilities, making black enclaves in urban areas economically infeasible. Koreans and other outside retailers drain the resources within insulated communities, and aren't bound by their race to demonstrate their community spirited nature by giving back to the community.

Some blacks prioritize advancing themselves over the advancement of their race, developing an individualistic egoism and lack of altruism, which more directly aligns with integrated American culture. This kind of selling out causes culture-based conflict in the black community. Success in conforming to capitalist rules reinforces a lack of empathy for other blacks who blame their own failures on the capitalist system and who may actively reject entrepreneurial practices as a way to preserve the black culture. Inherent characteristics of individual blacks and the choices they make, and not general class or economy characteristics explain failure.

The separatist structure fails because the isolating minority often is not self-sustaining. The decisions black separatist groups made in the 60s to gain economic independence within their own neighborhoods achieved group identity but led to seclusion and closed boundaries, blocking new ideas of better business methods from suffusing into the community.

One way to return profits to separatist groups, according to Oscar J. Coffey, president of the National Black Chamber of Commerce, is for cities to "establish enterprise zones in urban areas that nurture small black-owned businesses with low-interest loans and business expertise." Local governments have attempted to work with the separatist pockets in society, providing enterprise zone tax breaks to encourage self-determined, legitimate black businesses to move into depressed, self-secluded areas. Some blacks expect government, based on government's past support of slavery and denied civil rights for blacks, to make special concessions to minority-owned business rather than treat all businesses alike in the granting of government contracts. It is expected that the government select the most impoverished businesses to deliver services and products rather than the most successful. It is expected that government charitably support poorly performing minority-owned businesses rather than non-minority-owned businesses that are doing just as poorly.

Rather than demand conformity else feel the economic brunt of such failure, governments offer socialistic incentives to get separatists to embrace capitalism, a contradiction of economic philosophies that cannot work together.

Minority segregation in business and education may promote unethically misleading reporting procedures so that the segregated establishment can maintain an illusion that it is offering products and services that are comparable to the products and services of integrated establishments. For instance, in predominantly black, state-funded educational institutions, some segregationist administrators request that their faculty change non-passing grades for a quota of students. This practice presents a deceptive picture that the university is adequately serving the public interest, is earning support funds supplied by the government, and can successfully educate minority students as well in a segregated environment as students who attend integrated universities are educated.

The entertainment industry has answered requests that blacks in film and television programs be depicted within a black culture, doing away with integrated casts; Judd Nelson was the token white character in the movie, *New Jack City*, for instance. It used to be that being a black actor wasn't economically feasible in Hollywood when the cost of casting all-black films wasn't expected to pull enough theatergoers to turn a profit. To pick up the black audiences and satisfactorily rebut the charges that the entertainment industry produces entertainment only for whites, producers create programming that appeals only to blacks, creating all-black cast television programs as a means of employment for black actors and a means to satisfy black viewers. It turns out that blacks in all-black television sitcoms get into the same silly situations that whites do in white sitcoms—that's parity.

Including an integrated cast of characters gets the ratings numbers up. Racial discrimination isn't an issue for blacks auditioning for a role that's written for a black, though colorism is often cited, meaning that film and TV producers feel that white viewers are more likely to accept light-skinned blacks in roles with integrated casting. Integration alienates some black and some white viewers; fewer black viewers are expected to care what goes on in white culture, and whites are thought to have little interest in black culture, or the conception of black culture through the eyes of the entertainment industry. People who don't care, don't buy tickets, and the asses don't make it into the colorblind seats.

Show business and the general reporting media has to be portrayed not as stereotypes, but as typical people in the context of black culture and integrated situations. The mass media do shape the way people perceive one another; if the only blacks that film goers ever see are gang banger stereotypes, that inevitably affects opinions about their own race. Black viewers focus on negative character traits associated with blacks in film and novels, and unreasonably demand that blacks be drawn as more heroic and noble, else the entire race will be negatively affected by the impression of the characterization, which undermines the black race's objective of changing negative perceptions. Giving in to demands to create black role models equates with censorship of artistic freedom, subversion of art to political agendas.

Racial offense was the focus of protests early in 2005 for portrayals of fictional characters in the Fox Network television serial *24*. Members of the Council on American-Islamic Relations (CAIR) were outraged by the heartlessness of a terrorist Muslim family living in a sleeper cell in America. Says CAIR spokesperson Rabiah Ahmed, "'There's danger in ... Muslims constantly being portrayed as terrorists.'" "Fox executives and *24*'s producers are addressing the concerns. They met with CAIR's leaders, and, as a result, agreed to distribute to all 182 Fox affiliates 'I Am an American Muslim,' a CAIR-produced [30-second] public service announcement that depicts Muslims in a positive light" (*TV Guide*, February 6, 2005, p. 8). Frequent portrayal of ethnic minorities having singular character traits, such as Italians being Mafia gangsters in the movies, influence public opinion and create stereotypes. Black leaders invoke hyperbole to describe their outrage that a thug in a movie was played by a black man: "It's tragic." No people of any race are like those portrayed in most movies and in television shows; characters aren't real people, and minorities need to learn what's real and what isn't.

Disney's revision of *Fantasia* was intended to obliterate all record and all association of stereotyped images of blacks with the Disney studio. The removal of scenes of racial stereotypes in old films actually obliterates the fact that American filmmakers have a history of dropping racially stereotypical metaphors into their work, erasing all indication that racism in films was intended to teach children white morals and values. Disney also hoped that revising *Fantasia* would let it reach the broader audience of blacks who may have objected to the way blacks had been previously depicted in it.

"In the years of integration, black actors and black themes began to be integrated into mainstream films. A new generation of black filmmakers is determined to tell black stories from a black perspective, to black audiences who have been largely ignored by Hollywood. They want artistic and financial control" (Lawson, *Dayton Daily News*). The 2005 Oscars may have satisfied the need in Hollywood to embrace black-oriented, integrated movies, while desperately attracting minority viewers through the show's multicultural sensitivity. "[Chris] Rock did his usual riffing on black culture, Beyonce Knowles warbled two songs, and the camera cut obsessively all night between African-Americans in the audience...." (*The Week*, Volume 5, Issue 198, p. 19).

Black children internalize a negative self-image based on how they see, usually in the media, other blacks treated. The media shows actual mistreatment of blacks and editorializes about the degree of this mistreatment, and they also represent blacks as violent, poor, and uneducated, which the media bases on statistics. Direct, positive experiences with members of minorities "tend to be overwhelmed by second-hand sources of information: stories picked up from parents, things on the news, particularly relating to crime and violence, and our political practices" (Horwitt, *Dayton Daily News*, August 1992). It is just as irrational to generalize from a single first-hand experience with race as it is to generalize negative traits seen in the media to the whole minority.

Blacks and whites remain largely socially separate, but the reason for this separateness is only partially due to a previous generation's proscriptions against integration. The races remain separate by personal histories, identities, and emotional attachments of each group to its own race. Each group cites its personal attachments as culture and refuses to give up the culture that they have instilled with such emotional value. They will not integrate, thereby losing some of their habits, routines, and practices to accommodate the demands of larger, integrated groups. If a gap can be prized open in these groups, many of the reservations against allowing different races into groups could be resolved.

The races are not in the same boat. Though we're all in this together, the destinies of whites and blacks aren't intertwined on either a general or individual level. For many of us, our destinies aren't even intertwined with those of our parents, not to mention our own race. And there is no proof that an entire race's destiny is controlled by or linked to the destiny of another race's success or failure. Individuals control their own destinies and the destinies of a few others who may allow themselves to be controlled. Substantial numbers don't want to mix with other races. Whites don't want to throw their lot in with blacks, risk becoming emotionally involved in the black dilemma. Whites see so many ways that integration by blacks and the acceptance of even low-paying employment, rejection of regressive rap music sentiment, and consistent use of birth control methods would prevent the tragedies they see in the black community. They don't understand non-assimilation, especially when they witness rude black youths who seem to become disruptive only after entering integrated theaters and restaurants, seemingly flaunting their right to be discourteously loud and obnoxious because they paid for the privilege. Blacks who have been led to believe that whites will oppress them spend their lives looking for opportunities not to take orders from whites, and consider this attitude a virtuous crusade that they easily reinforce every time they antagonize whites.

A consequence of continued separatism, paired with demands for special treatment, is prolonged negativity among the races.

Hyphenated Americans

Blacks who have always lived in the U.S. and have no current or former dual citizenship in any African country imply a false affiliation when they identify themselves as African-Americans. Hyphenation is about a separate, distant nationalism and heritage, not race. African-American isn't color-neutral; generations of whites have been born in Africa and live out their lives as African citizens. African-American doesn't conjure images of African princes and royalty; American blacks who wear the dress of royal African tribal leaders are more likely descended from hunter/gatherers who warred with other tribes, lived in grass huts, had primitive technology, and exerted no princely powers.

African-American is a pretension to something that people imagine as their racial homeland, giving American blacks something bigger, something illusionary to cling to, an exclusive quest for ascendancy that American whites can't participate in or take away. Differentiating people born in the U.S. as African-American fulfills a desire to highlight one's separateness and national allegiances.

"I think the notion of a hyphenated American is un-American," Daniel Boorstin notes to *Parade* interviewer Tad Szulc. "I believe there are only *Americans*. Polish-Americans, Italian-Americans or African-Americans are an emphasis that is not fertile" (Szulc, quoting Daniel J. Boorstin).

Hyphenation is an impediment to acceptance of people of other races and cultures. Hyphenation implies that the name of the country in the initial position is more important than the name in the second, subordinate position. Hyphenation says, "My country comes first. I give it my allegiance first. It will always be first in my heart." Hyphenation intends to emphasize not racial, but national segregation from American culture. Though thoroughly American, some blacks act as though their culture is stridently separate, ages old, to be respected. Many whites have long forgotten their ancestor's European roots because such connections are often completely irrelevant in an assimilationist society, except on ethnic-recognition holidays where there'll be music, food, and beer.

Habitual use of African-American may lead to negative conclusions about the degree of patriotism that American blacks feel, a value about which many Americans feel strongly. Fraudulent misuse of African-American, though fashionable, evokes feelings of ambivalence about black commitment to the support of integrated life. To some whites, hyphenation is interpreted as an intentionally obvious reminder to whites of where blacks lived before whites forcibly removed them from their homeland and enslaved them in America.

Legal citizens of the U.S. are simply Americans. American-born blacks aren't just visiting, having no intention of investing in American communities, taking all that America has to offer and leaving the country for the African continent. Spoiled by the protections offered in American democracy, freedom, opportunity, relative safety, civil rights, superior infrastructure, choice of entertainments, modern daily conveniences, and leisure time, it is unlikely that American blacks would choose to tough it out in arid Ethiopia, live under harsh military rule in Somalia or other African dictatorships, battle the legacy of apartheid in South Africa, fear for their lives in civil-war-torn pockets where genocide is a very real possibility, or live in barren deserts with little food, scant sanitized drinking water, traveling medicos, and substandard educational opportunities, while tending a small agricultural plot far from civilization in order to survive. American blacks do not live like African blacks in terms of culture, personality, motivation, or identity.

American blacks owe allegiance only to America, though they may acknowledge emotional tugs to the continent from which their ancestors were stolen, often with the help of African blacks who, confronted with the temptation of trinkets, raided other black tribes to round up more slaves for the Europeans. Hyphenation has its genesis in an emphasis on returning to only the positive African cultural roots, a selective and revisionist view of reality. Knowledge of one's racial heritage and connections and place in the world was expected to motivate blacks to feel more positive about themselves, raise self-esteem, and instill a sense of pride and larger belonging. For some, the courage of tribal leaders imparted assertiveness and confidence in the face of racial discrimination in America. For others, comparing their lives with the lives of Africans made them appreciate where they came from but appreciate more where they are–in America.

Africans "had many tribal pasts, and it was virtually impossible to identify one's own particular historical roots. [H]ow were they to symbolize their past? What flags, anthems, religious heroes and heroines were they to claim in asserting their ethnic identity?" (Fuchs, 178). So, American blacks adopted Pan African colors to encompass all of Africa, since Europeans had split up the tribes across geographical areas, making it difficult for American blacks to claim a specific tribe.

We all have the option of tracing our heritage and enjoying the interest inherent in the mystery, the research, the facts, the insight into discovering what kind of people contributed to our eventual birth. We all also have the right to advertise our separate ancestral descent through hyphenation.

"I object to the belief that it is more important that we belong to some particular small group than to the human race.... The separate groups in our country are concerned about their power—whether it be black power or white power ..." (Szulc, quoting Daniel J. Boorstin).

The hyphenation convention, taken to its thematic limits for an American black who takes up citizenship in France, for example, would be African-American-French or French-African-American. Further regionalizing and alliterating, Atlantan-African-American. But this isn't right, either, because Africa is a continent, not a country. For consistency, hyphenation should be country-country or continent-continent; African-North-American. Such specification is not possible for black descendants who cannot trace their lineage to a specific country in Africa, so leeway is extended for the inconsistent hyphenation.

Some believe that developing a homage mindset is virtuous, but who we are now, in the present, and not our heritage, defines us. Americans must see superiority and strength in being American, accepting and forgiving its heritage of racial oppression in much the same way that blacks selectively discount the negative aspects of African culture. Racial delusion about the royalty of one's heritage is unproductive. Hyphenation fosters divisiveness; rejection of hyphenated nationality promotes American nationalism.

Separatists and Adoption

Black separatists condemn the adoption of black children by whites. Black children raised by white parents will inevitably gain a different, non-black set of beliefs about life. Undoubtedly, these black children *will not* hear that black poverty and poor education and lack of employment opportunities are the result of whites keeping blacks down. White parents won't describe their race's participation in classic AIDS and drug conspiracies against blacks in the inner cities. The black child will serve as an instrument to dilute the black race's group cohesion, never to learn about his African heritage. How can blacks as a race gain power if black children adopted by whites are corrupted to reject black culture, which is one of the alleged conspiratorial goals of white adopters? In an unforgivable betrayal of one's race, black children adopted by whites will embrace white ideals, and may not develop racist beliefs at all, neither against blacks nor whites nor against any other racial or ethnic minority. Such children would find it disadvantageous to hate their white parents, as racist black separatists would prefer.

Adoption agencies that base placement of black children on segregationist policies may deny black children a stable family with white parents for the questionable offsetting value of installing black heritage concepts, though this stated desired result cannot be guaranteed in any race's household. Agencies that operate from separatist philosophy may tacitly support the tendency of blacks quietly adopting black children from relatives or from foster homes because there are no fees, rather than from agencies, though such back alley practices receive no oversight to ensure that the children are going to qualified parents. Blacks also adopt in much fewer numbers than whites, who are more likely to adopt white children than black children, and thus leave a glut of black children that stay in the system with foster parents an average of 60 percent longer than white children.

Because of the outcry by black separatists against whites adopting black children, 300 families in British Columbia, Canada adopted the overflow from the Open Door Adoption Agency in Georgia. The U.S. appears to be exporting black babies to circumvent resistance by black separatists.

A Minnesota law gives preference to same-race families in adoptions–and similar policies exist in other states, making children pawns in a game of racial politics. Lou Freeman, president of the NAACP's Minnesota-Dakotas conference, "likens Minnesota's law, called the Heritage Preservation Act, to apartheid. 'It's emotional, racist, ethnocentric foolishness. We are trying to become one society. The test should be what is in the best interest of the child" ("Racial match in adoptions debated," *Dayton Daily News*).

Steven Belton, an attorney for the black grandparents of Baby D, who had been a foster child to Steve and Janet Sharp, a white couple who had filed to adopt the 3-year-old girl, stated that "'Part of the legacy of slavery is that they took away your children. That heritage can't be ignored.'" Jacqui Smith, a family coordinator, feels that the white parents' love isn't enough for a black child. "'We have to save our children. If you've never spent any time where you're the outsider, you don't know how that feels.'" Leora Neal, who heads the adoption service for the New York chapter of the National Association of Black Social Workers, states that black children "'have already lost their biological family. To lose their race and culture is just another blow to their ego and their self-esteem.'" "Many blacks say racial tensions in the United States make it even more important to preserve the cultural identity of minority children." Blacks have called interracial adoption "cultural genocide" ("Racial match in adoptions debated," *Dayton Daily News*).

The argument by adoption segregationists is like homosexual guys pouting when they learn the hunk they're eyeing is lost to the "straight" team (oh no you di'ent just go there, SNAP!).

Flawed generalizations are evident in the issue of whites adopting black infants and children. Stating that only black parents can indoctrinate a black child is an example of blacks stereotyping blacks as having a single black culture, ignoring those blacks whose life focus might not be in the passing of the racial heritage baton, ignoring those blacks who, like subpopulations of effete whites, appreciate the opera and foreign art films and literary book club discussions and Barry Manilow (okay, not Barry Manilow). The argument that whites are incapable of instilling black heritage generalizes that all black families who might otherwise adopt black children have the same black heritage and culture in common and that those black adoptive parents have a compelling drive to instill this black heritage as a programming initiative for the adopted child.

Separatists also distinguish "black" love from "white" love, as if love knows color and race, can be better or worse, or can be felt more strongly from blacks than whites. Such false, generalized distinctions that one race's love in general is superior or more desirable than another's prejudice children against interracial romance and any hope of harmony among the races.

It's understandable that parents and grandparents want to perpetuate tradition in their children, but if black tradition can only be imparted in black families, this suggests that heritage is supremely delicate and easily lost if not constantly nurtured. It implies that children won't seek other sources of information outside of their adoptive parents, that they never meet other kids of their own race at school, on the basketball court or skating slopes, and that they can't find books and videos on the subject of black heritage in libraries. It also ignores the concept of open adoptions in which the black biological parents are invited to spend time with their offspring.

Another implication of the generalization that only blacks should be allowed to adopt black children is that white adoptive parents may maliciously refuse to educate the black child fairly and impartially about race, or will distort historical facts about black heritage and tradition, or purposely misinform. The generalization also suggests that all white cultures are devoid of valid heritage and values. Opponents of interracial adoption advance a number of other insulting, unsupported accusations:

- whites are more likely to mistreat and abuse black children than adoptive black parents are (no child protective service organizations have been able to verify a disproportionate number of confirmed reports of abuse by white adoptive parents of black or other minority children)

- whites will teach black children that white racism for blacks doesn't exist, and the black child's innocence will make him more vulnerable to racism and less able to identify it in later life
- whites can't appropriately mentor black children, won't address the black children's identity problems or answer the black child's questions of Who am I? Where do I belong?
- whites can't teach racial strength and pride in black children
- whites will turn black children against the black race, making them ashamed of being black
- whites buying blacks through adoption is too reminiscent of slavery.

Advocates of separatist adoptions speak in refutable generalities about the benefits of raising children in a stable family, as if anyone would feel it was preferable to raise any child in an unstable environment. They imply that for black children, only a black family is stable. Being reared in a black environment lets one feel good about one's racial group identity, even though racial heritage can't be escaped–color, along with differing physical features, are distinct identifiers. They state that the child's full knowledge of the black experience builds a positive attitude about its cultural heritage, but this positive identification is often achieved by prejudicially demoting and defaming white racial heritage, making the heritage-installation argument a veiled demand for segregation. Children who are repeatedly told to feel good about their race may even develop doubt, feeling that they must be inferior, else why all the reminders?

Separatists argue a general principle that self-identification begins early in the preschool years and that it's essential to be surrounded by nurturing persons and an environment that can shape a healthy identity and a productive person. But this principle applies just as validly to white Americans as to black. Identity isn't more important, or at least it hasn't been proven to be more important, for black children than for whites. A predominantly black environment can be as hostile for a white child as a predominantly white environment is for a black child. However, discomfort for black children in white school environments may be escalated because black children have been told so often by black parents to question their racial equality when they enter a multiracial environment. If white parents focused so much teaching about the whiteness of its race, white children may feel just as uncomfortable about their racial heritage in predominantly black environments.

In unity of thought and purpose, there is greater strength to press for group self-interests; unity in strength is the meaning of an African saying that sticks in a bundle can't be broken. More adherents and their added voices in groups can more effectively get the group's word out and promote the group's interests. The message for black separatists is that black children raised in a black household are more likely than those raised in a white household to be recruited to embrace the separatist ideology. Black parents are recruited by black separatists and asked to emphasize to their children how their race makes them different. To achieve this emphasis, black parents must consciously select points of contrast that support their own orientation against another race, selecting stereotyped characteristics of the race they wish to attack, contributing significantly to the perpetuation of racist attitudes. Whites run the same risk of instilling racist attitudes.

Children of separatists will actively interpret every social interaction in terms of how its racial heritage controls the way the interaction proceeds. They have learned all of the stereotypes from their parents and have had precious few experiences to the contrary. They nurture their beliefs and refuse to consider that a person from another race can be trusted, which would mean that the child's parents were lying, an unacceptable option for children who know how to deny their own positive experiences to continually substantiate and validate their parents' pronouncements. Decency by whites is seen as an ulterior motive, and the separatists' suspicion, which is evident, is correctly attributed by the white participant as the product of racism. Whites see racism. Whites see it, and many deplore it, regardless of which race commits it.

Separatists advocate separate neighborhoods, separate schools, and separate cultures, though separation by race into secluded societies has been shown to limit equal distribution of and access to public resources. They hint that their children will be able to experience success only within closed, uniracial cultures, though seclusion prevents opportunities to meet and expand individual growth potential, and brings frustration and longing for general praise and recognition for excellence in the society of humankind. Removing children from the mainstream of society and placing them in self-enforced segregated cultures isolates them from the success–and the failure–they might encounter in the broader society. Children lower their expectations because they are told to. They lose hope of gaining broader recognition for their talent because they are told to. They blame the people their parents tell them are responsible for the different set of standards, when they should instead be indignant about the artificial restrictions their own culture has placed on them. When they are finally introduced to a broader culture and higher standards, secluded children will feel inferior, unprepared, and lost.

Teaching black children that they must embrace only the black culture to experience success in life teaches hatred and vindictiveness toward whites for alleged injustices. It admits to a willful failure to integrate (desegregate) in society. These children are being taught a method of justifying self-defeat by blaming it on an entire race of people. They are not being taught how to use all of the available resources and opportunities. They are not being taught to accept social rules that humans live by. They are not being taught how to better their existence, only how to live with limitations. So, separatists would raise their children with the destructive ideology that praise and recognition must come only from blacks. This nearly effectively quashes any hope the child may have had of excelling in society as a whole rather than excelling in a small world shaped by the perceptions of parents—that blacks can excel only in a black culture. Some pessimistic blacks have adopted the catchy phrase, "as blacks, we have to work harder."

Separatists advise black parents to remind their children that they should be prepared to encounter more stressful situations because of their minority identity. Black children should learn that whites will refuse jobs based on race, will mistreat blacks because of their race, and will stereotype blacks so whites can retain their racist attitude. There doesn't have to be a tradeoff: the physical and emotional welfare of the child versus the preservation of racial hatred.

Some black leaders recognize the prevalence of separatist ideas in the black community and condone the excuse that integration has caused failure in black American businesses. If blacks fail, failure is unlinked from ability and linked to white control of the means of a black's success. They lump all whites in a class, which conveniently ignores the exceptions. Some white employers are racists. Others discriminate only by test scores or by their assumptions about a job applicant's abilities based on the applicant's experience in the field. Others discriminate according to the applicant's peculiar dialect and English pronunciation. Realizing that Black English is non-standard, some blacks go into interviews speaking standard English. Others refuse to change their speech, saying they're not going to change their heritage just to satisfy some white bread employer. They are rebelling against the business culture in which they want to assimilate. You just don't use jargonistic, culture-specific speech and abbreviated words in a business setting when you're trying to communicate clearly and impress customers into coming back again. It has little to do with race, and a lot to do with business. Blacks are not being singled out and forced to assimilate the ideals of the social or business culture whose acceptance is desired. All whites are not afraid of black success in predominantly white businesses.

Separatists disguise their racism by speciously exploiting the argument that blacks need to exercise the preservation of their cultural heritage. What has been the heritage of black Americans but slavery and oppression? What has been the heritage of white Americans but enslaving and oppressing, things which whites cannot take pride in? Why do separatists want their children to remember how white ancestors subjugated the black race except to preserve not the culture, but the hatred? And such facts are often presented in in-your-face fashion, tauntingly.

A black child who becomes accustomed to living in an integrated environment will be more comfortable with either race than a child raised in a uniracial culture. This isn't tantamount to rejecting his own race, and doesn't indicate that the child who feels comfortable with either race lacks strong identity with his own race.

Whites have been playing longer on the capitalistic field, an economic system that does not exclude players based on race, though other players may, so whites have an advantage, knowledge of how to use and bend the rules which they can then help adopted black children to understand. Whites feel there is no dishonor in giving black children the advantage of a middle-class education, economic opportunity, and game skills in a competitive environment. Black customers may have different demands, but until then, mutual communication must be maintained using the most accepted standard: English. Keeping black children in foster care isn't preferable. Reproaching economically strapped single black mothers who've put their children in a foster home, thus giving whites the opportunity to turn black children against blacks, isn't productive; vilifying poor, single and divorced black mothers is even a little hypocritical since it is often because black fathers who've shunned their familial responsibilities that gave mothers little option but to take the adoption route.

Successful adult blacks who've been raised in white adoptive families and who oppose segregation are poster-child exceptions to black segregationist propaganda. Exceptions to belief systems must be justified or discounted. The greater the number of exceptions, the more effort is required to justify segregation not just to oneself, but to those from whom the group wishes to be taken seriously either for recruitment purposes or for monetary solicitations. For instance, every successful exception who comes out of the projects is proof of the possibilities; such success deflates arguments that the condition of impoverished inner-city blacks is hopeless in the face of racist government policy and corporation. It is easier to sabotage an inner-city black's attempts to succeed than to explain away such success when it occurs.

Rather than tell their children to fight every characteristic associated with a different race, parents should tell their children that all humans don't perceive other humans as having equal rights, though they should for the sake of humanity. Meanwhile, should white couples be deprived of the joy of loving a child, caring for a child, and ending a child's suffering and hunger simply because the child is black and carries the baggage of separatist outcries? Should children become the victims of racially divisive vindictiveness? Should children be deprived of a stable, nurturing environment where one could not be found in their own cultural circle? Interracial adoption will not change a black child's curiosity about its heritage. The child will quickly realize that it is different from its adoptive white parents and will want to explore that difference. It is hoped that the type of people who would adopt a child of a different race would teach that child that being different doesn't mean being inferior.

Anything interracial irks separatist blacks, but also hits a nerve with separatist whites who think that black males date white females only for the social status of doing so (and disdain the white female for allowing herself to be used). Are couples of different races coming together conjugally to create light-skinned babies, to antagonize neighbors who don't cotton to that sort of thing, to prove commitment to integration and the benefits of close association with whites, or to dominate a white more personally in a relationship? Do the stereotypes of the black man's large penis ruin attractive white women for having interest in white men again, reducing the pool of available women for white men to date? There is always a question of ulterior motive. Are interracial relationships about exploration, attempts to appear liberal, or brainwashing other races one person at a time to cross over? Maybe it's only about economic advancement or social elevation by association. Maybe it's about love of the underdog or the more powerful. What are the personalities of interracial couples? Are their same-race hatreds involved in such pairings, attempts to distance, low self-esteem issues? Why such interest in other cultures?

Is an interracial couple's love really anybody else's business?

5

The Impact of Culture

Culture is the art, behavior, intellectual force, manner of living, values, habits, and shared political, religious, and philosophical beliefs that are typical within a particular community. Often, when people complain about other races, the resentment isn't based on race, but on cultural components in the race that its members embody and manifest. Race is a distinction that simply eases identification for those who want to direct their attacks.

The broad American culture is based on reason, science, individualism, free will, political liberty, private property, technology, and customary patterns in art. Its traditional values include family, work ethic, duty to country and respect for parents, self-control, and respect for authority in maintaining social order. Black subset culture is typified by a "competing set of insurgent values, the focus of rights-oriented political ideologies, of the rights revolution, and of the civil-rights movement...." Black culture "has been largely concerned with the rights of the individual–with freedom from oppression, from confinement, from hierarchy, from authority, from stricture, from repression, from rigid rule-making, and from the status quo" (Edsall and Edsall, p. 60).

Black communities control their own value systems. Values are not given to a group of people. Liberal policies or liberal-minded people who offered free love, illicit drugs, welfare, Planned Parenthood programs, ideologies about raising children and reductions in competitiveness didn't mandate participation or incorporation of these values by others. They offer choices that anyone can either accept or ignore. The cause of problems cannot be blamed on the offer of choice, but upon the making of bad decisions when choosing among the offered alternatives. If a white person physically forces a black to submit to nonconsensual "free love," that is rape and should be dealt with on an individual basis. If a white person physically restrains a black person and injects the black with an illicit drug, that is attempted murder and should be dealt with as such. But offering "free love" and drugs doesn't force others to choose these over other alternatives. It is the demand for drugs that maintains that alternative. The initial decision to try drugs, knowing of their addictive properties, is also an individual choice among offered alternatives.

Social anthropologists, notably Lawrence Harrison, compare the imperatives of various cultures and conclude that some cultures are superior to others based on the degree of adherence of those cultures to humanizing value systems. Harrison makes a case that cultures are either progress-prone or progress-resistant, not inherently, but through nurturance of political and economic systems that, in progress-resistant cultures, oppress experimentation, criticism, and self-discovery of creative abilities. People living in progress-resistant cultures incorporate values that impede their progress, progress being defined within the democratic-capitalist model that presumably liberates and financially rewards people for discovering their creative capacities. So, based on the criteria espoused by comparative culturists, behaviors and values can be said to be superior, though individuals, regardless of their race, who demonstrate these behaviors and values, among many others, cannot be judged as superior. Other characteristics of progress-resistant cultures include female genital mutilation, honor killings, junk science as medicine, and scientifically debunked superstitions that dictate routine behaviors.

Behaviors and values are race neutral, since both may be adopted by any race. However, anthropologic declarations about culture receive extensive and perversely slanted media coverage, and the social scientists who advance them are thought to be racist. Self-appointed and self-proclaimed spokespersons, often iconoclasts like Louis Farrakhan, the leader of the Nation of Islam, with extremist political views who claim to represent a race, challenge culture-denigrating concepts, seek forums to represent their race, and counter the negative assessments made about cultural values held primarily by a sole racial constituency. However, it is not a race that such spokespeople represent, since all members of the race may not agree with them. It is the countering point of view that these spokespeople represent. It is each individual audience member's decision to accept a speaker as his or her representative. For audiences that attend lectures by people who bask in media attention, support of the speaker's viewpoint is generally implied.

If spokespersons criticize cultural anthropologists for being racist, rather than debate the cultural values in question, some moderate-thinking adherents may tag out of the meetings, while radical-thinking fans may tag in as the speaker's new proponents. The group gains attention from the impugned race, members of whom find it difficult not to vengefully and mindlessly reciprocate with hate not for just the spokespersons, but for the race the spokespersons allegedly represents. The cycle is vicious, a terrible drain of emotional and intellectual energy.

Acts of regressive civility, even if occurring only within generally denounced sub-subculture minority populations, such as the systematic gang rape of female members as initiation rites and defilement of the corpses of rival gang members who've trespassed turf, must not be concealed by the media simply to avoid the risk that others will misapply the barbaric behavior more broadly as a characteristic of the race.

Premise: Culture does not excuse crime or barbarity.

In daily dealings with people of other races, we form impressions, many prejudicial. Compounded with other knowledge about a culture, when we see people in jobs who are obviously ill-equipped or slow and unresponsive to customer needs, some whites attribute the poor performance to the race of the employee, rather than to the employee's culture. Such poor performance by minorities may be the result of a conscious effort to rebel against the authority that employers assign to customers, which exceeds that assigned to the employee. It may be from racial animosity. It may be from hatred of the job. It may be from failed education and training.

Education is seen as a white thing by blacks who have been brainwashed by black separatists that education will not advance them in the white man's world, so blacks shouldn't even try to conform to the controlling institutions of another race. The black culture is one that "disparages academic seriousness as 'acting white' and celebrates destructive behaviors" (Will, *Dayton Daily News*). Educational success in integrated schools is seen by some fellow black students as an act of racial betrayal, as is having white friends; white students are not immune to being called nigger-lovers for their attempts at interracial friendships. Somebody will always be willing to pass judgment.

Some blacks believe that Eurocentric school curriculums and business models compound racism by reinforcing Eurocultural superiority in a multicultural world. Educational systems have been borrowed and improved, made more flexible to permit expansive applicability. Those who have worked to improve the system have a paternal/maternal responsibility to see that other cultures do not break the educational order and institutions. Some in minority communities are attempting to replace proven systems which have demonstrated value for all races, with culture-specific systems that separate rewards from the criteria of performance and that underplay the importance of written language and reading in favor of an oral tradition.

Some blacks feel that being smart and being black are culturally conflicting roles and that smart blacks are trying to buy into the white world, since it is white people who so frequently emphasize the importance of education in a competitive economy. This attitude is the strongest hindrance to black achievement. The backlash is that many blacks are trying to convince themselves that lack of intelligence is a good thing because it is a predominantly cultural trait. Therefore, they accept lack of intelligence as a part of being black: it is an unfortunate definition of themselves, and they accept the risky tradeoff by hoping to be superior in sports, which is a more social activity and gains more attention from one's peers than being holed up five hours a night studying alone in a room.

Structural explanations for cultural groups' failure to thrive in general, according to Blauner, "tend to attribute racial stratification to imperatives of social and economic structures, including racial discrimination. Cultural explanations emphasize internal characteristics of the ethnic group, such as family patterns, values, and other traditions" (Blauner, p. 5). "Whites tend to explain the racial crisis in personal terms, emphasizing the motivations of individuals, rather than looking at social forces and group relations" (Blauner, p. 42). The cultural characteristic of blaming individual failure and individual acts on the economy, the culture, self-segregation, external forces, social conditions, poverty, and group relationships allows individuals to disavow accountability. The next step is a demand that external forces throw tax money at conditions, though improved conditions will not influence individuals who will always choose to fail or commit crime.

Liberal whites do focus on culturally based characteristics when examining why more blacks have failed to advance at a rate equal to that of whites in similar economic classes. The demands to curtail culture-based barriers to economic success—poor education, poor motivation and work habits, lack of discipline, and deteriorating family cohesion—are judged by many minorities to be unreasonable compromises. Characteristics inherent in black culture counter the characteristics required in a capitalistic society to advance. Businessmen don't care about the "black" way to do a task or to view a condition. They want to do something the best way, financially, most efficiently. People don't judge the way of doing something as being superior because most whites or most blacks do it that way; a way is superior if it profits all concerned.

Blacks are not automatically installed in the capitalist culture, and capitalist culture doesn't seem concerned about changing rules to accommodate racial needs, unless a profit can be made. Blacks blame whites for tempting blacks with material (as shown in the Tracy Chapman song, "Material World"). Some blacks claim that the nature of the capitalistic scramble for profit betrays the black culture and family values, causing blacks to become greedy and self-centered. If they are to participate, however, some blacks would like every facet of every culture to include specific black cultural presence, meaning, black people in high positions in corporations. The culture argument—"Let's inject a little color culture into this business"—is a tactic to pry open white sympathies to jobless blacks. Blacks cite their racial differentness rather than lack of ambition and compliance with capitalistic rules for failure. They would rather claim that their culture requires a different system of rewards and punishment to motivate blacks to succeed, and that they need a different definition of success.

> **Premise:** A culture does not become superior based on the degree to which its members commit to their culture and their group identity within it.

The greater success of blacks who assimilate into integrated business mocks the refusal of those who don't participate in mainstream cultural endeavors. To be clear, many blacks want material, want power, want to succeed—simply not according to the rules that everybody else plays by. The success of black immigrants in business provides a model that doesn't depend on demanding trappings without putting in the hours:

> "The fact that [black] migrants are not socially and culturally 'American' is critical for understanding their success compared to the African-American poor. For one thing, they have not been socialized into the materialism of the consumer culture. Their self-worth does not hinge on how much they possess. Thus migrants tend to be quite frugal—they spend less and save and invest more. Their emphasis on the collective ethos of the extended family allows a pooling of resources and a sense of collective responsibility that is often anathema to the highly developed individualism of many African-Americans.
>
> "Coming from societies where persons of African descent constitute the majority of all classes—elites and poor alike—black migrants do not associate blackness with failure as part of their cultural and sociological experience. They are therefore far better equipped to fend off the psychological weight of racism in the United States than their African-American counterparts.
>
> "Coming from societies where there is less emphasis on the market and more on the household, family, and community, they rely heavily on their subcommunities for food, clothing, goods, entertainment, restaurants, and services." (Hintzen, pp. 127–128).

From a sense of tradition and indoctrination within segregated communities, the young generation of blacks often maintains the paraphernalia of culture even though they would benefit financially, socially, and psychologically choosing alternatives that are available to them. The behavior of young black males in 2007 greatly contrasts the behavior of black grandparents, is much less respectful, and much less informed by reason. Many young blacks have a belligerent attitude, refusing to work low-wage McJobs, lack desire, demand undeserved respect, and glorify violence and mistreatment of black women through self-destructive depictions in gangsta rap music (sales of which often fund gang armories). Minority subcultures outwardly reinforce their racial stereotypes of violence to instill fear and panic, which substitutes for respect.

Many whites fear that negative aspects of black culture–poverty as a badge of oppression, a culture of silence, promiscuity, drugs, gang violence, out of wedlock births, lost respect for life–might slip into the mainstream culture. They've seen rap/prison clothing styles come into vogue, rappin' white boys who listen, copy, and steal rap and hip hop, not in an attempt to understand the problems of black urban youths, but to piggyback on the thrills of violence and to make fast bucks making counterculture music. Crossover appeal in entertainment and fashion refers to the appeal to both races equally. Some whites adopt black culture because they don't want to be seen as racist by blacks. Allowing the opinion of others so much control over their lives signals both a need to belong somewhere and a profound feeling of being lost in the bigger culture, unable to gain attention and recognition except by being part of a smaller culture. This is why cliques form in school.

Blacks who live in violent communities see the success of violence in resolving roadblocks to resources. They are taught that being a strong user of violence solves problems and that cooperation and compromise and bartering don't solve problems. The success of blacks in violent sports like football and boxing may also promote violence. Blacks learn that militancy meets political goals.

In many respects, black methods and culture require less effort–truncated language and imprecise pretend language (Ebonics) that avoided learning standard English; citing racism for failure instead of working within the system of gaining rewards; selling illegal drugs; committing robberies; egotistically posturing to dull but violent rap lyrics; demanding racially preferential lower standards of achievement and then barely meeting them; and attacking testing instruments as culturally biased to explain failure. Blacks who cry racism, sell crack, commit crime, speak music and steal rhythm, and decry bias in standards don't care about the negative long-term psychological and cultural effects, or the negative image that these easier routes to success promote. Using the excuse of culture reduces the work they must do, so they use it to excuse their own personal failure not to acquire skills required to get desirable, high-paying jobs. What conclusion can be drawn from such evasions of effort: people with regressive values and few moral compunctions will opt for the easiest route to achieve desired goals.

Misconceptions about blacks and black culture, or absolute ignorance of black culture and lifestyle, does not in and of itself constitute racism in whites or other ethnic groups. Being ignorant of another group's culture does not presume racism against that culture. Unless you specialize in comparative cultures, there are undoubtedly many groups of people about whom you will know little or nothing. You should not be considered racist because you lack knowledge of another's culture, but because you feel your own culture to be superior to all others. Lack of knowledge does not presume that you also believe that your own culture is superior.

Blacks don't kill blacks in inner cities because of anything inherent in black culture. Killing is one reaction to adversity and being poor and uneducated and morally ungrounded. But the choice to commit violence distinguishes the individual, not the situation. Reaction is less determined by cultural than by personal values and experience in situations.

Failure to accept homosexuality and sexually transmitted disease among black males created a culture of silence. A gay black man in a recent television special decried the lack of public attention received by blacks infected with HIV, underplaying the general consensus that stigmas in the black culture prevent blacks from admitting to homosexuality, bi-sexuality, unprotected sexuality, and intravenous drug use. Culturally, blacks choose to remain silent about diseases that are shamefully contracted. The black church discourages talk of homosexuality, and blacks have had a general historic aversion to public discussions about black sexuality. The gay black in the TV special declared that gay white men received disparately greater political attention not because they frequently marched en masse on Capitol Hill and banded to demand medical research funding, but because the sons, daughters, lovers, and constituents of white politicians could more conceivably be gay and infected with AIDS. So, it could be a white thing, too, the politicians may have thought. Active misattribution of a subordinate, less likely cause meets the agenda of being race related, in addition to being easier and less embarrassing than organizing a march of black men campaigning for more AIDS research funding.

The True Value of Multicultural Diversity

A number of corporations offer seminars in cultural and multicultural diversity, professing that people of diverse cultures bring divergent perspectives to how problems have been traditionally solved, and others must learn how to be respectful and tolerant when working with people who bring unfamiliar behaviors into the workplace.

Many courses in culture studies are offered at colleges and universities with these business-related goals and the goal of appealing to a broader prospective student body. The Wright State University library was renamed the WSU Paul Laurence Dunbar Library because "'Naming the university library in Dunbar's honor reaffirms our commitment to multicultural diversity and to meeting the needs of the Dayton metropolitan community,'" WSU President Paige Mulhollan said (*Dayton Daily News*). The symbolism of changing a name actually does little more than appeal to and appease blacks. Self-serving reasons for the name change were to convince blacks who intend to attend college to consider WSU for its sensitivity to blacks, and that black students at WSU are likely to find a dorm community of other blacks with whom to connect.

A video-based exhibition called "The Kids Bridge" presented for a six-month period at the Smithsonian Institution and originally presented by the Children's Museum of Boston was aimed at making children aware of their commonalities with other races and the diversity of ethnic groups and cultures in their world community.

When Bill Gates of Microsoft made a "Digital Divide" video to show at a Tavis Smiley-supported symposium, highlighting the value of cultural diversity in his business accomplished by using MS PCs in grade schools, he did so less from civic humanitarian motives than from concern about future commerce and purchases by blacks of his products.

Many apply evolutionary metaphors to educational and corporate diversity, viewing a diverse workforce as a good hedge against the sameness of homogeneity, which may restrict solutions to problems to a certain ineffective mind set. Diversity in investment portfolios is good because it provides a safety factor that isn't available in investments of single-business or single-industry sectors that may collapse. Diversity in biological environs is seen to serve a complex function in the preservation of the stability of nature, resistance to disease being a prime example. Genetic diversity in mixed race offspring, or heterozygosity, is associated with a lower likelihood of genetic congenital diseases than in less diverse, single-race offspring. Facial symmetry is an indication of good health, that the infant didn't encounter pathogens or toxins in the womb. Hybrids are good.

However, the concept of diversity in and of itself is neither good nor bad. The decisions about what is included in a diverse mix are either effective or ineffective in meeting desired objectives. Biological geneticists are experimenting with inclusion and exclusion of genes to strengthen the phenotypic traits of organisms that humans feel are most desirable. Investment brokers determine which market segments and which instruments will provide the best buffer against various stock, bond, and securities declines. If they make good choices, the diversity serves a valuable purpose.

But sometimes people carry disease that others must become inured to or accommodate or inoculate society against. Some cultures are primitive, superstitious, and have rituals that are illegal in American culture. Some cultures discourage individual success, education, well-being, science, honesty, equality among its members, literacy, free speech, voting rights and human rights in general, and democratic freedoms, including freedom of the press and a right to a fair legal trial for the accused. When diversity introduces excessive negative variations that are far from balanced by their few positive contributions, homogeneous populations question the value of that diversification. They wonder whether it is desirable to introduce diversity based on metaphorical logic (that is, because multicolored flowers are more interesting than unicolored flowers, then multicolored people will benefit society because of the increased interest they bring). Multicultural diversity's value is uncertain because different people have different definitions of what is valuable to society and in business. Diversity does not significantly increase the quality of everyone else's life and, in fact, may diminish quality in concretely identifiable areas.

Corporations institute cultural diversity programs that make them appear progressive, and therefore, more desirable to shareholders and culturally diverse people whose talents the companies want to exploit after attracting them with the image of the company's formalized, politically correct programs. Most companies promote cultural diversity programs to protect their asses against suits brought by minority job candidates whose inadequate job skills were, perhaps, the primary reason they weren't hired or promoted. Multicultural diversity programs are de facto extensions of affirmative action policies, helping corporate attorneys fight lawsuits that falsely allege systemic corporate discrimination based on race, culture, age, sex, or physical inability. In a suit-happy society where little proof is necessary to support allegations of discrimination, companies can point to their progressive cultural diversity programs and show that they are doing everything they can to ensure fair employment.

Companies would rather not be concerned with spinning their image and defusing specious racial discrimination lawsuits. They don't need multicultural diversity; they need diverse skills and ideas, which can be cultivated in the absence of racial, ethnic, and culture diversity. Through diversity programs, however, companies show they have tried and been unable to hire qualified people of culturally diverse backgrounds in proportionately sufficient percentages to that race's population occurrence in society. The programs demonstrate an earnest attempt to meet legal requirements. Publicity about cultural diversity programs within companies has multiple effects but one implicit purpose: that of creating awareness that the company is spending a lot of money (which the companies can figuratively write off as necessary charity) on training programs tailored to culturally diverse people, to recruit them, and to keep them on staff whether or not their productivity matches that of non-minorities. Awareness shows non-minority workers how not to create low morale by mistreating people based on their race and culture. It's still okay for managers to harass minorities for not meeting performance criteria, as long as these failings are well documented and the minority has been counseled.

Though the term "cultural diversity" does not directly denote special privileges or attention to any one group, it is used by corporations to show culturally diverse groups that they are being selected for treatment not given to non-minorities. Programs of cultural diversity are the initial steps in recognizing that there are socio-cultural differences in employees and that decision-makers must take these differences into allowance when scheduling day-to-day operations. This means that minorities must be treated differently than non-minorities would be treated.

The purpose of awareness of other cultures is, ultimately, rank and file acceptance of the ways of the other cultures, not the inculcation of majority cultures into members of the minority culture. However, knowing that someone else's needs, understandings, beliefs, and behaviors are unique and shaped by a different heredity, heritage, rearing, educational background, and experiential background should have no impact on general and specific criteria for quality standards of job performance. Though non-minorities meet the criteria of having a culture influenced by all of the same factors as minorities, non-minorities are expected to meet a static criteria for performance. If the criteria for performance acceptability must be changed to accommodate culturally diverse populations and is applied only to those populations, then it should be changed for all, not just for a group who cannot meet the criteria based upon mainstream educational or philosophical backgrounds. All should be just as miserable meeting the standards, without cultural concessions or exceptions. If a minority wants a job in a corporation that requires a specific ability, that person had better get that ability or has no reason to expect to get the job.

> **Premise:** Acceptance of cultures does not suppose acceptance of inability to perform a job based on cultural norms and mores. If some behavior or value in a culture is counter to productivity, the corporate employer must train in that behavior.

No group should receive special dispensation simply because its members have different, minority backgrounds. Perhaps they haven't learned how American business and capitalism work, but that's something they'll have to learn on the job, just as all employees must learn a specific company's corporate culture. Everybody should have the same opportunity to learn.

True assimilationalists know that to gain the rewards offered in a larger group to which one belongs, one must take on the values, language, methods, and beliefs of that group. Accepting the beliefs of the group may mean making personal sacrifices of ones belief structure. Exploitative assimilationalists mimic the values of the group to gain rewards offered to the group's members. For instance, people will tolerate working at a place whose processes and values they abhor just to earn a living. It is the responsibility of the person who wishes to belong to a certain group, such as a capitalistic, profit-seeking, business organization, to become more like the group to realize its rewards (capitalistic culture is taught in core required business and economics classes in college). It is not the group's responsibility to conform to the individual ideologies of every one of its members, though the leaders of the group may state that such acceptance is a corporate goal just to appeal to more employees with broad-based ideologies.

When the member fully assimilates the group values and attains the reward of high reverence within the group, then that individual can seek out those who conform to his/her views, and all who refuse to assimilate, for various reasons, can object, form counterfactions of the group, or leave the group. There would be very little group cohesion if the group attempted to cater to the minute background differences of each of its members. The principle for organizing in the first place—to make money—is of primary concern to business groups, and those groups have an agreed upon, stated path for achieving the objective of making money.

The fact that so many aspects of daily life are being turned into racial issues by multiculturalists is a major cause of racial tension. Hypersensitivity results. The Crayola Crayon company re-packaged eight colors from its 64-crayon box and named the resulting package Multicultural Crayons. The colors in the new box are mahogany, peach (changed from flesh in 1962), tan, sepia, burnt sienna, apricot, black, and white. The Crayola Crayon company had received requests from teachers using a multicultural curriculum to provide a reduced number of specific colors so that children would become more aware of the skin tone of the multicultural figures they colored. With the 64-crayon box, all of the colors in the multicultural crayon package are available, but the students, the teachers allege, were not using the colors appropriately to separate figures by color. The curriculum was geared toward forcing children to recognize cultural diversity rather than toward sharpening perceptual acuity or fine motor skills. The crayons subvert the goal of achieving color perception to ideology. The Crayola Crayon company probably kicked itself for not taking advantage of the opportunity to exploit ideology and sell re-packaged crayons earlier.

In an effort by Diamond-Star Motors Corp. to demonstrate sensitivity to the various cultures on staff, the cafeteria operators and company executives agreed to expand the variety of foods to include traditional southern cooked meals. The cafeteria chef, a black man, decided on barbecued ribs, black-eyed peas, grits and collard greens. Almost immediately, two black employees protested the menu to the car company executive, saying it was a stereotype of black dining habits and insulted the memory of the Reverend Martin Luther King, whose birthday was to be honored the following Monday. The menu was changed to meatloaf.

Multicultural programs never train minorities in the needs of non-minorities. Multicultural markets, for instance, is a euphemism for being a market primarily for blacks and other ethnic minorities, a market occasionally visited by whites who want to feel exotic but don't want to take a trip to Lebanon for Lebanese cuisine and harassment customarily reserved by the native population for American tourists. Oddly, blacks in cultural studies classes at college never learn about the suspenders worn by German or Polish peasants to keep their britches up, and black children participating in school-sponsored multicultural festivals are rarely asked to portray geishas, Native Americans, Mexican banditos, or Afghan sheep herders. Each ethnic group in multicultural festivals portrays its particular culture, and each race celebrates only its own racial culture. The goal in multicultural diversity programs is not to teach about many cultures, but often just black culture, which is a telling sign of the purpose of corporate seminars in multiculturalism.

On a personal note, this author has attended several cultural diversity seminars in sizable corporations. I was **not** convinced of the value of seeking employees who were qualified based on skin color. A lot of theoretical value was offered (metal alloys are stronger than iron by itself, for example), but no concrete numbers were offered about how ethnic diversity affects the bottom line. I brought this point up during a feedback period and was met with verbal agreement from no fewer than six of the other employees in attendance. The issue was discussed for half an hour, but no hard numbers were forthcoming. When the facilitators prompted for other potential roadblocks to acceptance and implementation of cultural diversity "awareness," I mentioned that for those who are already aware, there will be a general apathy about formalizing this awareness.

I reviewed some of the more interesting exercises with my manager later and she reminded me that this program was being implemented as a means of meeting legal requirements for proving non-discriminatory hiring practices and non-abusive treatment against black employees. So, it really didn't matter what legitimate objections I foresaw concerning acceptance and implementation of the diversity program. My objections provided fodder for the consultants to dispel future objections (for example, "Oh, data are indeed available").

One of the interesting exercises we did in the seminar had four white attendees get together and try to find five similarities and five differences among our team members. We had absolutely no trouble finding differences, but commonalities across all team members were very hard to identify. I think these results had the opposite effect expected by the seminar facilitators (both black). If there is that much diversity among white males from the same midwest area, explain why that isn't enough to achieve the alleged "results" of cultural diversity. Whites from the city have a different culture from whites from the suburbs or from farms. So, really, the word *culture* is a misnomer for the purpose of the program. A more honest name would be race diversity, which is politically incorrect.

The facilitators also divided us by social class, education, and gender (just a few of the traits by which others tend to group people). Those groupings were interesting. The only members in the "no college degree" group were the only two black employees in the seminar.

The documentation provided at the seminar was such complete propaganda that I was surprised that corporate management allowed it. For instance, "Integral to an environment of Acceptance is recognition of the presence of systemic oppression and discrimination." "To achieve full inclusion, each new identity group in an organization must be accepted individually. In many ways, the process is a return trip on The Path, starting at the Symbolic Difference stage, with the new members becoming pioneers." It all sounds like an insidious cult initiation that presumes corporate illegality in hiring and treatment practices.

It is hoped that corporations don't become driven by the unproven processes, idealistic drivel, and other race-baiting recommendations made in this cultural diversity seminar.

Celebrating racial differentness implies that the differentness–minority status– is inherently positive, though individuals have no control over their race. Race is circumstantial. There's no reason to celebrate a genetic toss of the parental dice. Race isn't an accomplishment. People are born into cultures; children have no choice to switch teams. There's no reason to have pride in one's racial composition alone, or have pride in a stranger of the same race who's achieved something notable, high-fiving and affiliating with statements like, "those are my peeps," and in a hard stretch of logic considering the success of others to be one's own success. Racial pride attributes moral worth and extends associative qualities to individuals based on the irrelevant physiological similarities shared by race. Rather than referencing racial pride to instill self-esteem, commendations should be conferred for persevering and overcoming by using one's abilities, creativity, temperate emotional control or other personal characteristics, despite hardships, since these are actual behaviors that one can cultivate and improve. Exhortations to minorities to have pride in their race make majority populations resent the implication that minorities have more reason than non-minorities to celebrate, some special license. The double standard is that whites are accused of racism if they celebrate their white culture. Whites are left to celebrate their heritage, such as their Irishness to skirt accusations of racism, opting to be stereotyped as heavy drinkers, instead.

It may be a fortuitous double standard that discourages whites from having pride in their race, since to have such pride is irrational. Unfortunately, the pride will likely be irrationally transferred to one's vehicle, which the owner simply made enough money to purchase.

The premises of this study regard racial distinctions to have little real importance in life, laying responsibility for thoughts and actions directly at the feet of individuals. Those who emphasize the importance of race and culture in adoption, education, and marriage do so to maintain segregation by race, a policy that angers those who feel that integration is in the best interest of the races.

Heritage, racial and cultural traditions, and one's racial past are only as important and valid as individuals perceive them to be. People imbue experience, events, and circumstance with meaning. The degree of importance subjectively assigned to heritage and culture is neither right nor wrong, though acts based on them can be right, wrong, illegal, ill-advised, etc. People do not have to respect your race, your heritage, your traditions, your culture, nor anything you stand for, and you don't have to respect theirs.

Though different races within different regions and with different backgrounds may have separate and distinct concepts of culture, all races share similar life experiences within their cultures and want many of the same things in life. So, race is not the problem, though it seems so intuitively; we are more than just our race. At appropriate times, we are patriots representing our country, entrepreneurs representing capitalism, a varied people who represent at various times and under specific circumstances our families, our churches, our colleges, our way of life. Racism isn't the problem; hatred of the unknown is irrational. Fear and caution are more likely responses. The legacy of racism is a reasoned evaluation of benefiting from oppression—overt hatred is inevitably self-serving. It is rational to protect economic interests from competition. It is rational to be careful in cultures about which predominantly negative stories circulate. Minorities are as capable as non-minorities at being racists.

Though it is often persons of color who lobby that racially preferential treatment be backed by law, our government representatives who, for whatever reason, surrender to irrational demands and draft unfair race-based laws should be the ultimate target of non-minority resent and anger.

6

Language Barriers and Education

Language can be wielded as a kind of weapon, and a refuge if multiple meanings can exist for individual words; for instance, if confronted for using insulting language, someone can respond: "I was using this other meaning when I said you were fat or bad or a bitch." The intent behind language can be to gain rights, such as whites wearing T-shirts emblazoned with the phrase White Power, signifying the right to bust double standards and use racially provocative emblems. Such language displayed by whites can be interpreted as hatred, intimidation, and the flaunting of historical mistreatment of blacks, and blacks can defend their use of Black Power insignias as a means to bolster their self-esteem. Blacks rationalize racist slogans against whites by citing facile interpretations of the slogan, black power, rather than meaning superiority, meaning self-empowerment, self-respect, and independence. Language is flexible and vulnerable to abuse.

The nearly trademarked phrase, "that's hot," can be uttered sarcastically when someone is told, "I farted." It can also serve as a signifier of acknowledgement to show that someone is listening, but just barely, and it can mean it's most exact meaning, such as referring to an iron skillet handle on a hot stovetop. Or as a new meaning, "that's hot" can just exude trendiness and fashionability. Any sublanguage that depends on inflection, context, and knowledge of the speaker and what the speaker considers to be cool is a lazy language with limited functionality. Separate languages are an impediment to economic growth and social cohesion.

Separate language is maintained for the sake of being separate; people tend to associate with those who have communication styles complementary to their own. When words are assigned multiple meanings so that fewer words will have to be learned, which is the easiest way to create coolness, and when differentiating syllables are dropped and not enunciated, communication suffers from the confusion. Language would then depend almost wholly on context. For some outsiders hearing blacks talk in a rap culture, they're speaking English as a second language. Listeners feel that the speakers are either incapable of speaking proper English, or that they choose not to in a mixed language social situation. Choosing not to speak a language that all can understand is a sign of arrogance and dismissive derogation, splitting those who are worthy from those who aren't.

Often, however, misuse of the language is intentional. Slaves were forced to speak a variant of English so that they could secret their seditious thoughts from their masters. Today in subcultures, differing language keeps more cultured speakers (teachers, counselors, parents, clergy) out of the cool kids' grills. Rappers create new words from pieces of existing words because they don't want to learn existing English words and neither do the audiences to which they want to appeal. Syncopated tough talking is easier than getting voice training to sing. Using sampled music that other performers created is easier than creating original music, which requires a knowledge of music. Hard beat, nontraditional vocalizations are copied, making many rap songs indistinguishable from other rap songs.

Some people speak with a dialect and rhythm specific to a subculture or to make themselves distinctive, using speech as a pretension that gets them attention or allows them to fit in.

Poor pronunciation and enunciation give the impression of substandard education. Many blacks make their feelings about education known when they convert Ts to Ds in their speech: Sidney becoming Sitney, David becoming Davit, would becoming woot, "she cault me and I tollt them," with becoming wid, earth becoming eart, "So, whud I getd?", borrowed becoming borrote, neighborhood becoming neighborhoot, and headlines becoming hetlines. Th becomes d: true dat, dis bitch. Clipping Gs, softly pronouncing all vowels, speaking with an indefinable slurry accent of any region and garbled dialect and mispronouncing words are all reliable indications of the speaker's level of education. People, whether prejudiced or not, key in on communication ability as a standard criteria for making judgments about the speaker's ability to think and the speaker's competence levels.

Some infractions include mackin' to mean being successful with women; failure to use adverbial endings and clipping Gs (steady mobbin'); subject/verb disagreement (we be chillin' and she don't know shit); contraction abuse (she goot lookin'); profuse use of double negatives; and unclear pronoun references. In the late 1990s, such offense against standard English usage was termed Ebonics, and serious consideration was given to teaching Ebonics in the public school systems, which is what happens when education systems try to legitimize mediocrity for the sake of cultural diversity.

Socially coded language protects blacks who congregate to discuss racial issues. Whites can't decipher the words that fomenting malcontents devise in devious schemes to get back at whites, or to console one another for their victimization and to develop programs to become empowered in the face of enormous odds.

Larger than the racial issue is the tendency to look at people as insiders and outsiders. The insiders experience we-ness based on similar physical characteristics, language, and religion. Linguistic and cultural unity causes less stress than disunity. Many use language as their identity within groups:

> "For white male teenagers who are in the process of forming their identities as young men, the urban black male represents someone who knows how to pick up women, who knows how to handle himself on the street, who perhaps knows how to handle a weapon and can take care of himself. His kind of way of walking, talking or dressing can give one the trappings of a kind of masculinity that doesn't perhaps exist in the safe white suburbs" (Cutler, quoted by McNiel).

The crossover appeal of rap culture confuses cultural boundaries. Blacks criticize whites for parasitism, telling whites to pick a race. Whites don't have the same cultural philosophies and can't plausibly fake racial discord from a black rapper's point of view. Some whites feel that rapping flatters blacks for creating art that joins cultures, though hip hop practiced by whites doesn't create a common ground. When black females adopt Valley Girl speech patterns to fit in, they lose their unique culture through assimilation, and degrade their individuality. Some aspects of subcultures have never been a good idea to adopt.

The mainstream culture is intended to be tolerant of all cultures until violence erupts or someone is influenced to coercive suppress people. Inflammatory and abusive language, such as rappers calling women bitches, advocating murder, and disavowing responsibility for killing, reflects subcultural attitudes, prompting SCLC marchers to use slogans like "Up with Hope, Down with Dope" and "Stop the Killing–End the Violence."

Rap lyrics are the ultimate in politically incorrect speech. Their authors consciously include racist and sexist language, bashing all values held dear by those in the larger culture, citing the rebellion of music as a tradition. The success of such music is one more indication that even the most offensive elements in culture and those who commit those offenses are no longer oppressed and need no more special treatment, affirmative action, or quota systems.

In contrast to intentionally vile lyrics, blacks who aspire to separate themselves from such subcultures demand that both whites and blacks monitor their speech when speaking about race. Demanding politically correct speech is a measure of power within a special interest group. Proscribing language conceals true racists, who will cloak their attitudes in a parody of conscripted speech. They will still be able to ridicule groups of people using politically correct terminology, pairing their speech with condescending tone, harshness, body language, and the context of speech. Being forced to call blacks African-Americans doesn't engender in racists a new respect or understanding or help embody the sympathetic views that language police ask whites to model, or make them more liberal and kind toward other races. Politically correct language also obscures historical context. For instance, changing the term, midwife to midspouse doesn't convey the fact that a recently pregnant woman's job is to suckle a baby for another man's wife.

Language skills are directly tied to education, or the lack of the proper focus in priority subjects. Rather than language, cultural knowledge is prioritized. Teachers at the private W.E.B. Dubois Academy school in Dayton, Ohio, formed by the Afrikan-Amerikan Institute for Positive Living Inc. community organization use an Afrocentric approach, in which African and black history are part of the traditional curriculum. The school's main source of revenue is a $200,000 grant from the federal Drug Free Schools and Community Act Fund (Clark, p. 1A). The Academy also incorporates the Golden Legacy series of 16 comic books featuring historical black figures. Margaret Peters, a teacher at Colonel White High School, also in Dayton, believes that blacks need the historical perspective offered by the comic books because black kids need to see "'what their own people have done.'" Bertram Fitzgerald, author of the series, feels that black "'history and the achievements of African-Americans have not been well disseminated throughout the educational institutions, leaving black youngsters to feel left out of the development of America and the world.... I thought it would help develop greater pride and self-esteem in black youngsters and adults'" (Rhodes, p. 1E).

Dayton Opera officials and members of the board of trustees are shaping up a plan for an African-American task force that will involve African-Americans in both operations and programming. The education and opera insiders will help to develop a curriculum pairing adults and children to learn opera history as it parallels African-American music history. The program is being added to the company's long-range plan to foster the sharing of heritages in operatic and African-American art forms. General cross-sectional training in techniques of art are subverted to lessons about the technique of African art, specifically. In a cooperative effort between Resurrection School, an almost totally black school and St.

Charles Borromeo School, mostly white, an artist-in-residence supervised twelve students from each school who created a woven banner. "The weavers got together to paint African 'Dahomey' murals on their 5-by-5-foot banners." One mural depicted animals in a jungle setting, and the "other will depict characters from a sequel to *Mufaros*, an African story...." The artist, Meg Guyton Dickason, also "spent hours in each class at every grade level in both schools–teaching everything from African mask-making, to African sculpting, to African tie-dyeing. They made papier-mâché animals that told African stories, and they decorated doors with African designs." "'We have so much to learn from African–about family, about art work, about self-esteem,' she said. 'I believe it is a connection to learning a lot about ourselves. We find that everything is a connection'" (Babcock, *Dayton Daily News*). Teaching African art fits in a curriculum in which Indian, Japanese, French, Danish, Incan, and American Western arts are also taught.

It should be understood that newspaper reporters will not find an interesting angle in covering English classes, so the absence of such stories should not be inferred to mean that such classes aren't also a part of school curriculums.

Interest in culture-specific curriculums is increasing. "The National Association for Equal Opportunity in Higher Education, an umbrella group for historically and predominantly black schools, show that enrollment at its 115 member schools increased 3.5 percent, or by 10,300 students, from fall 1989 to fall 1990" (Clark, "Black-college Ranks Growing," *Dayton Daily News*). "The number of black college students increased from 340,000 to more than a million between 1966 and 1982. In 1980 some 80 percent of black college students were attending predominantly white institutions. From 1980 to 1984 black college enrollment dropped 3 percent nationwide" (Blauner, p. 166). Blacks want to go to black colleges so they can become more thoroughly indoctrinated in African history and black American culture. However, courses in racial and cultural pride have no transferable application in business life.

A spokesperson from Wilberforce University, predominantly black, stated that it is harder for the college's graduates to get jobs and repay government student loans in hard economic times: "'There aren't as many jobs for our student population.'" Fewer jobs for their students, though not for students of other colleges? The implied reason is that blacks are more discriminated against in the job market. More likely it is because the college has a strong reputation for graduating students with substandard job skills and knowledge, which prevents them from competing as strongly for the available pool of jobs. In some predominantly black universities, the practices of elevating poor grades and lowering standards for passing general proficiency tests are common. This results in false evidence that the graduate from a black university has equivalent knowledge with a graduate from a university that did not elevate grades, lower standards, or pass students through attrition.

Allowing black colleges to stay open though their graduates fail to meet state requirements for intellectual competency is the politically correct thing for state legislators to do, especially if they want to continue getting the black vote. Central State University, a troubled Dayton-area black institution, has faced many legal charges: enrolling phantom students to get more government educational aid; lying to black foreign students to get their tuition; re-electing demonstrably corrupt presidents; lowering grading and passing standards to boost the appearance of their students' achievement; and tolerating a dangerous and violent campus. If CSU were closed by the state of Ohio, there would be cries of racism by blacks, accusations that would all be in spite of concrete evidence that CSU cannot meet the education, legal, or campus safety standards demanded by the state of other higher education institutions.

The focus in black colleges on black studies is inevitable and defended as a necessity since mainstream colleges give short shrift to historical black figures. The lessons of history emphasized in schools are not black or white, though it was rich white male politicians who acted upon the course of the nation, dealt with national problems, made laws, instituted systems of government, and started wars that succeeded or failed. History texts acknowledge that southern state economy was founded on slavery and catalogues uprisings, and war, to abolish it. Black historical figures impacted primarily social change, heading social and civil movements, and the very act of making people aware of minority hardships becomes history, but history texts must cover a limited global cross section. History offers universal lessons about diplomacy, negotiation, leadership, the impact of inventions and advances in transportation on daily life, and government. American government has permeated every aspect of life, and white males in government consigned blacks and women to support positions that restricted them from meeting criteria for historical significance. White males have been racist and sexist, but the race or gender of the historical figure doesn't invalidate the principles underlying the criteria on which to judge a person's historical impact.

As sidebars to the strategies in military campaigns, new history books mention women factory workers and army nurses in WWII and the tenacity of black soldiers in segregated black army units in the Civil War or against the Germans in WWII. Individuals making up the support network are not described, whether they are white male, female, or black. Actions taken by minorities to modify social structures and racially insensitive government restrictions, the economy, and institutional policies and systems are of secondary importance. Inventions by blacks are also cited as accomplishments and major contributions to technological advancement. However, determining the race of "inventors" is difficult since the Patent Office doesn't require race information on its forms. Further determining the extent that one person "invented" something is difficult because the Patent Office considers an improvement or contribution to an existing product to be a "re-invention" of the product. For instance, Alexander Graham Bell has patents on the "invention" of the airplane, but all he did was improve on a previous design.

It is not the intent of textbook authors in science, art, social sciences, mathematics, law, civic government, or history, to provide role models for black children; less significant figures, black or white, cannot compete in terms of the importance of their philosophical, intellectual, and political contributions. Small-scale actions that do little more that shape opinions cannot take precedence over benchmark catastrophic and cataclysmic events that have a lasting effect on a large number of people. With equality and equal civil rights, women and blacks can meet criteria in the same way that white males meet it.

The attention span of children is a limited resource, as is their ability to synthesize and understand complex issues. Elective curriculums can offer more comprehensive descriptions in biographies and special focus, non-text books about people in sports, entertainment, and music, for instance. Many books focus on the contributors as special classes, such as all women, black women, or all blacks. These books, because of double standards, aren't considered as equally sexist and racist as books written by white men, for white men, and about white men. When the criteria for inclusion in a history book becomes the race of the person making a contribution rather than the significance of the contribution, then that book is racist.

How can the need to include blacks in history books be met without lowering the standards for significance? We can look at achievement in different ways, based on the context and circumstances within which the act was performed, examining the difficulty levels. Relative achievement. But then history would be based on people achieving rather than the value of their contribution. Multiple histories—one for blacks and one for whites, one for men and one for women, one for straights and one for gays, one for liberals and one for conservatives, one for vegetarians and one for carnivores, one for Republicans and one for Democrats, one for pro choicers and one for anti choicers, one for animal rights activists and one for humanists, one for environmentalists and one for resource developers—

aren't the answer. Blacks refusing to learn as a means of protest for the absence of blacks in history books also isn't the answer.

Teachers attribute the "high failure rate [of black students] primarily to absenteeism, which runs about 20 percent daily at Dunbar [High School, a black, Dayton, Ohio inner-city school], and lack of effort by the students. Teachers also said that many students display problems with math skills they should have mastered long ago–such as basic operations, fractions, decimals, and negative numbers." Calvin Miller, one of six math teachers at Dunbar, argues that some students "'do not have the ability to learn the subject–Can't everybody handle it, so I don't think it's fair to them'" (*Dayton Daily News*). In the math portion of the Ohio high school proficiency test in 1992, 69 percent of the state's black sophomores weren't able to pass on the first attempt, compared to 25 percent of white sophomores and 52 percent of Hispanic sophomores. Education department and school officials say the test is not racially biased. Then superintendent of Dayton Schools, James Williams, stated that he didn't see a bias in the math: "You either know it or you don't know it" (Fisher, "Math trips area students").

In the high school group in 1990, 53.3 percent of black males were either behind or dropped out, compared with 52.8 percent of Hispanic males, 44.4 percent of Hispanic females, 42.7 percent of black females, 37.4 percent of white males, and 26.3 percent of white females. The TV is on in black homes close to 70 hours a week, compared to 48 in others, tempting students home from school in the afternoon to be distracted from homework. Other important factors in the explanation of differences between blacks and whites might be that blacks earned only 23 of the 3,310 doctorates in physical sciences and 28 of the 1927 doctorates in engineering that were awarded in 1990. Blacks "in their final year of high school score only about as well as white seventh-graders on tests of math and geography" (Mona, p. 210). "In five subjects–mathematics, science, U.S. history, civics, and geography–more than half of the black high school seniors scored below basic" (Mona, p. 211).

In teacher communities, it's a truism that black students who are failing based on their grades are often passed ahead to the next class level because teachers feel that forcing black students to meet "white" standards is unfair (culture can't be transcended argument), that the subject isn't really necessary for the black student (reduced expectations argument), and that high failure rates makes blacks look bad educationally (need to protect/spin racial image argument). Relaxed standards hurt the cause of blacks to prove directly how smart they can be, and it is left to employers to develop skill assessments because they cannot trust the education that job applicants received.

Knowledge doesn't depend on culture; students from every culture can read and memorize facts, rehearse mathematical processes and language, and be taught to think clearly and interpret and analyze defined situations that will be sampled in achievement tests. Schools whose curriculums teach to achievement tests to both improve student knowledge in foundation areas and assure higher passing rates for their school districts should not have high failure rates on achievement tests. Such tests under such conditions truthfully cannot be characterized as being biased toward middle- and upper-class knowledge. It's likely that students in high schools that don't emphasize core studies and aren't exposed to fundamental courses lack the knowledge to pass college-level tests, though a majority of white and other ethnic group test takers pass. Some claim that the test of bias in a test is the racial proportion of those who pass the tests. The conclusion that a test is biased against blacks based on those who pass is invalid because some blacks belong to the group who passed. All achievement tests are discriminatory–they discriminate against people who don't know the material, don't read well, don't know scientific and mathematical principles, and don't analyze or recognize complex relationships between concepts. Individuals also fail from a lack of targeted training and preparation.

The criterion for competence has deteriorated. Adjusting tests to require less specific knowledge, thereby giving poorly educated minorities a better chance of success, makes high school and college degrees increasingly more meaningless. National intelligence tests now require evidence of knowledge about more general, neutral topics. However, those who do not speak the English language well, who are unfamiliar with sentence structure, who cannot read and understand questions on standardized achievement tests still perform poorly even on culturally neutral test questions. Federal mandates force schools with high percentages of poor performing students to spend a proportion of their budget on special counseling programs, restricting federal funding flexibility for those schools that don't comply by instituting recommended programs. Many poor performing students are minorities. So the federal mandates result in special treatment for minority students at the expense of students who perform well but for whom the school cannot afford to develop more enriched educational programs to challenge their potential for learning.

There are effective and ineffective learning styles. The styles used by the poor and disenfranchised are often ineffective, usually due to time conflicts and employment requirements and neighborhood distractions, regardless of race. Variations in how people process information or perceive the world can be attributed to learned habits and cultural, environmental and social pressures and conditions. A learning style is an information processing habit which represents the learner's typical or usual mode or perceiving, thinking, remembering, and problem solving. The question for educators is how to best impart information to accommodate the learning styles of the ethnically diverse student body while not detracting attention from other students in a mainstreamed classroom when all students have not attained the same education acquisition ability. Teaching styles used in integrated facilities focus on academics, while technical training facilities focus on life and employment skills. Few schools focus on cultural and social skills alone.

Limited resources and budget make it impossible to consider the specific needs of everyone in a mainstreamed group, meaning the placement of all students, regardless of their special education needs, into the same classes as all other students. Theoretically, classrooms that are integrated to include students of every mental level reduce the stigma that those students with special needs feel when they are physically separated from the general population of the school and labeled learning disabled.

Mainstreaming lumps all students into the same class, hurting the chances of each to receive a quality education and diluting teacher efforts to educate every student with equal enthusiasm and energy. It is difficult for one teacher to reach less mentally able students in a classroom while also meeting the needs of average and exceptionally gifted students. Forced by budgetary constraints, and even limitations of teacher ability, teachers must strike a balance between which class of people will receive attention. Each student suffers because the teacher attempts and usually fails to equally educate according to the student's needs.

In their attempts to meet each student's needs in a mainstreamed environment, teachers sub-classify students within the same classroom. They place students of differing mental capacity into different groups, consequently spotlighting below average students and defeating the purpose of mainstreaming, which is to prevent stigmatization and self-fulfilling prophecies for students with below average mental ability. To reduce the stress to members of groups that have been singled out for their lower level of mental ability, some teachers label every group non-descriptively. The labels aren't paired with either negative or positive values: the bluebird group, the orangebird group, the greenbird group, but not blackbird, yellowbird, or redbird, designations that are too close to minority colors. Teachers must label the groups something, or it would be hard to refer to them: "Hey, that group, I'll be with you as soon as I get this group started on its task."

It is hoped that students could act maturely and responsibly, accepting that others have special needs. It is hoped that other students would sacrifice their time to help provide for those needs. But do they? More likely, they resent that their own education is compromised by the teacher's need to flit around the room to keep each group working independently. Brutes in the classroom will make fun of members belonging to below average groups, bullying that main-streaming has made more convenient for them. Some below average students may be emotionally scarred by this derision. Some may be strengthened by accepting the reality of prejudice toward below average students.

It is not enough to question the methods by which learning is measured. Information is either processed with emphasis on meaningful content or it is not. Focusing on and rebelling against what society determines to be meaningful fails to address the effectiveness of one learning style over another. Some blacks want to think that blacks learn differently as a race in a further attempt to preserve the black races' uniqueness as an identity, or to dumb down tests. Trying to change society to accept the standards of a minority races' less effective information pro-cessing style will result in failure, especially when the major difference between the learning styles is that the ineffective styles are characterized by less effort in learning to process information.

It is true that some teachers use teaching styles that do not maximize learning, the lecture method, for instance, but this is changing. To reach all students would require individualized learning modules which would best be accomplished through computer-assisted training materials. These materials will be tailored to black learning styles and must ensure that blacks will learn the same facts and information that is learned by whites who may use a different learning style. The outcome of acquired knowledge must be the same as measured by standardized tests. This means that ethnic groups cannot believably blame their failure to learn facts based on their differing learning styles. However, this solution does not address the excuse that the facts that society determines to be important are racially biased toward white culture, thereby giving blacks the right to indig-nantly refuse to learn the facts. Engineering, physical, mathematical, astronomi-cal, biological, manufacturing, and music principles are not racially loaded.

One solution to requiring multiple teaching styles in classrooms is to allow each student to determine, from a laundry list presented by teachers at the begin-ning of each year, how he or she would best learn the material, and provide pre-packaged material in that style/format, in addition to a single method that the educator decides will most efficiently and effectively impart knowledge to the greatest number of learners in a common, efficient, predominant delivery format that is shown to be effective and subject-content oriented rather than student oriented.

It is asking too much for teachers, who are paid a pittance relative to the importance that American society places on education, to take into account the data processing habits of each culture's members and to plan, implement, evaluate, and give and receive feedback in ways that are consistent with the individual learner's style. Though all instruction should be geared to the needs of the individual child, this ideal is not feasible. If people who are considered minorities are taught based on some preconception of how minorities learns things, that wrongly presumes that all minorities within the same race learn in the same way. Teaching techniques that allow exceptions may exclude valuable information which all need to cope in society as a whole. Grading methods based on criteria that differ from other educational systems make it difficult to determine qualifications for ability to perform paid tasks. However, different teaching methods are being used and different subjects that account for student culture are being taught. Cultural training has little applicability in American business life at present.

Inner-city schools spend more money per student because cities have larger tax bases than suburban schools and city unions have the power to demand that more money be spent on special programs. More money is needed because inner-city students are more likely than suburban school students to be in special-education programs. They are more likely to require bilingual education programs. They are more likely to require special attention for learning disabilities. The reasons behind who is placed in each of these special programs vary tremendously. Poor diet and chemical toxins in the environment, and genetic diseases may account for those with learning disabilities. Many students may require remedial reading assistance. Sometimes, parents make conscious attempts to get their children classified as special-needs so that the children can be in smaller classrooms. There is little evidence that special programs yield students who are any more successful on achievement tests than those mainstream method programs from which the funds are diverted.

Extra money does not address the problem of students who don't want to learn, regardless of teaching approach.

"'I think it's part of the reality that blacks generally leave school with weaker education backgrounds than their white counterparts do. Until we can equalize the quality of schools, that disparity will be an issue,'" vice president for research at the Joint Center for Political and Economic Studies, Milton Morris, believes (Walters, *Dayton Daily News*). The logical fallacy in Morris' statement is that integrated schools of unequal quality cause weaker education only in blacks. Multiple community and home life factors are involved: refusal to learn because learning isn't cool, laziness, lack of inspiration, poor self-esteem that causes despair about learning, absence from school to earn money for family, poor diet, family life anxieties that interfere with concentration, and the student's rejection of white institutions in general. Some minority students feel that education makes blacks white, and refuse to excel, though excelling makes them more competitive intellectually for society's rewards. Education is seen as a tool of the whites. Some blacks have little incentive to become educated, they say, because they weren't offered the jobs they were promised for getting the education. Other blacks *were* offered jobs, and therein lies a telling differential that requires further study in individual cases and emulation of those who landed jobs.

Public schools shouldn't resemble a daily tourist itinerary through cultures, while integral hard sciences, mathematics, engineering, physics, general history, and life skills through social studies courses suffer. Parents can school their children in fluff courses. Schools should hire the best qualified teachers, and if those are teachers do not belong to the race of the students being taught, that makes a difference only in the minds of the rebellious students and their parents. Andrew Hacker feels that black students must be taught by black teachers from texts written by black authors, and in a school run by black administrators (Hacker). To think that a difference in the educational results would be substantially improved by a same-race teaching environment, that teaching negrocentric histories rather than general subjects deemed by whites to have greater importance for a rounded knowledge base will capture a black child's interest more, is a call for segregated classrooms. Establishing racial rapport with students is not important to educating them, but only plays into the agenda that race trumps everything else of interest in education and life. There is no evidence that teachers of the same race as their students use any secret techniques to motivate their students to learn better than they would had they been taught by teachers not of their race. Decisions made on the basis of one race that don't apply to all races are racially discriminatory and detrimental decisions.

The purpose of education is to expose children to a wide range of knowledge about different subjects so that they may find an interest into which they want to exert their productive energies. It is not intended that education should preserve individual cultures or be limited to a single culture, be that culture black or white or Asian or Indian or Puerto Rican or Mexican.

7

Class Differences and Economic Realities

Economic classes are divided by arbitrary maximum levels of the wealth, income, and asset value of their average members. The typical classes are lower, middle, and upper. Often, the single factor of wealth has predictive value in how people will behave in given situations, though predictions must be general. Societies throughout time have used class division to maintain group wealth and control of large quantities of material and power. Those in lower classes often have had little recourse but to revolt or accept the crumbs that came their way.

Lower classes accept that they may at times need social hand-out programs to survive, swallow their pride, and roll with the punch to their self-esteem. Regardless of race, the poor experience the same stress of staying at home unemployed and of waiting in line for interviews for low-paying, unskilled labor positions that have little chance for promotion or to give employees a chance at independence. There is little racial disparity within classes whose classifying criteria is wealth.

Lower economic classes scramble to keep every employment and monetary advance, resentful of any lost footing. What seems to separate, seen in contrasts, black minorities from other immigrant minorities is differentiating culture. Blacks who fought to establish civil rights and equal opportunity legislation resent that other minorities who weren't involved in the fight are able to use these same laws to raise their standards of living even higher than blacks. Many blacks are selfishly interested only in bettering the black race, preferring that other ethnic groups and whites remain in an underprivileged underclass. However, whites, with their history of enslaving blacks, cannot be seen as conscientiously neutral to the plight of blacks and uninvolved in the cause of blacks to gain equal footing. The concept of equal opportunity is a virtuous one no matter who has to fight for it to become fully realized.

Blacks resent that other minorities are beating blacks out of the limited welfare benefits, special privileges, the affirmative action job slots, and funds that are earmarked for special, college tuition grants for minorities. Blacks resent that whites cite the successes of Koreans, other Asians, and Hispanics as evidence that people can succeed against the odds. "Segregation was imposed far more rigidly on blacks" (Fuchs, 138), though this imposition may have been offset by laws that prohibited immigrants from opening businesses. Immigrants often have the same low-skill jobs as blacks and were denied the same civil rights that blacks were denied. Blacks cite that Asians are less obviously different from whites than blacks are from whites, and are seen as more servile, and therefore less threatening in the job market than blacks. This made whites more prone to giving jobs to Asians than to blacks, is the contention. Asians and Hispanics worked cheaper than blacks, left their families at home in another land, and would do seasonal work, such as picking crops. Asian immigrants who were entrepreneurs worked for slight profit margins while earning enough to keep themselves fed. Immigrants succeed because of their cultural values and their belief that work, frugality, lack of materialism, and saving are rewarded.

Minority success and ethnic pluralism threaten the power and economic security of the majority; employment opportunities are limited and majority groups must either reduce their perception of need for the rewards, reduce their selfishness, or increase their diligence and dedication to their careers if they want to preserve their current status. What whites "resent most is people paying attention to the ideas and attitudes of minorities within the country. It seems to me that the not-very-hidden agenda of the far right is to keep minorities as second class citizens" (Maybury-Lewis, p. 93).

Lower classes find it difficult to compete when playing by the rules of the middle class. The middle class has received parental modeling, education, and training in the rules, benefits that aren't as readily obtainable by those in lower socioeconomic classes. Blacks feel that standards of advancement in a capitalistic society are a poor criterion when applied to the very different black culture, a culture that promotes the expectation that accommodations must be made based on sensitivity to this differentness. What blacks encounter is whites who focus on the cultural characteristics of blacks as the *reason* that more blacks fail to advance at a rate equal to that of whites with similar backgrounds, in similar economic classes, and with similar opportunities.

The black underclass urban dweller was born when well-paying, unskilled jobs and middle-class blacks left the cities for the suburbs in the 1960s. "This out-migration left the poorest elements of black society behind—now isolated and freed from the restraints the black middle class had imposed. Without jobs and role models, those left in the ghettos drifted out of the labor market" (Kaus, p 38). Poor blacks are stigmatized for their poverty by both whites and blacks in middle income classes.

> "Overall, a much smaller proportion of blacks than whites has arrived in the middle class, and blacks are more concentrated in the lower middle class. Compared to whites, employment in the public sector accounts for a much higher (and increasing) proportion of the black middle class. Even in professional occupations, blacks tend to be in the lower-paying, lower-prestige fields.... A higher proportion of married black women work than married white women, and their average earnings more nearly equal their husband's, since black women have reached parity with white women in occupations and earnings, whereas the gap between black men and white men remains extremely wide. In the nation's one thousand largest companies there were only three black senior executives in 1979, four in 1985. [As of 1989] there are no black-owned firms in Fortune's list of the five hundred largest corporations, and none of these corporations has a black chief executive officer (Blauner, p. 166–167).

People with more money have to step on someone else to remind themselves of how much better they are than the people under their feet. We all need somebody to shove. We cheer for whoever is most like us and our class, having pride when someone from our class becomes successful and wanting to see that person become more successful than anybody else in other classes so we can enjoy the success vicariously. We will always be a society of classes, and attempting to legally bring down the top classes to raise the lower classes admits to the desire to continue having classes, just not the desire to be in a class that has less advantages or is less likely to become wealthy.

Economic Differences

"Poverty is increasing faster among white people who are not Hispanic than among blacks," the authors of the Center on Budget and Policy Priorities wrote in a report titled *White Poverty in America*. "Non-Hispanic whites constitute a majority of the poor in 33 states." In seven states, non-Hispanic whites constitute the greater number of poor among the group of poor. "'Poverty among non-Hispanic whites has received scant attention,' the center said. 'Poverty debates in this country frequently become ensnared in controversies about race and ethnicity.'" Half of the "'nation's 35.7 million poor people are non-Hispanic whites....'" The report concludes that "51 percent of the 4.2 million people added to the ranks of the poor between 1989 and 1991 were whites other than Hispanic. Blacks and Hispanics each accounted for 22 percent of the growth of poor people. The number of non-Hispanic whites living in poverty increased 14 percent while the poor black population was increasing 10 percent. Despite the overall statistics, a black or Hispanic person was much more likely to be poor than a white individual, since population percentages differ. The report said nearly 1 in 10 whites were poor in 1991, but the poverty rates among blacks and Hispanics were nearly 3 in 10. This report used the Census Bureau definition of poverty, which is based on an income level varying by family size. For 1991, a family of four with income of $13,924 or less was considered poor" (*Dayton Daily News*, October 10, 1992).

In 1990, working black couples made only 85 cents for each dollar earned by similar white couples. Black men and women were nearly twice as likely as whites to work in low-paying service jobs. Black families in general had median incomes of $21,548 in 1991, amounting to 57 cents for every dollar earned by white families. "Almost one-quarter of all black families had incomes of more than $25,000 (in constant dollars) in 1982, compared to only 8.7 percent in 1960. Among employed blacks the proportion who hold middle-class jobs increased from 13.4 percent in 1960 to 37.8 percent in 1981" (Blauner, p. 166).

Between 1967 and 1991, black families earning $25,000 to $35,000 increased from 10 percent to 15 percent, according to adjusted income figures from the U.S. Census Bureau. Between 1967 and 1991, black families earning $50,000 to $75,000 more than doubled from 4.3 percent to 10.3 percent. "The average family income of blacks today [1992] is some 60 percent that of whites.... Twice as many blacks continue to be unemployed as do whites.... 44.8 percent of black children live in poverty today [1992] compared with 15.9 percent of whites ..." (Gergen, p. 76). "In 1986 [the black poverty rate] was 31 percent. **Worse yet**, the number of poor blacks increased from 7.1 million in 1970 to 9.7 million in 1982. **Although** the majority of poor people are white, the proportion who are black rose during the sixties and seventies, from 25 percent to 31 percent. According to a *Miami Herald* analysis of 1990 census data, the percentage of blacks in the U.S. work force did not change from 1980 to 1990. In 1980, 'blacks were **under-represented** in the nation's executive ranks by 50 percent. Today, despite a near-doubling of the number of blacks in executive jobs, the study shows that there still are 40 percent fewer blacks in such positions **than should be expected by their share of the work force**'" (*Dayton Daily News*, August 16, 1992). Note that added emphasis in the media accounts is intended to bring awareness to value-loaded language and the media's misplaced emphasis on race proportionality as a significant criteria in hiring.

Poverty rates in America are high, at 30 percent for blacks, 26 percent for Hispanics, and 10 percent for whites according to 1990 Census Bureau numbers. In 1988, 60 percent of black Americans 15 to 24 years old lived in poverty, as did 25 percent of those 25 to 34 years old. In 2003, overall, whites "with an advanced degree had the highest average annual income with $74,122. Asian Americans had the second highest with $72,852. Hispanics and African Americans had the lowest annual incomes among those with advanced degrees averaging $67,679 and $59,944 annually. The largest racial inequity was between [whites] with a Bachelor's degree who made $53,185 [and] Hispanics who made $12,263 or 29.9% less with an average annual income of $40,949" (U.S. Census Bureau report, 2003). Note that the positioning of the difference in dollar amount in the U.S. Census Bureau report is intended to momentarily mislead readers into being shocked by an earnings disparity that would be dispelled further along in the sentence; other salary comparisons in the report were paired between amounts earned, not between amounts earned and differences in amounts earned.

"In 2001, over half of African American households of married couples earned $50,000 or more. Although in the same year African Americans were over-represented among the nation's poor, this was directly related to the disproportionate percentage of African American families headed by single women; such families are collectively poorer, regardless of ethnicity" (McKinnon, April 2003). "The poverty rate among African Americans has dropped from 26.5% in 1998 to 24.7% in 2004" (DeNavas-Walt, August 2005).

A contributing factor to poverty among black families is the desertion of black males as head of households, which often impoverishes black women and children. Fewer than half of black families have a husband and wife living together today (*Dayton Daily News*, September 25, 1992, p. 1A). In the mid-eighties, 43 percent of all black families were headed by a single parent, and one-parent families accounted for 73 percent of black families below the poverty line (*Dayton Daily News*, August 16, 1992). Only six percent of black children in the 1980s were living with both *biological* parents. Of the approximately 1.4 million children born to unmarried women each year up to 1992, 67 percent, or nearly 2 out of 3, are born by black women (*Dayton Daily News*, September 25, 1992, p. 1A).

Possibly due to poverty and the prospect of raising children in a single-mother household, black women have 635 abortions for every 1000 babies they bear, compared with 274 for white women (Gergen, p. 76). The high rate of abortions performed on black women may explain why do so few blacks turn out to picket abortion clinics or march in anti-abortion rallies.

The one bright spot is that studies confirm that white employers feel less threatened by black women than by black men and are therefore more likely to hire black women. Anita Herbert feels that in black cultures, a lot "'of black families dissolved because it was easier for a black female to obtain a job. So it put her in a stronger position'" (Terkel, p. 50). The shortage of eligible black males makes single-mother households more likely: 1) few of the black males have legal jobs that would make them attractive as mates, 2) most are already married, 3) many are in jail, 4) few are not on drugs, 5) few are monogamous, 6) few are sensitive to females, 7) few are disease free, and 8) few can provide mental and emotional stimulation.

More numbers of whites live above the poverty line than blacks. Generally, people who have more money have higher education levels, work longer hours, are in jobs that require higher education levels to perform, come from stable home and family environments, have parents who were financially well off (middle and upper-middle class), make sounder business decisions, live in low crime suburban areas, invest their money wisely, and don't abuse drugs and alcohol. The number one predictor of upward social mobility is not ambition, intelligence, or persistence, but the socioeconomic status of one's parents. Poor parents present a role model of being poor and wealthy parents model behaviors that encourage monetary success.

Clarence Smith, the publisher of *Essence* magazine believes that "many blacks don't enter business because they grow up in ghettos and have few positive role models.... 'You have to be extraordinary to be able to overcome the negative life there and go forward to become a doctor, lawyer, businessman or anything. Life in the ghetto has to change substantially and people have to perceive opportunity at a very early age. That's what the middle-class black community is working so hard to do: reach in there and help out'" (Dillon, October 28, 1992).

Joseph Lowery, SCLC President, said, "black Americans must not succumb to materialism and greed but become involved in making positive change." This attitude opposes the call by minorities for markets to provide blacks with more products and non-essential luxury items. Lowery went on to lash out against economic oppression, presumed caused by whites: "'Until we condemn economic violence with the same intensity that we condemn street violence, we shall be compelled to endure both'" (Clark, August 10, 1992).

Commentators wrongly conclude that the income differences between races are evidence that employers, health care practitioners, and law enforcement agencies are practicing racial discrimination on a massive scale. To the contrary, fitting a profile of success is unrelated to race. Greater percentages of whites fitting the success profile shows only a race correlation, not causation of racial discrimination against those having less money. Hostility between the races may be the result of class distinction rather than race distinction. The bad tendency to generalize negative traits to entire groups applies to economic classes as well as racial groups.

The economic differences between blacks and whites also contribute to a feeling that blacks are being victimized. In 1990, black men and women were nearly twice as likely as whites to work in low-paying service jobs (Blauner, p. 166). Of the more than 14 million small businesses nationwide, blacks owned about 450,000 in 1992. Black Americans represent more than 12 percent of the population, yet control only one-half of 1 percent of the nation's capital stock. Black men in professional occupations tend to be in the lower paying, lower prestige fields. According to the 1990 census, of the 756,000 lawyers and judges in the country, 25,704, or 3.4 percent, are black. 2.6% of engineers in the U.S. are African-Americans (*Dayton Daily News*, August 16, 1992). Black entrepreneurs owned 3 percent of the nation's businesses while white males owned 64 percent, according to 1987 data released by the U.S. Commerce Department in July 1992. These statistics make blacks less an economic and legal force than whites, though reasons for racial differences in various professions are only hinted at.

Billy Tidwell, a social scientist at the national Urban League in Washington, offers a metaphor of black economic potential that accuses whites of making blacks commit crime by racially discriminating against them: "'Imagine the Los Angeles riots laying waste to America day after day. That's roughly how much the U.S. economy misses out by not providing more opportunities for the nation's 30 million blacks'" ("Racism's End Could Boost U.S. Economy," *Dayton Daily News*, August 1992). In the same slanted news piece, Stuart Butler, an economist at the conservative Heritage Foundation, states, "'Racism always leads to a reduction in the GNP in any country.'" The fear of bad publicity from such implied charges of racism is a major incentive for employers to change their focus from making a profit to providing jobs to minorities, some of whom may be unattractive as job candidates.

Also according to Tidwell, if the per capita income of blacks was on par with whites, there would be an additional $93 billion earned, though this prediction doesn't address how customer demand for services or products worth $93 billion could be generated, and doesn't mention whether unemployed, low-skill blacks were being counted in the forecast. Tidwell also seems to make law enforcement systems responsible for the price tag to jail the 25 percent of black men and teenagers, which is about $7 billion, rather than the criminals that make jail necessary (*Dayton Daily News*, citing Billy Tidwell).

Blacks spend $22 billion each year going to and arranging conventions and vacations (*Atlanta Journal*, October 1992). Sample products directed at black consumers are finding their way into the hands of blacks using creative business outlets. Companies are "distributing millions of product samples through such unconventional venues as black churches. They're importing merchandise from Africa, broadening product lines, and creating specially targeted marketing departments. And they're using research on black tastes and values to make established ad campaigns relevant and fresh." Those who want but can't afford these new products may go further in debt and become a further burden on society when they default on their loans for products. Researchers are studying black tastes and values to construct their campaigns to get more of the black dollar. Rappers scouting for bling have been the best thing to happen to the jewelry business since unbreakable glass displays, video cameras, Liberace, cubic zirconium, and navel piercings.

Money is the great equalizer. The more money that minorities earn, the more businesses and advertisers want their money. The pursuit of equality has led some blacks to change their focus from gaining rights to squeezing money out of the capitalist society.

Blacks are buying less from the small black businesses in black neighborhoods because they can get the same products cheaper from a better-capitalized integrated competitor. Larger integrated businesses use the technique of lowering prices to successfully compete with one another, and all customers can benefit from the lower prices. Small black businesses in depressed areas cannot offer as much variety or as low a price (and won't if competition doesn't exist), so blacks realize that it is economically more sensible to shop at larger integrated businesses.

> "As a purely factual matter, prices do tend to be higher–and the quality of service and products lower–in stores in low-income neighborhoods. But the knee-jerk assumption that this represents 'exploitation' or 'racism' ignores the economics of the situation.
>
> Many of the ghetto stores charging high prices are struggling to survive, while supermarkets in other neighborhoods are very profitable charging lower prices.

[C]rime, shoplifting, vandalism, and riots have raised the costs, both directly and by causing insurance rates and the costs of security to be higher in ghetto neighborhoods.

The costs of delivering goods to small neighborhood stores are also higher than the costs of delivering goods to huge supermarkets. Delivering a hundred cartons of milk to a supermarket is cheaper than delivering ten cartons of milk to each of ten local stores scattered around town.

Selling a customer $50 worth of groceries in a supermarket takes less time than selling ten customers $5 worth of groceries in a little neighborhood store." (Thomas Sowell, August 25, 2006).

Blacks also shop at larger integrated businesses because they recognize the name of the business through broader advertising, and because they perceive that the more visible large companies are, the less likely they will be to rip customers off due to tighter restrictions and a stronger need to maintain a healthy reputation between itself and its customers. This name brand perception and the association of the ill-affordability of the business to rip off its customers compensates for the blacks' flawed perception that a black businessperson is less likely to rip off a black customer than a white businessperson is to rip off a black customer.

Blacks who lobby for the inclusion in predominantly white businesses of products and services that are used almost exclusively by blacks encourage blacks to shop at the integrated products and services stores. Every time a black purchases a product or service at an integrated establishment, that same product is not being purchased at a predominantly black establishment, meaning reduced revenue for black-owned small businesses.

Class and poverty greatly impact medical care. Blacks are more likely than whites to be poor and, therefore, more likely to be affected by the inability to acquire the health insurance required for treatment in the general health-care delivery system instead of hospital emergency rooms. Blacks receive fewer heart transplants because they are likely to be poor and poor people are more likely to have medical problems on top of heart ailments that could make a heart transplant unworkable. The American Medical Association recognizes that blacks and other minorities tend to die younger, see doctors less, and have more illness than whites. Average life expectancy for blacks at birth is 75.3 years, with black men overall having "6.4 fewer years of life expectancy than white men" (Lamb, *Dayton Daily News*, October 26, 2006, p. D5). Studies by the federal Department of Health and Human Services show that 139,000 blacks died before age 70 between 1979 and 1981, a rate 42 percent higher than for whites. For black males, life expectancy was 65 years in 1992, a figure that is impacted by high death rates of young black males rather than the shorter life span of black males over the age of forty-five. The homicide rate for black males from 15 to 24 years old increased between 1985 and 1989 by 74 percent to 114.8 deaths per 100,000. The death rates for blacks as a group aged 25-44 were 2.5 times that for whites. Reported HIV infections in 1989 were 40.3 per 100,000 for black men, three times the rate of 13.1 per 100,000 for white men. For black women, the rate was 8.1 per 100,000, nine times the rate for white women ("U.S. falls short of health goals," *Dayton Daily News*). Black gay men are the primary sufferers of AIDS in the United States, making AIDS increasingly a disease of blacks. By the end of 1991, blacks were 3.6 times more likely than whites to have the disease. Between 1985 and 1990, the rate of syphilis infection among blacks increased by 150 percent, while it decreased by half among whites. Nationwide, blacks are fifty times more likely to have syphilis than are whites (Taylor). Around a billion dollars a year is spent treating gunshot wounds in America's inner cities, and blacks are ten times more likely than whites to require emergency-room treatment for the effects of cocaine abuse (Taylor). According to the General Accounting Office, 10.2 percent of blacks have diabetes, while only 6.2 percent of whites do (General Accounting Office, *Dayton Daily News*, April 7, 1992). Minorities die much more frequently than whites from high blood pressure and other cardiovascular diseases, cancer, diabetes, substance abuse and infant mortality.

Another problem contributing to quality medical care is the lack of good hospitals in black neighborhoods. According to Vernellia Randall in her book, *Dying While Black*, "black neighborhood hospitals have decreased by 90 percent over two decades," reducing suitable access to health care and forcing patients to overwhelm the fewer remaining health care facilities (Lamb, *Dayton Daily News*, October 26, 2006, p. D5).

High infant mortality rates among blacks is related to a lack of maternity information and advice. According to a June 1992 study by the National Center for Health Statistics, black babies are almost twice as likely as white babies to die in their first year of life, even among college-educated parents. Black babies are nearly twice as likely as whites to die in their first year of life, even among college-educated parents, according to a study published in the *New England Journal of Medicine* and a June 1992 study by the National Center for Health Statistics. Black babies died more often because they were more likely to be smaller at birth, whether premature or full term. Black mothers are more likely than whites to give birth to dangerously undersize babies because of a wide array of pregnancy problems, not any single health factor (*Dayton Daily News*, p. 1C). In a study by Dr. Allison Kempe and others from Harvard Medical School, it was found that infection or rupture of the amniotic membranes in black pregnancies accounted for 38 percent of the extra low-weight births among blacks. Premature labor for no apparent reason accounted for 21 percent, high blood pressure 12 percent and hemorrhaging 10 percent. Black women were three times as likely as whites to experience these difficulties during pregnancy. The researchers said they believe the racial differences between white pregnancies and black pregnancies "are rooted in profound social inequities." Social conditions of poverty that complicate black pregnancies include malnutrition, lack of prenatal care, maternity ignorance in teen and preteen mothers, former and current botched abortion attempts, abusive relationships with fathers, and drug use during pregnancy. Among babies who were normal size at birth, blacks survived just as well as whites. Dr. James Collins of Northwestern University, who has conducted similar studies in Chicago, said researchers should start trying to learn whether the stress of racism plays some role in the premature delivery of black babies. The Ohio State Legislature in 1987 formed the Commission on Minority Health to try to reduce the health gap between whites and minorities in Ohio.

Poverty is related to most of the social and medical ailments that distinguish minority races, though former registered nurse and author Vernellia Randall writes that blacks "'are quite literally dying from being black.... Without focusing on race, the problem never will be fixed'" (Lamb, *Dayton Daily News*, October 26, 2006, p. D5).

8

Minority Crime, Profiling, and Hate Crime Legislation

For many Americans, the law-and-order issue is intertwined with unspoken, though often warranted fears about young black men in inner cities committing a disproportionate amount of violent crime. At some point in their lives, twenty-five percent of black men and teenagers end up behind bars (*Dayton Daily News*, August 1992). Nationally, nearly a quarter of all black males between 20 and 29 years of age at any given moment are in jail, on parole or on probation; "1 out of every 5 black males spends part of his life behind bars" (Gergen, p. 76). In 1992, "James Williams, superintendent of Dayton schools, said 750,000 African-American men in the United States are incarcerated, while only 400,000 are enrolled in higher education. 'We need black men if our race is to continue,' the superintendent said.'" The FBI reported in August of 1992 that 1,429 of every 100,000 black youths were arrested (though not necessarily indicted) for violent crime in 1991, a rate five times that for white youths. "The fear is greatest of inner-city youths in high tops and gang colors. But all blacks are tarred to some degree" (Mabry and Thomas, p. 37).

According to the 1990 Sourcebook of Criminal Justice Statistics, blacks account for 46 percent of arrests for rape; 56 percent for murder and 65 percent for robbery" (Juan Williams, May 5, 1992). While blacks make up only 12.3 percent of the population [in 2006], they committed 60 percent of the murders and over half of all rapes and robberies in 1992 (Taylor, 1992).

"Earlier acts of violence against whites ... gave many blacks a feeling of controlling their own destiny, of power, even pride. Violence ... did not lead to more repression, but to thoughtful reflection by white and black leaders about the corrosive despair of black Americans" (Fuchs, p. 176). Neither pride nor a sense of controlling one's destiny, however, leads blacks to assault whites; black criminals prefer to steal from white victims because whites generally have more things to steal than others in minority groups have. Liberal white Americans reflected, while others in the white community emphasized law and order, demanding more policemen, even considering a police state where black crime was concerned.

Crimes against whites by blacks are largely ignored or vastly under-reported by the mass media:

> In 1986 and 1987 whites committing crimes of violence–robbery, rape, and assault–chose white victims 97.5 percent of the time and black victims 2.5 percent of the time in those incidents in which the victim could identify the race of the offender. Blacks committing violent crimes chose white victims 51.2 percent of the time and black victims 48.8 percent of the time. For the specific crime of robbery the figures are similarly striking. In 1986-1987, of those robberies in which the race of the offender was identified by the victim, 95.1 percent of robberies committed by whites had white victims and 4.9 percent had black victims; 57.4 percent of robberies committed by blacks had white victims and 42.6 percent had black victims (Edsall and Edsall).

In Dayton, Ohio within the first 10 weeks of 1992 "12 whites [were] assaulted for no reason by black teen-agers in the area of Fourth and Main streets downtown. Police confirmed that the first 10 weeks of the year saw a trend of attacks against whites downtown, usually those who were by themselves" (Bray, *Dayton Daily News*). For "no reason" in the report should be amended to read, "for no reason that the reporters cared to determine or speculate about for fear of libel suits if they hinted that the cause may have been race-related, possibly hate crimes."

National statistics for 1980 attribute 51 percent of all violent juvenile crime to blacks youths. "Black men constitute [approximately] 46 percent of the prison population, and blacks are jailed at a rate eight times higher than that of whites" (*Dayton Daily News*, August 16, 1992).

Stated another way, statistics show that blacks are primarily victimized by blacks. Two-thirds of the homicides in the first six months of 1992 in Dayton, Ohio had black victims (Clark, *Dayton Daily News*, August 11, 1992). "African-Americans are 70 percent more likely than whites to be victims of violent crimes" committed by any race (Mabry and Thomas, p. 37). "Blacks commit more violent crime against whites than against blacks. Forty-five percent of their victims are white, 43 percent are black, and 10 percent are Hispanic. When whites commit violent crime, only three percent of their victims are black" (Stix, October 6, 2005, quoting from *The Color of Crime*). The homicide rate for black males in the 15 to 24 year age range increased between 1985 and 1989 by 74 percent to 114.8 deaths per 100,000. The death rates for blacks as a group aged 25 to 44 were 2.5 times that for whites (*Dayton Daily News*, p. 8C). More than 90 percent of the victims of all, not only violent but also theft, check fraud, shop lifting, and property, crimes committed by young blacks were other blacks; homicide has become the leading cause of death for young black males *and* females.

According to FBI records:

> "By race, 70.7 percent of all arrestees in 2002 were white. The offense for which whites were arrested most often was driving under the influence. The offense for which blacks were arrested most often was drug abuse violations.
> By race [of 14,054 homicides in 2002], 48.7 percent of murder victims were white, 48.5 percent were black, and 2.7 percent were of other races.
> Data from single victim/single offender incidents indicated that 92.3 percent of black victims were slain by black offenders, and 84.7 percent of white victims were slain by white offenders" (www.fbi.gov accessed 12/31/06). (See the explanation in the following paragraphs of how white is deceptively defined.)

According to New Century Foundation in a study entitled *The Color of Crime: Race, Crime, and Justice in America*, "… between 2001 and 2003, blacks were 39 times more likely to commit violent crimes against whites than the reverse, and 136 times more likely to commit robbery. Blacks committed, on average, 15,400 black-on-white rapes per year, while whites averaged only 900 white-on-black rapes per year. Of the nearly 770,000 violent interracial crimes committed every year involving blacks and whites, blacks commit 85 percent and whites commit 15 percent" (*The Color of Crime: Race, Crime, and Justice in America, Second, Expanded Edition, 2005*, American Renaissance, 2005). Rape statistics for prison populations, in which black inmates rape white inmates as an institutionalized sport, are not included in the black-on-white rapes cited here.

Statistics should not be accepted on their face value. For instance, the

> "feds inflate white crime statistics by counting Hispanic offenders as white.… If someone attacks a Mexican for racial reasons, he becomes a Hispanic victim of a hate crime. However, if the same Mexican commits a hate crime against a black, he is classified as a 'white' perpetrator. Even more absurdly, if a Mexican commits a hate crime against a white, both victim and perpetrator are reported as white. Thus, the number of white perpetrators is exaggerated, while the number of white victims is constricted by the federal double-standard" (Stix, October 6, 2005).

Statistics don't tell the entire story. For instance, the reason so many more blacks are arrested for crimes may be that police and the justice system are more diligent, based on a minority's known proclivities, about arresting and locking up young black males, people who have the best chance of having been productive members of the black community. Perhaps the higher arrest rates indicate a higher failure of blacks than whites to evade arrest, either intentionally because those committing crimes feel that their lives are worthless and they don't care if they lose their freedom, or because they have a shabby support network to shelter them, or because they don't know how to evade capture. The statistics may have something to do with the neighborhood's efforts to curb crime, such as an organized effort to watch over one another's property and to phone the police when they suspect crime. The residents of one neighborhood may be more concerned and involved in the protection of the entire neighborhood.

Premise: Sometimes crimes involving participants of more than one race aren't racially motivated.

The issue of crime has been a divisive element among political parties. Willie Horton, the Massachusetts prisoner who committed rape and assault while on furlough, was used by the Republican Party as a symbol of what could go wrong if prisoners were thought to be reformable:

> "For years liberal Democrats were afraid to talk tough on crime, lest they be branded racist. As a result, Democratic leaders were accused of coddling criminals. Republican politicians have pandered to white fear, but they have been deliberately coy about it, using code words and thinly veiled messages like the GOP's infamous Willie Horton ad in 1988" (Mabry and Thomas, p. 37).

Many blacks complain that police are too tough on black suspects, while other blacks in the same neighborhood, often victims of crime, complain that there aren't enough cops in the when crime occurs.

Rioters like those causing havoc in Crown Heights, Brooklyn, NY in 1991 are more brazen, but no less easy to deal with. A Hasidic Jewish man ran over two black children pedestrians, and an uprising of black males countered with violence, condemning all in the Jewish religious group for the act of one driver. Riots like the one that broke out on August 11, 1965, in the Watts section of Los Angeles usually have at their foundation a charge of oppression or injustice. In the Watts riot, blacks threw rocks and bottles at policeman, shouting

> "'Burn, baby, burn!' as television cameras rolled. By August 16, after the National Guard had been called in and order slowly restored, there were thirty-four dead, more than 1,000 injured, over 800 buildings damaged or destroyed, and nearly 4,000 arrests (Edsall and Edsall).

Crimes committed by blacks against whites receive much less media attention than crimes committed by whites against blacks. For instance, at the Chapel Hill campus of the University of North Carolina, Dr. Khalib Muhammed stated, "We are tired of the blond-haired, pale-skinned blue-eyed buttermilk-complexioned cracker Christ or peckerwood Jesus." In 1990, Yankel Rosenbaum was stabbed to death by a group of blacks in New York who chanted "Kill the Jew." One of the murderers identified by Rosenbaum before his death confessed to the police but was acquitted by a jury. The media did not indignantly spread this unjust verdict as it did with the hyped Rodney King verdict. In 1989, a white man was badly beaten by a gang of blacks in Cleveland, and as he was lying in the street, one of his attackers got into the man's truck and ran him over to the cheers of the others. "In January 1991, four blacks agreed to kill the first white person they saw. A Northeastern University student in Boston was unlucky enough to be the first; he was stabbed to death. In 1991, a black man was arrested for murdering seven white people. He explained the murders by 'a deep-rooted hatred for white people.' In 1989, Gus Savage, a black congressman from Chicago, responded to a reporter: 'I don't want to talk to you white motherfuckers. Fuck you, you motherfucking asshole white devils'" (Walter Williams, "Racial Double Standards Threaten a Civil Society"). A 29-year-old white man in Dayton, Ohio was beaten by about a dozen young black men as he pumped gas. A witness, who is black, made the following statements: "'As I was passing the gas station, I noticed this crowd of black guys. It was about 12 to 15 at least,' he said. 'I saw them beating this white guy like they were losing their minds. He tried to crawl away, and they kicked him some more. He was kicked and punched in the mouth. He was bleeding from his mouth and nose.' At one point, one or two appeared to be helping the man get up, the witness said, but then they too joined in the beating. 'They were standing in a circle around him. They were just hitting and kicking. Man, it makes me gag,' the witness said" (Russell Carollo, "Young Blacks Beat White," *Dayton Daily News*).

In Knoxville, Tennessee,

> "a young white couple, Channon Christian and Christopher Newsom, were victims of a brutal crime. They were carjacked, kidnapped and raped. Cleaning fluid was sprayed into Christian's mouth. She was stuffed in a trashcan

and apparently suffocated. Newsom was shot and set afire. His body was dumped. Five blacks, one a woman, have been arrested. The story made headlines around Knoxville. It was unnoticed nationally" (Pitts, *Dayton Daily News*, June 3, 2007).

However, according to Pitt, at least one report shows that "blacks and Latinos are underrepresented in news media as victims of crime and significantly overrepresented as perpetrators" (Pitt, June 3, 2007). Newspapers have limited space, and the preponderance of black victims of black crime makes such stories too common, too pedestrian to clog up news columns day in and day out. When there's a white victim of a black criminal, the story has the added punch of race controversy.

Black community leaders don't want fair and objective reporting of black crime. Leaders have convinced or intimidated news establishments to downplay crimes by blacks so that campaigns to create a positive black stereotype don't go off the tracks. Black community leaders want the appearance of a different reality, an image that is contradicted daily by violent black criminals.

Racism does not cause riotous behavior; people's emotional responses to what they believe is racism leads them to riot. Racism cannot be used as "a legitimizing rationale for violence, crime or the endemic problems of the urban poor" (Morganthau, p. 28). As with any psychological and emotional state of mind, until the racist translates his feelings into written, verbal, and physical action such as the beatings of whites, those feelings are difficult for external observers to prove or prosecute. Racist thoughts can't be prosecuted. Only recently, and when connected with a crime motivated by racism, has racist thinking been made legally punishable by longer prison sentencing through hate crime legislation.

When asked by a reporter what made a black police force new hire qualified for the position, a black police captain in Dayton, Ohio, answered, "He knows diversity." Knowledge of diversity in any city is the least important aspect of policing, but having a captain who wrongly prioritizes diversity as a qualification is a bad sign for any city.

It's difficult to prove or disprove every possible explanation for a condition. However, comparing the statistics for the police arrival times in black communities versus white communities, the police seem more reluctant to answer calls of black-on-black violence in predominantly black communities, showing less diligence, and, some would say, a greater desire to be part of the clean-up crew after allowing blacks the time to decimate themselves. In areas of high gang activity, police understand that gang members shoot and stab members of rival gangs, and that gangs, in general, gun for the police. Rivals hate by tradition and to justify taking property. They get power through violence. Gangs are like sports teams—there are rules, there are signals, there is coordination of effort, and there is a definable objective.

Many theories are floated to explain the high crime rates by blacks. Additional police presence in black neighborhoods may lead to higher profiling of blacks, and it is hypothesized that similar rates of presence and profiling in white neighborhoods would uncover higher, comparable rates of white crime. (The probability of catching more whites by exercising greater police diligence in white neighborhoods might be true, but such speculation doesn't change the actual number and type of crimes committed by blacks caught because of accurate and successful profiling.) Some cite the greater sophistication of whites to commit and then avoid detection or apprehension for white-collar crimes. High incarceration rates are explained by automatic presumption of guilt for blacks and the financial inability of poor blacks to obtain good legal counsel and representation. "Legal experts argue that [fear of black crime] may account for higher conviction rates and harsher sentences for black defendants" (Mabry and Thomas, p. 37). Some excuse theft crimes as a necessity by the poor in minority communities, though the single greatest indicator of an area's crime rate is not poverty nor education, but race and ethnicity. Even when one controls for income, the black crime rate is much higher than the white rate" (Stix, October 6, 2005). Some liberal apologists overlook all drug possession crimes as harming only the drug abuser. Blacks take drugs to escape their harsh reality, and they consider their reality to be more harsh than the white person's reality. Sellers of drugs receive much harsher prison sentences than buyers, irrespective of the seller's race. If a greater proportion of drug dealers on the streets are blacks, more black dealers will be arrested on drug distribution charges. This accounts for the statistic that blacks in the U.S. are four times more likely than whites to be arrested on drug charges.

Homeowners in neighborhoods that experience frequent crime are apologetic for other members of their race who are shown to be criminals, or lie to reporters, saying "this type of crime has never happened in this neighborhood before, to my knowledge," when they know it has. The lies are meant to protect racial image, so that readers or viewers won't get/keep the negative impression/association of blacks and crime in the neighborhoods. White criminals don't get as much publicity as blacks, blacks contend, so there is less likelihood that whites will develop negative stereotypes about whites based on the frequency of media coverage of white crimes.

Profiling

Profiling is the practice of identifying potential perpetrators of specific crimes based on conspicuous characteristics that these subjects have in common with criminals who have been apprehended in the past for similar crimes. Though profiling isn't officially sanctioned in many of the nation's police departments, and is actually illegal in some states, unofficial profiling allows law enforcement officers to identify those people who should receive more than a cursory inspection. Race is often a characteristic in profiles. Other associated factors also inform law enforcement profiles, such as gang tattoos, pimped vehicles, clothing style, music style and volume, nervous behavior, the known criminal history of a profiled individual or individual's associates, and the inconsistent composition and reputation of a neighborhood where blacks who fit a specific criminal and residential profile are reportedly seen. Such composite factors raise suspicion.

Charges that profiling is based only on the controlling criteria of race are rarely valid. Arrested suspects often make charge of profiling offenses in preparation of an anticipated defense strategy, highlighting suspected bigotry in police departments. Such charges also encourage law-abiding blacks to refuse to cooperate with suspected racist police officers in their investigations, which insidiously aids black criminals in evasion of future apprehension when black witnesses refuse to come forward. Though decried by some as discriminatory and undemocratic, such charges are self-serving, having the potential of discouraging police to inconvenience accusers in the future to avoid internal department investigations into the unwritten practice of criminal profiling.

When police profile black suspects, they don't rely on easy generic stereotypes. Inaccurate profiles would focus law enforcement resources in the wrong direction, leading to ineffective policing. Profiling experts in police departments continuously monitor the compiled criteria that comprise profiles, recognizing counterprofile measures by criminals who have learned which characteristics in profiles police key on and adapt by disguising those traits in themselves. Profiles are evolving instruments.

Police question blacks who cruise predominantly white suburbs, asking what they're doing even if the black is on his own property. It is better policy to be secure than to risk hurting the feelings of innocent parties who fit the profile but who have committed no crimes and don't intend to in self-reports, as long as civil liberties are not abrogated and abridged beyond what might be claimed as mistaken identity. Citizens with weapons who haven't received training in proper profiling techniques are a far greater danger than law enforcement personnel who have, if only tacitly. Citizens often let fear dictate their reactions: "'Imagine how it feels to walk down a street and by your very presence, you evoke fear'" (Terkel quoting Bob Matthieson, p. 164).

Police, overcautious to protect communities, operate on the basis of criminal element profiles, allowing police to err on the side of safety. It's the action taken by police that people object to on racial grounds. Sometimes, police don't use the greatest sensitivity when they question suspected criminals, and their conduct comes into question. Some officers assume that everyone who meets several criteria in a profile is a criminal, assert excessive force against these people, and fail to conscientiously apply presumptions of innocence or perfectly observe principles of civil rights. Police are not racially neutral and react based on experience in comparable situations.

Black customers are profiled in stores because owners have experienced that black customers steal more than white customers do. Better to be safe and risk insulting honest black customers, who may not return after such presumptive attention. Shopkeepers depend on the honest black shoppers to be cognizant of the reality of black shoplifting rates to accept the need for special security.

The safety argument carries a lot of weight. Told that there was a 75 percent chance you'd be mauled by a lion when placed in a cage with it, you'll likely avoid that cage. If whites in minority-dominated neighborhoods knew they had a 50 percent chance of being harassed by a minority, a 40 percent chance of being mugged, a 30 percent chance of being carjacked, a 25 percent chance of being shot at, they'd be more likely to stay out of those neighborhoods. The man on the street trying to stay safe can't see liberal excuses. He doesn't question what makes someone potentially violent and morally unrestrained in his upbringing–poverty, past reward for violence, attitude, values, opportunity, suppression of conscience and other rationalizations. What he can see is race, posture, clothing fashion, and gang paraphernalia. He may commit flawed racial profiling based on a higher statistical occurrence of black criminals, but he is rational to want to feel and be safe. The logic he uses consists of a basic syllogism learned in logic or rhetoric classes:

a) Personal safety is imperative for the survival of the human race.

b) Violent crimes are more numerous, more liable to result in fatality, and more likely target non-minority innocents in poor minority neighborhoods than in mostly white neighborhoods.

c) Therefore, avoiding poor minority neighborhoods increases a non-minority's level of personal safety.

The first two statements in a syllogism are premises, whose truth is always debatable. At any given moment and in a given situation, personal safety may be less important to an individual than gaining a risky thrill. Also, the race will survive even if a billion people are killed. A white's avoidance of minority neighborhoods doesn't guarantee his personal safety, since crime can occur anywhere at any time, and most often in one's own home by someone known to the victim. Probabilities are true in very limited instances and often only in vacuums of statistical intellectualizing.

Ethnicity and religion aren't the primary factors in profiling guidelines for airline passengers. Trying to be politically correct where terrorists are concerned can get people killed. Airport screening/profiling is valid discrimination based on attire, attitude, nationality, whether a one-way ticket was purchased with cash, apparent nervousness, and the wrong questions asked about the flight.

Complaints of racism in profiling have led police to soften their diligence in complying with standard operating procedures regarding profiles. Police

> "have been exercising racial bias on behalf of blacks, arresting fewer blacks than their proportion of criminals: '… blacks who committed crimes that were reported to the police were 26 percent less likely to be arrested than people of other races who committed the same crimes….' "[A] 2002 study by Maryland's Public Service Research Institute found that police were stopping too few black speeders (23%), compared to their proportion of actual speeders (25%). '… the only evidence for police bias is disproportionate arrest rates for those groups police critics say are the targets of bias. High black arrest rates appear to reflect high crime rates, not police misconduct'" (Stix, October 6, 2005).

It is generally a safe bet for cops, lacking direct evidence, to rely on statistical and experiential knowledge to develop crime suspects. Such profiling decisions are based on experience of proven allegations of crimes by blacks who manifest certain criminal behavior. Police don't care if blacks resent that police automatically think that blacks are more dangerous than whites based only upon the preponderance of news stories about violence and crimes committed by blacks and on the stereotypes these stories create. Fear that members of another race are likely to cause harm causes car windows to be rolled up in bad neighborhoods, and innocent minorities walking by may laugh at how stereotypes have caused such white paranoia. That's okay to most whites who don't become victims.

Hate Crimes Legislation: An Argument for Repeal

On July 7, 2005, a 19-year old male was sentenced to eight months for spray painting KKK on the home and car of a black family in Fincastle, Virginia, a destruction of property felony hate crime based on race.

A boy in a street gang is tragically gunned down in a struggle for inner city dominance and territory. His parents don't grieve less when they learn that a member of their own race rather than another shattered their family.

A gay man is intentionally infected with the AIDS virus by a vengeful male lover. The victim's relatives and friends watch him waste away and vow to see justice done for the carrier of the killer virus.

Several obese women are attacked by a skinny man who slams their ankles with a lead plumbing pipe and laughs as they struggle to stand. He's convicted of multiple counts of simple assault and receives the standard prison sentencing.

The full weight of the law doesn't apply to the victims in the last three hypothetical crimes because either the tormentors or the victims don't fit the discriminatory hate crimes provisions set forth in the Violent Crime Control and Law Enforcement Act of 1994 or in new amendments before congress. To be eligible for enhanced sentencing that is generally added to existing statutes for criminal conduct motivated by hate or discrimination, convicted defendants must have intentionally selected a victim based on "the actual or perceived race, color, religion, national origin, ethnicity, gender, disability, or sexual orientation of any person." This hate crimes statute and others like it at the local and state levels benefit only members of particular victim groups, if the premise is incorrectly accepted that enhanced sentencing is a benefit to society. The goal is to correct presumed inequality of legal recourse for these groups by legalizing unequal treatment for everyone else.

Everyone else includes most victims of gang violence. Most gang violence is judged to be a result of societal rebellion, generalized and institutionalized territoriality, mob conformance behavior, revenge for past wrongs wrought by opposing gang ancestors, drug dealing collateral damage, and any number of reasons that can be happily provided by sociologists and psychology professionals. Though gang-related killings are abhorrent and often based in senseless hatred of opposing "colors," they generally are not considered hate crimes because members of gangs are overwhelmingly of the same racial composition. National statistics show that more than 80 percent of the victims of violent crimes committed by blacks are other blacks.

An angry homosexual carrier of the AIDS virus is presumed not to target homosexuals because of the victim's sexual orientation. People of the same sexual orientation congregate and infect one another with deadly diseases for reasons that don't meet the conditions of hate crimes legislation. Also excluded from enhanced sentencing are defendants who attack obese people of no particular gender or race, single teen mothers for being immoral parasites of the welfare system, boy band members whose singing really sucks, lawyers, abortion doctors, U.S. Post Office managers, bald guys, people with phony southern accents, the elderly who reject the label of "disability," kids of any gender victimized by pedophiles, the mentally deficient, the homeless, prostitutes of either gender if attacked indiscriminately, environmentalists, politicians, and numerous categories of people because of their employment.

Theoretically, if the *criminal's* race, national origin, ethnicity, gender, disability, or sexual orientation is the same as the victim's, then the crime is less likely to fall within the definition of hate crimes statutes. For instance, a healthy white male who attacks another healthy white male in a bar presumably doesn't do so because the victim is white or male or non-disabled. However, what if the white attacker is racist, and the white victim has co-opted slang, speech patterns, clothing, and swagger associated with black gangster rap culture? Might hate crime provisions be invoked in this case? Could it be possible that one could hate one's own race, ethnicity, gender, disability, and sexual orientation, and express that hatred in violence toward others who possess those personal and demographic characteristics?

Because of the heightened, if unfounded, awareness of race as a key factor in social relationships in the U.S., prosecutors believe that they can safely categorize white-on-black and black-on-white crime as hate crimes, if any evidence points to the victimizer as generally racist. As a result, most black victims are afforded application of hate crimes sentencing only when the victimizer is not black.

Disparate sentencing places a variable value on the lives of victims, placing less on minorities victimized by minorities of the same class than on those victimized by people who possess differing personal and demographic characteristics. Hate crimes legislation tends to promulgate such racist and categorical assumptions. The inexhaustible matrix of varying personal characteristics that victims and victimizers possess make it impractical for any law to fairly and justly accommodate all shades of targeted hatred, or racial and religious intolerance. Supporters of hate crimes legislation, like Stephen Clark, a staff attorney with the Utah chapter of the ACLU, concede that exclusion of many victim classes from enhanced sentencing protections is unavoidable, and that special rights for members of some groups will be created (Denton). Freidrich A. Hayek, a socio-political economist, points out that beneficial effects of laws are realized "only if they are applied to all cases to which they refer, irrespective of whether it is known, or even true, that they will have a beneficial effect in the particular case" (Hayek, p. 16).

The existence of exclusions and special rights in any law discriminates against those for whom the law cannot be equally applied, debatably in violation of the equal protection clause of the United States Constitution. According to a report by the Anti-Defamation League, the "statutes unconstitutionally benefit minorities, because minorities are more likely to be victims of bias crimes, or … the statutes unconstitutionally burden majority members because majority members are more likely to be prosecuted" without direct evidence that race factored in the criminal intent.

To minimize the exclusion of victim classes, many local and state statutes contain versions of hate crime legislation that attempt to broaden applicability of sentencing enhancements. In Utah, for instance, anyone who "commits any primary offense with the intent to intimidate or terrorize another person or with reason to believe that his action would intimidate or terrorize that person" is charged with a third degree felony. Federal statutes like the Hate Crimes Prevention Act are intended to extend the federal government's ability to investigate or prosecute incidents of hate violence. However, under Section 245 of Title 18 U.S.C., only racial and religious bias-motivated interference, by force or threat of force, in another's pursuit of a Federal right or benefit, such as voting, may invoke penalty enhancement, and only if the government can prove both that the crime occurred because the victim belonged to a protected group and that the victim was attempting to engage in a protected federal activity. Instead of drafting complicated qualifications and limitations, the public might be more comforted if the law applied, without discrimination, to anyone who interferes, for any reason, with another's legal pursuit of a Federal right or benefit.

Crime victims who are ineligible to receive equal presumed protections under hate crimes legislation, that is, black victims of black criminals, for instance, are justified in feeling indignant about the unfairness of legally sanctioned discrimination. Taking offense at hate crimes legislation, however, is an equal opportunity option. Members of a class that the government feels need extra protection are insulted by the insinuation that they can't protect themselves, or that they're assumed to be entitled to something extra because of their race, gender, or sexual orientation. Otherwise deserving of equal treatment, members of the "protected" groups may gradually become perceived by society as actually *needing* special consideration due to some inherent weakness associated with their personal characteristics. Such hand-outs are humiliating. A backlash of sentiment against hate crimes legislation is predictable considering the precedent set by affirmative action, which is increasingly recognized as a bad idea, with the imprimatur that it had it's place in a different time when minorities weren't protected equally by laws.

So, in a legal system with perfect adherence to hate crimes sentencing guidelines, the black gang banger who murders another black gang banger gets a lighter prison sentence than he would had he been white and demonstrably motivated by racial hate. Conversely, enhanced sentencing for hate crimes appears to implicitly presume that the same crimes committed for any reasons other than those specifically identified deserve less punishment. Lawmakers justify this sentencing disparity by invoking the principle that society at large is less threatened by roving gangs of gun-toting killers than by members of hate groups who intimidate those in minority communities, leaving their victims feeling isolated and vulnerable. In a debate with Stephen Clark, Terry Kogan, University of Utah law professor and member of the Civil Rights Task Force on Hate Crimes Legislation, is reported to support enhanced sentencing because it sends a "symbolic message about societal standards and teach[es] a lesson about permissible conduct" (Denton). Symbolism and education aren't the primary objectives of lawmakers or of laws.

For horrendous crimes committed by racists, homophobes and sexists, the depth of the victimizer's moral depravity is thought to be less affected by rehabilitation efforts. Generalized hatred is likely to lead to repeated crimes based on the same criminal intent, so hate crimes legislation presumes incorrigibility–similar to the Three Strikes statutes for violent career offenders–and is a preventative measure against future crime. The goal becomes removing these criminals from society for longer periods to make society safer. Your average vengeful psychopath, husband, gang banger, or any other member of society who commits similar crimes for reasons unrelated to race, gender, disability, or sexual preference are perversely thought to be more malleable to prison reform methods.

However, inasmuch as theoretical threats based on a criminal's past pattern of crimes can't be accurately predicted or assumed, neither communities nor individuals in traditionally victimized groups can be "protected" as a result of hate crimes legislation. Just as spoken and physical conduct is unforeseeable, neither can laws guarantee protection or even swift and consistent punishment of offenders. An apparent primary premise behind the call for enhanced sentencing is the protection offered through crime deterrence. One form of crime deterrence is removing the criminally inclined and convicted members from society and detaining them (detention deterrence). However, detaining anyone who's committed any crime, not simply hate crimes, for longer periods ensures that the detainees will not commit crimes, at least not against citizens at liberty in society. So why not enhance sentencing for all convicted criminals, if the purpose of sentencing is both deterrence and longer protection of society? Racists will continue to practice their hate in prison, though embezzlers may have a hard time structuring such a crime behind bars.

Another principle of deterrence is the compelling of people, by threat of punishment, to decide against committing crimes (restraint deterrence). The validity of this principle is largely unsubstantiated by evidence. Arguably, little hard evidence exists that supports the notion that harsher criminal sentencing has a directly attributable reductive effect on a potential or admitted criminal's decision to commit a crime. The extent of the effect, if it exists at all as a deterrent against hate crimes, is unknowable since there are no statistics on the number of potential criminals who 1) consider committing a hate crime, 2) think about how enhanced sentencing might compound their misery in prison, 3) think about how the label of hate criminal in prison would identify them for retributive punishment from other inmates belonging to the victimized group, 4) decide against committing the hate crimes, 5) and call in their decision *not* to commit a hate crime to some hotline so that it can be documented in a national database. Every apprehended self-confessed hate criminal obviously wasn't deterred by the prospect of spending any time in prison, not to mention amended time. Then there are all of those who commit hate crimes who aren't apprehended, and consequently not counted as statistics which might further validate the case of hate crimes legislation as a deterrent. Any restraint deterrent effect is unknowable.

Additional time in prison has not been shown to reduce recidivism rates, because prison has a way of hardening criminal attitudes. Prison inmates are largely self-segregating along racial lines, and within racially segregated groups, cohesion is often based on hatred and fear of other racially based groups in the prison population. The nature of the prison environment encourages rather than rehabilitates hate crimes mentality. Given additional prison time in which to stew in racial hatred, and fully supported by one's Aryan Nation, Patriot, Nazi skinhead, and KKK prison mates, hate crimes perpetrators predictably gain little perspective on the value of committing crimes for other reasons when they're released on parole, despite any mandatory racial-sensitivity training the prison might offer.

The threat of capital punishment does not deter those who indisputably commit capital offenses. The reasons that capital punishment fails as the ultimate deterrent apply, in varying degrees, to the failure of enhanced sentencing for hate crimes.

Both law-abiding and law-breaking citizens see frequent stories whose authors are outraged that convicts rarely serve their entire sentence, that existing laws are unenforced, that the criminal justice and penal systems need to be reformed. There's time off for good behavior, and prison overcrowding that necessitates early releases of jailbirds. There're work furloughs and weekend work passes, lenient parole boards, and jailbreaks. There're legal technicalities, shifty defense attorneys, overworked and racist or misogynist prosecutors, plea bargaining, dismissals for lack of evidence, and great lapses of time (up to fourteen years) between conviction and execution in capital punishment convictions, which allows aspiring capital offenders to forget that there are murderers in prison awaiting the needle. There're the controlled substances abuse prisoner outpatient treatment programs, the short-time institutions for criminals determined to be temporarily insane, and liberal boo hoo defenses that reduce sentencing based on the criminal's sad childhood. There're the jailhouse snitch arrangements, witness protection programs for organized crime whistleblowers, reduced sentences for turning state's evidence on co-conspirators, financial penance bargains for reduced time, and juvenile sentencing length restrictions. Then there's the biggest blow to the concept of deterrence—the absence of high-profile and sustained publicity for each and every low criminal sentenced for every crime, the kind of public display that would instill fear of legal retribution, much as the public square stockades made an example of humiliated Puritan offenders.

The deterrent effect loses power when the criminal considers the fallibility of the legal and penal system. Even exact knowledge of sentencing hierarchies for various crimes doesn't deter criminals who live by the credo, "They have to catch me first." Worse is the criminal who becomes more vicious because the possibility of an enhanced sentence inculcates the attitude, "I might as well make the most of the crime if I have to do the extra time." Hate criminals who are thinking clearly, meaning that hate isn't blinding them, though stupidity reigns unabated in hate crimes legislation, may vilify and blame the victim for the success of victim advocate groups to gain flawed hate crimes legislation, inflicting additional physical harm to compensate for the unfairness of the expected sentencing. Society suffers when criminals, rather than the law-abiding, lose faith in the system's ability to exact punishment with unfailing consistency and fairness.

Disaffection with the criminal justice system isn't the only roadblock to enhanced sentencing in hate crimes as a deterrent measure. Tougher statutes for hate crimes or any crime don't deter people who fail to consider the legal consequences of their crimes, who are unaware of the specific legal consequences, or who do consider the consequences and decide to risk them, anyway. Granted, most hate crimes committed by hate groups are premeditated, the hatred having been structured, systematized, and regulated by group coordinators. Hate as a by-product of teamwork. For those racist, sexist, homophobic hate criminals who don't premeditate their crimes, however, committing them out of passionate, blinding anger or jealousy, the prospect of enhanced sentencing simply isn't a deterrent consideration.

Statistics are now being collected, as required by the Hate Crimes Statistics Act (HCSA) of 1990, for crimes in which perpetrators appear to demonstrate "manifest prejudice based on race, religion, sexual orientation, or ethnicity." Statistics, however, don't prove a correlation between hate crime incidents and a deterrent effect of enhanced sentencing, and they don't indicate that the punitive effect for breaking existing laws is strengthened in the minds of criminals by the prospect of additional prison time. Statistics, though helpful to law enforcement in identifying geographic areas of high racial tension and time of day for race or sexual orientation-motivated incidents, fail to offer proof that hate was a factor in a particular crime, just as the arrest of someone for any crime doesn't offer proof of the suspect's guilt. Isolated statistics on the number of people charged with hate crimes ignore facts in particular cases. They also exclude dismissals of charges as baseless, for insufficient evidence, witness problems, or due process problems. Also excluded are those appeals that result in overturned enhanced sentencing verdicts. Also not evident in statistics are undetected hate crimes, unreported hate crimes, or less egregious crimes that law enforcement knows about but for which victims are unwilling to press charges.

Since statistics can't be referenced as proof of an individual defendant's hatred as defined in hate crimes legislation, they can't be used in court to convince the judge to enhance a convicted defendant's sentencing. In the prosecution phase for crimes in which hate may factor as a motivation, to ensure the uniform application of unequal sentencing, attorneys are required to establish legal proof that a defendant committed a crime based on "the actual or perceived race, color, religion, national origin, ethnicity, gender, disability, or sexual orientation of any person." Two challenges exist for prosecutors: 1) identifying those crimes to be prosecuted as hate crimes, and 2) proving that hate was the motivating factor in the commission of the crime.

Prosecutors have difficulty distinguishing race-based hate crimes from religion-based hate crimes. It's also difficult to prove whether a particular robbery may be a pretext to commit gender-based violence. Crimes against homosexuals may be based in homophobic fear (personal fear of latent homosexual tendencies), rather than in hatred of the moral disintegration that homosexuals represent to some. Clearly, not all crimes against members of non-white races are racially motivated, and not all crimes against women are gender motivated, and rape, though often determined by gender, is not necessarily committed from a position of hatred of the victimized gender. The complex granularity of additional proofs demanded by hate crimes legislation burdens the legal system, all for the sake of applying disparate sentencing.

Some crimes are committed because characteristics of the victim ease the execution of the crime. For instance, a criminal who targets victims whose physical state or inability to evade the crime or give chase may not "hate" people with disabilities. The criminal's parents, whom he loves, may both be disabled. The criminal may simply target victims for the sake of efficiency and convenience. Did the suspect commit crimes against members of the protected class not because of the primary defining characteristics that allowed the victim to be placed in the class, but for unrelated reasons, such that the elderly make easier targets, or that needy and promiscuous homosexuals and women make easy targets for robbery after they willingly agree to meet in a hotel room. Did the defendant commit crimes against prostitutes not because they are female, but because prostitutes are less likely to inform law enforcement officials about crimes of rape and robbery? Should a black defendant be believed when he states that he attacks and robs white victims because, in his experience, white people in his neighborhood generally have more money than blacks, providing a greater reward-to-risk ratio. Does the presumed reduced ability of certain groups to defend themselves against attacks in itself trigger enhanced sentencing statutes against perpetrators? Does the appeal of certain people as victims indicate that hatred predominated in the criminal's motives?

Personal conduct is rarely dependent primarily on a victim's personal characteristics alone, so to base sentencing on a single contributing motive for crime is a disproportionate punishment.

To apply enhanced sentencing provisions, prosecutors must generate concrete admissible evidence that bias factored in the criminal's decision to commit a crime. Title VII employment discrimination law is frequently invoked as an appropriate precedent for proving a prosecutable hatred. Under Title VII, hiring and firing decisions are regularly questioned, and patterns or trends are analyzed and compared against the availability of employable candidates in a given industry and geographic region.

Methods intended for proving employment discrimination and policing employment practices may not be appropriate to apply to hate crimes. Additionally, clauses within Title VII are too narrow to address hatred. Prior to Title VII, there were no blanket laws prohibiting discriminatory hiring and firing practices. In contrast, many laws govern the conduct of human criminal activity. Standard sentencing for crimes that anyone, including racists and opportunists, might commit are applied in some fashion or another. Title VII attempts to define and protect civil rights to societal rewards. The civil right does not exist for people not to be senselessly hated by strangers.

One method of proving hate-motivation to a jury involves demonstrating a pattern of criminal behavior, an effort that's likely to violate the tenets of rules of evidence. Past acts are inadmissible as evidence of acts with which a defendant is currently charged, even if the defendant's patterns of behavior were attributed to hatred in previous criminal cases. While observing rules of evidence that govern the exclusion of reference to a defendant's previous convictions, prosecutors face a difficult task in establishing verifiable evidence of patterned behavior and premeditation that would make the defendant eligible for enhanced sentencing. Similarly, a defendant's pattern of association with groups linked to the commission of hate crimes doesn't automatically prove intent to harm or intimidate another person. Conversely, the lack of a pattern of acts committed out of racial hatred, or simply amicable association with people of other races, may be cited to avert hate crime sentencing. In the case of Channon Christian and Christopher Newsom, the Knoxville, Tennessee victims of a brutal rape-murder allegedly at the hands of four blacks in January of 2007, officials stated "that because the accused have had white friends, they weren't driven by racial hatred" (Parker, *The Virginian-Pilot*, June 29, 2007, p.9). Parker states further, "that seems a flimsy argument, but it does serve to underscore the potential errancy and misapplication of laws that rely on the subjective judgment of others' psychological motives" (*The Virginian-Pilot*, June 29, 2007, p.9).

Another proof can be built on evidence of the defendant's verbal or written intent to commit a crime because of the victim's race, gender, sexual orientation, or other protected status. The prosecution must show that the emotion demonstrated by the defendant was indeed hatred, perhaps additionally creating the impression that the criminal activity isn't causally correlated with some other emotion, such as envy, love, disgust, pity, or jealousy. Defendants who are unable to accurately convey in writing or verbal speech the true nature of their emotional state concerning a victim, either because they lack the education to attach a correct label to their emotions or because they experienced multiple conflicting and confusing emotions that defy categorization, may agree to a prosecutor's suggestion that the crime was motivated by hate.

Proving intent also may take a bit of mind reading–after a hate crimes defendant is told by his attorney to clam up (plead the 5th), the court makes the assumption that the real reasons that a defendant committed a crime can be learned by someone other than defendant. In proving guilt in the commission of a primary criminal offense, determining motive is of less concern than the gathering of a preponderance of forensic evidence and eyewitness testimony. Establishing opportunity may be more important than motive in some cases. However, motive or intent alone must be proved to make convicted defendants eligible for hate crimes sentencing.

Legal precedents unfortunately exist in which unrelated racial statements by a witness or defendant have been admitted into the court record as evidence to discredit character, veracity, and motive. Inherent attitudes, beliefs and values presumed to be associated with speech were admitted in the case of O.J. Simpson v. State of California, in which the testimony of Mark Fuhrman was unfairly impugned as that of a professed racist. Speech doesn't necessarily reflect underlying belief systems, and lies are frequently presented as truth. Race-baiting statements made to garner negative emotional responses and reduce self-esteem don't prove that the speaker is necessarily racist, since other situational factors, for instance, dispiriting opponent athletes prior to a contest to gain a psychological advantage, may be in effect. However, speech that accompanies prosecutable criminal conduct has traditionally been used only for the purpose of establishing the elements of a crime or to prove motive or intent. Only recently has it been used as evidence in the effort to enhance standard sentencing for crimes.

Speech, and even vaguely defined "fighting words," that is protected under the First Amendment is rarely criminalized under most local, state and federal statutes, meaning that racist words alone aren't normally prosecuted in lieu of some other prosecutable offense. Under hate crimes legislation, however, citing a defendant's speech as evidence of hatred compels people to restrain their free speech in general, or risk having it used against them in the future to determine additional punishment for crimes that may have nothing to do with any prior speech. If a defendant has been heard to say that blacks are generally untrustworthy, and later commits a crime against someone who happens to be black, the defendant's earlier statements may entitle the criminal justice system to bump up the defendant's penalty. Politically incorrect radio shock jockeys who regularly berate members of classes covered by hate crimes legislation may have some serious concerns for their programming choices.

The assumption that racist intent operates in crimes committed by anyone who uses bigoted speech, which may trigger larger fines and longer prison sentences, relies on the value judgment that one kind of criminal intent (racism) is worse than another (getting money to buy crack cocaine), which gets into the realm of enforcing thought crimes. To be fair, prosecutors should use the past speech of all defendants to assist in proving that the crime by a black defendant on a black victim, for instance, or by blacks against white victims, or by blacks against ethnic or multi-racial or non-white victims, or by whites against black victims or ethnic or multi-racial victims are racially motivated; that crimes by a male defendant against either males or females or the transgendered, or by a female defendant against either males or females or the transgendered are gender motivated; and so on, effectively grid-locking the courts with necessary distinctions.

A lot of questions must be asked to determine the viability of applying hate crimes enhanced sentencing in a particular case. Did the defendant commit other unrelated crimes in which no members of the protected victim class were involved, presenting an exception to a pattern of criminal activity? Is there a direct link between statements made by the defendant and patterns of actions against the protected victim class? How much time elapsed between evidentiary statements of racial, gender, sexual orientation, and ethnicity hatred and the commission of a crime against the object of such statements? How often did the defendant make bigoted statements and not follow such statements with violent acts against a protected group? Do others in the defendant's association regularly make similarly bigoted statements on which no prosecutable action follows?

Defendants have been known to lie. How much weight do protestations of innocence have when uttered by a KKK member who says he committed a crime against a black to increase the esteem of the white race rather than to satisfy a deep abiding hatred of blacks? Must a defendant's statements of intent be proven either to be lies or to be inapplicable where the law is concerned? Do appeals court judges consider claims that "bias-motivated crimes statutes violate the due process clause of the United States Constitution because the statutes are unconstitutionally vague," as Denton reports in her coverage of a debate between ACLU attorney Stephen Clark and law professor Terry Kogan? The due process clause requires that a criminal statute give clear notice of specific activities that are proscribed by law, and since the hate crimes statutes are vulnerable to arbitrary law enforcement actions, it's not clear to defendants when bigoted behavior will be punished by sentencing over and above that offered for the primary crime.

In states in which judges are not permitted discretion to modify enhanced sentencing for hate crimes, standardized punishments gag judges who might otherwise sentence based upon their principles, which are in disagreement with obvious and glaring inadequacies in hate crime legislation. Mandatory enhanced sentencing periods remove flexibility and dynamism from the process, creating injustice due to the uncertain truth in the "proof" that commits a defendant to enhanced sentencing. However, judges who are authorized to make sentencing judgments might face verdict appeals by victims, their families, and advocacy groups in which the major charge is judicial prejudice. Enhanced sentencing options under hate crimes legislation are simply another layer of prosecutorial bureaucracy that burdens justice.

Victims have the right to appeal judgments, just as they have the equal right under the law to be protected against criminals, to exercise civil rights, and to expect that diligent effort will be made to apprehend, prosecute, and punish people who violate those rights. However, at the risk of alienating victims in categories that don't trigger enhanced sentencing, victims covered by hate crimes legislation advocate differential, harsher punishments when crimes are committed against them. Greater civil remedies for victims who meet certain demographic, racial, gender, and physical disability requirements are intended to offer redress for historically undervalued people. However, legislating remedies for past injustices are not a suitable use of legislative effort, and ideally laws should ensure that criminals receive the same rigorous punishment for similar crimes, regardless of the criminal or the victim.

Disparities in sentencing may appease minority groups that advocate for more stringent victim protections, but they risk fomenting discontent among members of groups who aren't afforded the same presumed protections. Crimes against specific groups do not constitute a special social problem that the legislation has a duty to correct, and asserting that they do is a mere pretext for claims for privileges by special interests. Hate crimes legislation is a disguise for civilizing courtesy and decency in the commission of criminal offenses.

Exceptions exist to the principle of equality of punishment for equal crimes. Ashruf H. A. Rushdy in an article for *The Humanist* explains the reasoning for regularly giving criminals harsher sentences for the greater assumed depravity of victimizing public officials and law enforcement personnel: "the state recognizes that certain kinds of crimes against certain groups of individuals are indicative of a deeper level of depravity and a greater risk to society and hence, constitute a potentially greater level of crime" (Rushdy, p. 26).

Though it's generally understood that criminal acts against law enforcement personnel in the course of their work receive greater legal rebuke than crimes committed against other professionals in the performance of their work, law enforcement officials are not represented as a protected class in hate crimes legislation. A different standard applies, that of one's work or service value to society. In fact, hate crimes legislation doesn't include hate based on any form of employment as being punishable by enhanced sentencing. Sentencing is also regularly decided by extenuating circumstances based on intent and motivation, such as self-defense, defense of country, accidents, and mental incompetence. Judges are given flexibility in applying the principle of mitigation factors, justifying a reduction of penalties suggested by sentencing guidelines for particular crimes involving extenuating circumstances.

Law-making bodies don't admit to passing laws whose objective is to legislate tolerance among society's members, since attitude adjustment on a mass scale would never work in our culturally diverse society. However, any success that might theoretically make society a tad nicer may seem worth the headache of legalized discrimination via enhanced sentencing for crimes against favored groups. Over the long haul, as a result of generalized social peer pressure backed up by law, fringe members of society might change their thinking and come over to the good side, just as many employers did when affirmative action and racial and gender quota systems were enacted. If hate crimes laws can be wedged into existing constitutional protections of derogatory speech and made to seem not inconsistent with other constitutional amendments, perhaps populations in society can be re-engineered to reduce incidents of race prejudice, ethnicity xenophobia, gender generalizations, and sexual preference bashing.

The Anti-Defamation League supports hate crimes legislation as a necessary step to prevent social unrest and suppression of civil rights by powerful hate groups in targeted segments of society. Hate crimes are presumed to have an absolute emotional and psychological component that impacts victims and communities in a predictably devastating pattern. Though based on exceptional historical events, legislation that proposes to predict how each individual will choose to respond to intimidation by hate groups is intellectually unsustainable. As with all laws whose scattershot restrictions depend on reductionist generalizations about human behavior, individual differences and equality among individuals are quietly ignored as the rights of some groups of individuals are subverted to the rights of others.

The assumption that crimes against some people are more heinous than the same crimes against others, or that one group of victims is more entitled to justice than another, is fallacious and offensive. That enhanced sentencing will restrain future criminal impulses is an unproven and unprovable assertion. Placating certain groups of victims by providing greater "protection" or by appearing to have greater legal compassion in the design of criminal penalties erodes rather than supports individual freedoms. Laws that attempt to control the results of personal conduct rather than to secure conditions, or means, for lawful conduct in an orderly society undermine freedom.

Regardless of the intent of lawmakers in drafting hate crimes enhanced sentencing legislation, it is not the law's purpose to dictate morality. Legislation cannot stop hate, may not even curb it, and arguably offers no more redress for hate crimes victims than standard penalties offer. People can't be punished for their absolute beliefs, though their actions are punishable. Adjusting the value and significance of humans to society through differential sentencing for crimes is not the province of the legal system, and not rightly the place of society, since humans don't exist to promote society, but more aptly to promote their own interests within the larger context of society. Any law that purports to discount the importance of crimes against one segment of society while affording greater protections to another segment for the same crimes is ripe for repeal.

9

Solutions to Race Resentment

Race resentment is a major stalling point in most discussions about race. Blacks legitimately resent that their ancestors were enslaved, that their civil rights were suppressed, and that employers may be practicing covert racial discrimination in hiring and promotions. It is only when we understand the causes of racism and prejudiced thinking that we can develop ways to correctly address these causes and design solutions that directly relate to them. This final chapter looks at current solutions being used and suggests additional solutions. Clear thinking on race issues and speaking to issues and individuals can lead to negotiations and more harmonious coexistence of the races.

We must greet all people on an individual basis and not prejudge them based on the actions of others in their race or who belong to demographic categories. This does not mean that we suspend judgment and presume that the majority of humans we meet will be good-hearted and kind and rational and well intentioned. People are prejudiced and may hate you based on your race. Know that many minorities refuse welfare, value educated, become professionals. Many minorities are not drags on society, are not militant, not criminal, and aren't drug addicts. Many whites aren't Aryan rednecks.

Advances

The financial, educational, and political advancement of traditionally disenfranchised races in America would appear to be an endorsement for democratic, capitalistic societies. Now, more than ever, Americans are aware of the problems facing the black race, its contributions, and actions taken by blacks to transcend the historic discrimination and suppression that members of the race have endured. Whites who unthinkingly relied on contemporary social custom and who dismissed blacks are now aware of how their own behaviors are colored by racially prejudiced or discriminatory thinking. As a result of unified effort, predominantly black coalitions forced government legislators to draft and pass laws that attempted to ensure equal civil rights for all Americans.

There are now a Supreme Court judge, black mayors of major cities, black police chiefs, a current and former black Secretary of Defense (Colin Powell and Condelezza Rice), and many blacks in law enforcement, politics, and government. According to *Forbes* magazine's wealthiest American lists of 2006, Oprah Winfrey's net worth was $1.5 billion, making her the wealthiest black of the 20th century, the richest black person on the face of the planet, and the first black to make *Business Week*'s 50 greatest philanthropists list. Many millionaire black athletes and high-visibility actors and musicians, and comedians realize the monetary benefits of dislodged racial discrimination. Bill Cosby's Theo Huxable for years on *The Cosby Show* was an exemplar of middle-class black success. The largest number of blacks in middle and upper classes than ever before attests to improvement. Barack Obama, a mixed-race man, is a candidate for president in 2008.

Black cohesion and support for other blacks is evidenced by the honorary tribute given to James B. Parsons, the first black to sit on a U.S. District Court bench when he retired after thirty years; fifty-two of the sixty-eight other black federal judges gathered to honor him. They also exhort black law students and attorneys to further integrate and improve the justice system for other blacks.

Many cities have large and prosperous black populations. The population of Birmingham, Alabama is one-third black and the city has a black mayor. Atlanta, GA is primarily black middle class (houses average in the $800,000 range), and 70 percent of its residents were black in 1992 ("Hair's Hot in Atlanta–The Coiffure Capital for Blacks," *Dayton Daily News*). "Black households had $679 billion in earned income in 2004, an increase of 3.5 percent" over the previous year, according to U.S. Census Bureau statistics (Bailey and Hackney, *Dayton Daily News*, July 8, 2007).

There are over 8,000 black elected officials and 42 black members in congress. There is continuing legal removal of race restrictions: The Supreme Court ruled June 18, 1992 in a 7–2 vote that potential jurors cannot be excluded from service because of their race. Government departmental representation that addresses racial issues abound:

- Civil Rights Division of the Department of Justice
- The Equal Employment Opportunity Commission
- The Federal Contract Compliance Office of the Department of Labor
- The Civil Rights Division of the Department of Health and Human Services
- The Civil Rights Division of the Department of Education

- The Office of Special Counsel in the Justice Department (set up to enforce the anti-discrimination provisions of the Immigration Reform and Control Act of 1986)
- The anti-discrimination enforcement mechanisms established in amendments to the Fair Housing Act in 1988.

Social integration efforts have made great strides, and interracial color barriers have been mostly torn down. In Alabama, interracial marriage was finally made legal in 2000. Examples of interracial coupling on contemporary television programs bring greater acceptance of interracial relationships–Mekhi Pfifer and Ma Wing on *ER*; Noah Wyle and Thandie Newton on *ER*; Ashton Kuscher and the black daughter of Tim Reid on *That 70s Show* (which also offered biracial characters); Zach Braff and a black girlfriend, and a black and Dominican (Carla, who must continually remind her husband that she's not Puerto Rican) married couple on *Scrubs*; and David Schwimmer and Aisha Tyler on *Friends*. Many of the depictions of racial line crossing in these programs do not dwell on the interracial nature of relationships as a problem or topic of discussion among the characters. Other examples of high-profile celebrity interracial relationships include Seal and supermodel Heidi Klum, David Bowie and Iman, and the Dineros.

Blacks have better jobs, better schools, better representation in elective offices, better anti-poverty programs, and legal elimination of racial discrimination in public places, the workplace, and housing.

Advances in awareness and a desire for discourse leads to structured talks. Dayton's Black-White Clergy Dialogue is a group that sponsors the Race Unity Awards, an occasion to celebrate racial harmony. "The awards are intended for individuals and organizations that have made an 'important contribution toward building better race relations in the Greater Dayton community'" (Kepple, June 18, 1992). Community forums analyze race relations. Numerous stories in national magazines describe people becoming aware of their own and historical racial prejudices. In *Readers Digest* (Sherman, March 2005), the author describes a black Tuskegee pilot who flew an escort plane for bombers in combat missions but encountered segregated quarters and racism while in training at the airfield. In the same issue, Halle Berry writes "My mother was white, my father was black, and I've always felt different and sometimes out of place" (Davidson, March 2005). Same issue, a white woman tells of her new attitude, her new belief that racial harmony is possible after she moves into a multi-ethnic neighborhood in Highland Park, Los Angeles. She learns that she can overcome racial prejudice by learning who individuals are (Fischer, March 2005).

Multiracial activist groups who are focused on non-racial, multi-purpose goals and who meet regularly, because of their visibility in handling issues that are not related to race, create the conception that whites and blacks can work together toward common goals that in no way emphasize the manufactured conflicts between the races. Such organizations succeed in breaking racial barriers as by-products of their efforts, by showing the cohesion and positive interaction of its members, and by enacting solutions rather than talking about solutions.

The Campaign Against Discrimination was developed jointly by the Advertising Council of New York and the Leadership Conference education Fund. The group's strategy is to encourage people to face the reality of discrimination and encourage them to talk about it, said Ralph Neas, executive director of the fund. The campaign includes 20- and 30-second public service announcements for television (*Dayton Daily News*, June 4, 1992). Parity 2000 is a community organization dedicated to helping Dayton-area blacks achieve equality. Parity 2000 sponsors media announcements designed to show blacks doing positive things in the community. Family unity was emphasized in the Black Family Reunion in 1991, a celebration sponsored by the National Council of Negro Women that drew more than 200,000 people from five states.

Some feel that racial awareness campaigns are ineffective, gratuitous photo ops to dispel negative reports about minorities, and participants don't do enough to address real civil rights inequalities or to make real improvements. Often, awareness campaigns are interpreted by whites as verging of racism. Though people are free to spend money on race-related announcements, resources used in awareness marches might be more effectively used to train people in economics and job skills, if volunteer social organizers can be swayed to divert their efforts into these more constructive endeavors.

People who attribute actions to factors of race frequently see situations as racially involved. They may see three white police officers arresting a black man, but the other reality is that three police officers are arresting a suspected car thief. When we can look at the situation dispassionately, we will stop attributing causes of the action to the race of the people involved. We must also question facile arguments, such as the statement that the future of young black males is being written every time we turn down school levies and build prisons, insinuating that society is more willing to deal with the effects of a disease than the cure, the cure being education in this case. This thinking assumes that money isn't being thrown into both areas in a multipronged attack. It also assumes that only poor education is a key commonality of everyone in prison.

Within every race, there are special interest groups, such as black men versus black women. Too often, blacks and women work separately for their own good but not for the good of all. This attitude impedes the solution of working together for the common good, not just for the good of a narrow focus group. One example of special interests served by grants from the Ohio Job Training Partnership Act is as follows: "One hundred black men between the ages of 18 and 30 have the opportunity to attend Sinclair Community College tuition-free through a program jointly operated by 1000 Black Males Summit and the college's African-American Male Initiative Program" (Ali, November 18, 1992). Females of any race or ethnicity are excluded.

When whites try to understand the black race's predicament, or try to help, many blacks explain the impossibility of whites to understand blacks. Blacks no longer want the help of whites, help that blacks see as condescension and an exercise of superiority, which blacks must refuse else regress to a previous dependency relationship with whites.

There is a renaissance in black art, says Gerard Pigeon, professor of black studies at the University of California at Santa Barbara:

> "'You could call this a renaissance of sorts,' he says. 'but it has been growing for a long time. It goes beyond the black middle classes.... Writers from the black middle class are cyrstallizing all the fears and hopes and search for racial identity of everyone. Every 30 years or so there seems to be interest in black arts. There have been other periods of heightened interest in black literature: during the Harlem Renaissance, after World War II, and in the 1960's'" (*Dayton Daily News*, August 1992).

Problems of regressive and dysfunctional behavior identified by critics and paired with blacks are real. The problem isn't one of image, but one of human instinct to generalize a few instances to the entire race. Unfortunately, this generalization is made stronger by negative impressions, and a few positive experiences don't easily offset or balance negative attitudes. A minority's laudable model might be missed, mistaken, misinterpreted as unassertive, not associated with skin color. Good acts might be seen as common decency rather than a welcome rarity within minorities, and might be counteracted by five bad acts (or perceived bad acts) by other minorities. Those who are aware of good models may never be in a position to avoid racially discriminating in a hiring situation or never see a minority job applicant. Racially aware non-minorities might not be the type who generalize positive and negative experiences based on race categories, or might die before passing along an undiscriminating impartiality or positive story to friends.

The hope is that a positive impact, though incapable of being measured, can be made on enough potential power holders to translate into less discrimination in a pay-it-forward fashion. If you believe in poetic justice, you may accept that some other member of your race may benefit down the road from your positive model. Whether anyone will is unknowable since human psychology is complex, depending not just upon one experience, but many experiences for which there are many interpretations for how each imparts lessons. Does all this mean that it's hopeless to be a good model of your race or humanness? No. Does it add up? Disappointment is inevitable when a nonpublic citizen's attempts amount to a molecule in a bucket.

The variables and the stars must be in perfect alignment for the solution of offsetting negative impressions. However, if politeness is a person's style, or a style that a person wishes to adopt because he believes that a positive attitude leads to positive results, it couldn't hurt race relations. But it's obvious that the pay-it-forward philosophy is a load of bunk.

Some racial minorities feel a personal duty to dispel fears that are based on crime statistics that show overwhelming crime by others of their minority. Presenting positive role rebuttals works only on those people who have such a racist low opinion of minorities that the positive act retains a shock memory for them; people expect positive behavior as social status quo and are less apt to take note of it. Negative impressions, which people hold more tenaciously, are hard to dispel, and the positive must be overwhelming and clustered in time.

People of all races who try to dispel racial stereotypes by modeling opposing behavior are admirable but ultimately fail. Some within subcultures may not personally exhibit the negative behavior that has earned the subculture's members a well-deserved negative stereotype, and there's not much to be done about being incorrectly labeled by outsiders with prejudices. A black man who says, "I'm not taking a shit job," is one black man, not speaking for all black men, and it's hard to dispel the negative impression that comes from that attitude, no matter how many other black men model positive attributes, becoming a "credit" to one's race. No one should try to be a credit to his race, as this means futilely trying to please too many people with too many definitions of what makes people creditworthy. Told that you are a credit to your race is an intended insult by implication: 1) one person is expected to represent an entire race, which the recipient of the compliment must be brainless to believe; 2) the race needs more outstanding role models to counter balance the numerous bad role models; 3) creditable examples are so rare in the race as to require special recognition; 4) if held as a truism, then the opposite must also be accepted, that people can be a discredit to their race, and 5) that a neutral, incidental characteristic, such as race, can be the basis for praise. Try not to take such a comment personally, because the person making it is an idiot, though well intentioned.

Sometimes, it's enough to be aware of language. One wonders why statements like "my best friend is black" in defense of accusations of not liking blacks, and when asked to identify a black, "They all look the same to me," are offensive. Any accusation about not liking blacks should be ignored, since it calls for a racial generalization. Asserting that a best friend is black is simplistic, implying that the race of the friend is the most important criteria in the friendship, exploitable as evidence in case anybody wants to accuse one of being a racist, and seems to say that a friendship with one person means that you can potentially be friends with any person of the friend's race. Though it may be true, thinking about members of other races as nonunique in appearance shows an apathy about their appearance. This is offensive because the person doesn't think enough about the individual differences in members of other races to think that these differences are important. Such comments show dismissiveness of the importance of paying attention to people of other races.

The institutionalization and socialization of civil rights laws do not mandate attitude change, but laws force employers and community service leaders to accept different races into their closed worlds. Those in closed worlds are resentful that their power to make key choices about who they hire and with whom they associate has been taken away, and directed their recriminations at the races who embodied and pursued passing of civil rights laws. In some instances, personal knowledge about members of the segregating race etched away at the broadly applied bigotry, and members of ethnic culture or races were accepted as morally strong and good at work, which is what the capitalistic system demands. Not letting employers down, though having gotten a foot in the door with the help of a law that champions discrimination in favor of minorities, is a great way to gain acceptance.

People who have a stake in the community and its businesses are less likely to be seen by other races in the community as negative elements. Minority races within a disproportionately black or white community are accepted. Minority business owners become known. Knowing dispels some prejudices and stereotypes about *those* people. Integrated businesses provide relief from race relation problems, but integration hasn't experienced more success because community members have unrealistic expectations based on race. Minority-dominated integrated businesses don't necessarily keep money in the black community, as expected. Business is in business for money, first, the community, second.

Though integrated, these businesses must cater to their "bread and butter" customers, and when those customers no longer sustain, business must branch out to
other communities. Once they have satisfied the community's narrow needs,
both of minorities and non-minorities, they have to struggle to find new needs to
meet.

Integrated businesses in communities largely populated by minorities are often
integrated in name only. Employers at minority-owned businesses still actively
practice racial discrimination, harming race relations. Employment laws don't
affect the employment percentage of whites in predominantly black businesses
because whites don't often invoke attention to the breaking of discrimination
laws. As a consequence, minority-owned inner-city businesses have nearly 100%
black employees. Such segregated integration isn't the answer.

It's a false assumption that if whites could understand the problems that
blacks go through, then whites would feel compassionate and help the blacks
resolve their problems and make structural changes in the societal systems. People
blame the victim. People are unwilling to give their time to others. People are not
altruistic. People will not sacrifice their own lifestyles for others. People believe
that individual humans are the masters of their own destiny and that with free
will, blacks have made poor choices within a known societal and economic
framework and expect whites to help blacks pay for those choices. Some people
will always want something for nothing. The importance of personalizing suffering as a persuasive technique works on a temporary basis, but compassion fatigue
sets in, and a constant bombardment of pleas from people like Sally Struthers to
sponsor sickly third world children are soon ignored.

Like many of the covertly racist methods used by blacks to gain favoritism,
methods used by racist white organizations such as the Ku Klux Klan (KKK) are
also underhanded. The 1992 observance of the anniversary of Martin Luther
King, Jr.'s birthday was accompanied by a rally of 100 KKK members at the state
capitol in Denver, Colorado. After the rally, a crowd of about 1,000 people
throwing bottles, bricks and snowballs attacked the school bus on which police
tried to get the Klan members out of the capitol area. Of course, the KKK members knew that their presence alone would intimidate others and rile heated pas-
sions, though they exercised their right to express their views, alongside opposing
favorable views about Martin Luther King.

Blacks in the NAACP would prefer that civil rights laws of free speech and
assembly and freedom from revealing member identity, rights won in a five-year
Supreme Court battle by the NAACP in the early 1950s, apply only to blacks
and not whites in the Ku Klux Klan. In a high-profile case in Vidor, Texas,

Anthony Griffin, a black attorney with membership in the NAACP, defended the KKK's right not to reveal KKK membership so that all of its members could be investigated to determine who may have harassed a black family that had moved into the white town of Vidor by order of federal desegregation laws. Other blacks called Griffin a traitor to the race, stating that no man can serve two races, two causes. Griffin impressed upon his critics that he was not representing races, but the law. Members of the NAACP then cited the difference between the NAACP and the KKK, which should justify differential definition of the right to secret identity: the NAACP is a political organization that attempts to advance the good of black people, and the KKK is a racist, terrorist organization. Name calling aside, all KKK members and the organization should not be characterized for the actions of an aberrant few members who have been prosecuted and convicted for breaking state and federal laws.

The Ku Klux Klan has used charges of civil rights violations to express their agenda publicly. In Cincinnati, Ohio, the U.S. Knights of the Ku Klux Klan got a city permit to display a 10-foot-tall cross in the city's center, Fountain Square. This was in response to a Jewish group that received a permit to display a menorah during Hanukkah. When the cross was repeatedly knocked down, Ron Lee, the group's vice president, stated that he wanted to press charges of criminal damaging and civil rights violations. He also stated that the city should be sued for not doing enough to protect the cross, which was protected by a 4-foot-high steel barrier and 24-hour police surveillance. Three people were charged with disorderly conduct, and a fourth was charged with littering in connection with the cross ("Klan vows to go after vandals," *Dayton Daily News*).

Some blacks think the NAACP has lost touch with issues that affect young blacks. William H. Gray, head of the United Negro College Fund defended the work of the NAACP on July 13, 1992: "'If it had not been for the NAACP, we would not be voting all over the country today. If it had not been for the NAACP, you would not have 26 members in the House of Representatives from Africa" ("NAACP Called as Relevant in '92 as '42," *Dayton Daily News*, July 14, 1994). The NAACP was instrumental in passage of the Civil Rights Act, voting reform bills and minimum wage legislation. Gray also encouraged black Americans to participate in geopolitical, economic and democratic revolutions as solutions. However, membership in the NAACP is declining and it is fighting accusations that it is out of touch with its constituency. NAACP has traditionally focused on political appointments and legislation rather than on crime in urban areas, police brutality against blacks, the plight of young black males as jobless, criminal, and homicide victims, and other grass-roots issues in the black community (*Dayton Daily News*, July 11, 1992).

Making holidays and naming streets in honor of great black leaders are also not solutions to racial tension. A January 19, 1992 survey by the Bureau of National Affairs showed that 17 percent of private businesses give their employees Martin Luther King Day off. "The survey, which covered 545 major firms, also indicates that King Day ranks 14th out of 15 holidays honored by many of the businesses polled" (Owens, *Dayton Daily News*). Reverend Raleigh Trammell, the Dayton chairman of the Southern Christian Leadership Conference (SCLC) stated that Dayton, Ohio was one of the few cities that had not honored Martin Luther King's work by having a street named after King. Eventually, Trammell's efforts led to co-naming Third Street in Dayton, Martin Luther King, Jr. Boulevard within the city limits. Trammell offered no statistics on the number of cities that have named a street after Martin Luther King. Changing the name of a street depended upon whether property owners on the street supported the change, and a public hearing had to be held before the City Commission could vote on the change. How much honor is bestowed by naming streets? Renaming makes giving directions to city visitors who are unfamiliar with the streets more confusing. It breaks up the logical progression of parallel streets that are numbered sequentially as a means of helping motorists keep a bearing on their location. Renaming means that businesses on the street may want to consider changing their address in all their advertisements. It means that some customers who don't keep up on the current affairs of municipal meddling may think businesses have moved to places they've never heard of, and have those businesses risk losing customers to competitors.

It must be personally painful to believe that obstacles are put in the path of blacks because of their race. And people can't change their race. That must make things look pretty hopeless for blacks. So, what's the answer, what are some solutions? One solution is to change what blacks see as the attitudes of people they think hold them back. This is a commendable solution, but the method used to change attitudes, which is the constant exploitation of the race issue, causes resentment, not personal feelings of guilt, against blacks for taking the easy, vindictive route toward change.

Something else we can do is speak specifically about the differing philosophical and political positions taken by blacks, classifying thinkers by the ideologies they hold. This prevents incorrectly attributing the ideology of a single group of blacks to the entire group of blacks as a race. The ideological-oriented labels must also be applicable to non-minority citizens who may also hold views similar to the group whose main classification criteria is ideology. For instance, all races and nationalities, to differing degrees can be said to be leftist, conservative, militant, extremist, segregationist, separatist, integrationist, and protectionist of heritage and culture. There are also varieties of black leaders: "race-effacing managerial leaders, race-identifying protest leaders, and race-transcending prophetic leaders" (West, p. 39).

Progress in race relations does not come about flawlessly. Some of the methods used to gain headway lead to racial antagonism and resentment. To gain equality fast, diverse black interest groups have abused a number of methods to emotionally or violently extort gifts of success and power. With indiscriminate use, these methods quickly weakened and experienced backlash and compassion fatigue within white communities. Whites object more often to the method rather than the objective or outcomes that blacks wish to achieve.

Currently, there is an upsurge in what is termed the racial uplift movement. Leaders of this movement promote education and awareness of European traditions to prove minority equality with non-minorities in knowledge of economic systems. New books that discuss race "dissect issues that were once, and are still considered by an older generation, dirty laundry" (Jones, *Dayton Daily News*, February 18, 2007). NPR senior correspondent Juan Williams' book, *Enough: The Phony Leaders, Dead-End Movements, and Culture of Failure That Are Undermining Black America—And What We Can Do About It*, was "inspired by a controversial speech Bill Cosby delivered in 2004 in which he criticized social problems in the poor black community" and focuses "on blaming black leaders such as Al Sharpton and Jesse Jackson, who follow a form of leadership developed during the civil rights era, for present problems and dismisses the effects of racism as the cause of high dropout and poverty rates" (Jones, *Dayton Daily News*, February 18, 2007). Heightened self-esteem and self-empowerment movements that don't cast blame on others for lowering esteem or usurping power also prove helpful in race relations: "There are changes we can make to empower ourselves. We can start by refusing to support and promote artists that depict us a pimps, hos and hustlers, and stop giving our children burdensome names that create hurdles in their pursuit of a better life" (Barker, *Dayton City Paper*, August 2–8, 2006, p. 5). Unhelpful are unsupported comments like those made by Melissa Harris-Lacewell, Professor at Princeton: "Contemporary racial inequality is structural, it's undercover, it is connected with also … with sort of black achievement" (Harris-Lacewell, *Bill Moyers Journal*, May 18, 2007).

Solutions for All

Solution: Allege racial discrimination through legal channels only, and have evidence of its commission.

Solution: Challenge other races when invited, do so gracefully, without rudeness, abiding by civil rules of shared discourse and debate, and in appropriate circumstances and locations.

Solution: Accept that current generations of people cannot be held accountable to repay the debt of injustice that those in the past imposed on blacks through slavery and Jim Crow; don't seek revenge against whites who didn't commit past offenses against you.

Solution: Avoid efforts to elicit unearned rewards from whites through guilt, claims of victimization, calls for reparations from whites who are unrelated to offenses, and demands for special white-discriminatory entitlements based on race; do not grab for undeserved sympathy.

Solution: Push for racially fair laws from congresspersons that do not provide preferential treatment to blacks in employment (affirmative action and quotas) and in educational opportunities (quotas and black-only scholarships). Discourage another government handout and more specialized laws against black-only discrimination.

Solution: Do not equate disproportionality based on black or white population percentages with evidence of racial discrimination in employment, education, government office, etc.; there are many reasons that minorities don't fill slots in society in proportion to their population percentages. The answer, if one is needed, isn't as simple as getting the numbers up in race percentages in the workplace.

Solution: Demand a single high standard of performance for all races. Double standards—one for minorities and a separate one for whites—are often discriminatory to whites. Do not grant awards only to minorities; do not say that inflammatory black speech and display of black separatist emblems are protected, yet deny the same protection to whites, abridging speech by race; do not segregate and name groups by race and decry whites for doing the same; do not lower grading standards for blacks but expect whites to score higher; and do not expect differential evidentiary rules in law for proving discrimination.

Solution: Don't seek approval of others in your race if doing so makes you irrational.

Solution: Don't pretend false grievances against the white race to avoid accusations by blacks of being a race sellout; don't let the expectations and value judgements of others give them power over your thinking and actions.

Solution: Use normal capitalistic routes to success, and don't cite black culture as a legitimate backdoor to easy success. Buy into unadulterated and unfettered capitalism, big time.

Solution: Avoid violence and the threat of violence to criminally obtain concessions and material rewards; put more pressure on criminals to stop committing crime. Do not gratuitously alienate through indiscriminate violence those who might be your allies. Stop the violence, stop pushing drugs, and stop abandoning families. The old litany of jobs, education, and opportunity holds up.

Solution: Self-police personnel in predominantly black institutions and businesses who discriminate in reverse against whites.

Solution: Refuse to hire employees or elect politicians to government office who are incompetent. Conduct case-by-case testing to determine whether job applicants are qualified to perform a given job, regardless of race. Employers, damn the EOC and develop interview questions that assess the educational requirements required of applicants to perform the posted job; fight for full discretion in whom you hire.

Solution: Accept only jobs for which you are qualified, even if such jobs seem demeaning and require hard work.

Solution: Do not promote a separate educational curriculum that emphasizes black and African culture over American culture.

Solution: Take responsibility for problems in black communities, instead of blaming problems on whites without evidence; do not blame white conspiracies for poverty and social dysfunction in black communities, and take responsibility for the individual actions and choices of blacks.

Solution: Debate issues logically, removing emotional components. Talk candidly about racial fears, stereotypes and ways to get along with each other.

Solution: Demand respect and consideration only when it's deserved.

Solution: Do not ask whites to be concerned about black self-esteem and feelings of self-worth when concern is not forthcoming about white self-esteem.

Solution: Do not try to pair the success or failure of blacks with the success or failure of whites; a connection between blacks and whites, in a general sense, exists only subjectively.

Solution: Understand that more whites are as poor as the poorest blacks, experience all of the same setbacks, and have as many hardships as blacks as a group; avoid false comparisons. Stop treating issues faced by all members of American society as though they require only an Afrocentric solution or study. Know that whites, in general and because of their race, haven't gotten anything free in their lives, and many have worked hard for everything they have, without resorting to racial discrimination or benefiting from it.

Solution: Don't hide crime statistics and provide misleading positive information to the media to dispel negative images of individual black criminals.

Solution: Celebrate American culture; don't elevate continental ancestry over American allegiance. Don't focus on false nationality; white racists don't focus on nationality—they focus on color as the differentiating factor between them and others.

Solution: Stop asking blacks to stop killing blacks, the corollary implication being that it's okay to kill whites, and publicly censor extremist black spokespersons whose rhetoric is so outside rational discourse that it incurs only interest in the perversity of their statements, and who characterize whites as continuing oppressors and exploiters of the black population. Question word use and implications in every media report regarding race, and write to the editor to express disapproval for racial instigation.

Solution: Do not change rules of conduct, business, and social systems to benefit only blacks, requiring sacrifices only from whites.

Solution: Address the issue under consideration rather than a related issue. Use clear language to express multiple viewpoints in race-related topic areas and in examination of the validity of each viewpoint.

Solution: Focus on more probable causes for failure; attribute correct cause objectively, not racially and emotionally. Notoriously ask questions to determine alternate reasons for failure.

Solution: Stop being ultrasensitive, seeing racism where it doesn't exist, as a first resort in multiracial interactions.

Solution: Be specific in speech, thought, attitude, and conversation; don't generalize based on race.

Solution: Judge and reward people for their performance, not the "content of their character," since character is broad and should not come into consideration if performance toward objectives exceeds negotiated expectations.

Solution: Practice coalition, broad-based politics that benefit all constituents equally, not that favor blacks disproportionately to percentages of blacks in communities.

Solution: Be incredulous that only politicians who are minorities will help minorities, which falsely presumes that white politicians are not broad-based and will not serve minorities.

Solution: Be upwardly mobile and too preoccupied with personal advancement to worry about race relations or the disadvantaged; be selfish and guilt-free.

Solution: Seek colleges that have a good reputation for teaching business and other career skills; don't consider only predominantly black colleges whose curriculum emphasizes the teaching of racial pride.

Solution: Take steps to understand and see similarities between people, not races.

Solution: Understand that blacks and whites don't speak with one voice, so don't generalize the speech and advocated acts suggested by one black as the beliefs of other blacks. There are many voices and points of view within all races.

Solution: Look for excuses not to riot.

Solution: Don't stereotype a race of people. Personalize each person of a different race that you encounter. Don't group people based on race.

Solution: Feel good about being black, not about being not white.

Solution: Teach black youths that materialism is only one sign of success. Convince black magazines and media to stop appealing to the materialistic and poor health habits of blacks, reducing reliance on tobacco and alcoholic beverage advertisements.

Solution: Help to put people in jail when they break laws, and keep them in jail.

Solution: Send unemployed people who complain a newspaper with the Classifieds highlighted.

Solution: Don't expect people to do things for you. If you say you want equality, don't expect advantages. Don't be a hypocrite.

Solution: Know that you choose to be part of a wider family of fanatics to take up a cause. If you murder for your family, you will be prosecuted for your family.

Solution: Stop writing race-baiting media headlines and slanted, liberal-biased articles that allege race as the prime causal factor in all events involving more than one race.

Solution: Teachers, provide prepackaged lesson units targeted to specific learning styles. Parents, aspire to earn and save enough money to pay for both bad public education and private education.

Solution: Understand that people are entitled to their racist opinions and stereotypes. Racism is not illegal. Be prepared to illustrate the irrationality in statements made by racists; disabuse nonsense notions and replace with values of hard work, personal responsibility, earned rewards, correctly targeted anger, and capitalistic principles.

Solution: Lobby to get racially preferential laws changed. Don't sublimate anger onto the recipients of an unfair law's favoritism or onto the employers who are forced by law to implement hiring practices that favor minorities.

Though it is easy to say change the laws, it's more difficult in practice, primarily because someone or group with greater power petitioned to have the unfair laws instated. Local, state, and federal government democracies demand that 51 percent of local voters win, whether the desires of that 51 percent are fair to the remaining 49 percent or are based on rationality. Often, the desire is based on personal or group economic, social, and political advancement. Whoever's in power makes the rules, and often those rules favor those in power and those who mirror the desires of those in power.

Solution: Don't repeat silly slogans like, "for blacks to be recognized as valuable and intelligent, they have to be twice as good as the whites." What whites? The poor white neighbor of a black in a poor neighborhood where many are out of work and lack strong educational backgrounds? Better than a white wino, a white whore, a white pimp, a white drug dealer, a white grifter or hustler, a white waitress in a greasy dive? Generalizations are like elbows.

Solution: Embrace art from the past that faithfully captures how bad white racist attitudes were; In 1992, the song *Shortenin' Bread*, about a slave who steals bread to feed his children, was banned in Spokane, Washington schools as racially insensitive.

Solution: Don't stereotype and depersonalize.

Solution: Don't demand that successful members of your race return and share their wealth else be branded a race traitor.

Solution: Help the less fortunate as you wish, but don't try to force others to.

Solution: Eschew relative achievement as a way to revise history to include lesser black figures.

Solution: If asked "Do you like black people," or variations of this question and you as a white, suspect you're being baited to make a racial generalization, answer "Could you be more specific?" If the questioner says black rappers, for example, answer, "Which in particular?" If you don't know the celebrity, say "I don't know him/her, personally." Add, "But I do/don't like his/her work/ music/acting style."

Solution: If confronted by a member of another race with, "Are you racist?" indicate the presumption of such a question and make the questioner aware of his/her own focus on race: "Unless someone brings it to my attention, I don't think about race," or "Most of the time I don't think about race unless somebody brings it to my attention."

Solution: If confronted by someone who asks to be addressed by his citizenship, for example, "Call me African-American," when the topic of neither race nor citizenship has been broached, respond politely and ingenuously as follows: "Oh, you have dual citizenship, both in America and Africa?" The answer will probably be, no, or something fatuous like, "I am a citizen of the world. Respond, "Oh. I'm surprised, then, that you would enter such a request to falsely address your citizenship into the conversation." When asked to be called an American of African descent, reply "I don't have that kind of time."

Solution: Speak out against those who show sentiments designed to divide the races.

Solution: Analyze the logic of every statement.

Truths to Keep Us Race Sane

- Expectations of equality of service in the absence of cash do not jibe with capitalistic realities.
- Most problems attributed to current government policies described as racist stem from expectations that people aren't responsible for their poverty, but that government is.
- Perception isn't reality, though perceptions influence decisions.
- People who do bad things are responsible for doing the bad things, and other people or society in general, or the capitalist economic structure, or the past shouldn't be blamed.
- Anger for being poor, jobless, belonging to a traditionally beaten down race, or for the perception of deserving more is not an excuse for committing crimes.

- The past does not dictate the future, but only influences the acts of people living in the present. People and their actions in the present determine the future.
- For the consistent application of logic, anyone who rationalizes that advocacy of one's own race isn't racist should also apply this rationale when race advocacy is made by other races.
- Religion ≠ race. For instance, Jews and Muslims aren't a racial category.
- People lie to gain benefits and downplay negatives. They actively misinterpret and misattribute cause and effect where racial accusations are concerned. Understand this and deny it.
- Poor people of all races have less political clout than wealthy people have.
- Class and culture differences, not race differences most often explain differences in treatment.
- Gender and race are neither qualifications for nor indications of quality education.
- It's a black and white and red and yellow and tan thing, and people will never be metaphorically color-blind.
- Knowledge about any culture isn't naturally acquired or instinctual; it must be taught.
- People represent themselves the way they want to be seen.
- Don't discriminate against the friend of the bouncer at your favorite night club.
- Perspective is not black or white, but experiential.
- Provocative statements gain attention; ignore them and deny attention.
- Rational, thoughtful responses are more helpful than strictly emotional responses.
- Only personal and honest efforts toward a goal deserve it.
- Race in government doesn't represent, elected people do.
- Some people say they want equality when what they really want is an advantage.
- Racist attitudes are the result of individuals, not entire races.
- Everyone should resent the use of deception by any minority to achieve social and economic parity with non-minorities.

References

"4 Whites Tried to Spark Riot, Looting, Police Say," *Dayton Daily News*, November 18, 1992, p. 10A.

"*24* in Hot Water," *TV Guide*, February 6, 2005, p. 8.

"Activist Delegates Seek Tougher, Angrier NAACP," *Dayton Daily News*, July 11, 1992.

"Ads ask Americans to end racism: 'Life's too short; stop the hate,'" *Dayton Daily News*, June 4, 1992, p. 7A.

"Alabama Oks slavery apology," *Dayton Daily News*, June 1, 2007, p. A10.

"Amos 'n' Andy Record, *History Detectives*, PBS broadcast, Season 5, Episode 1."

"Author Wambaugh Says King Case Baffles Cops," *Dayton Daily News*, February 29, 1992.

Keith L. Alexander, "GM's minority suppliers worry," *Dayton Daily News*, November 29, 1992, p. 1F.

Derek Ali, "Program to Help Black Men Attend Sinclair," *Dayton Daily News*, November 18, 1992, p. Z7-1.

Byron Allen, host, "We Had a Dream," broadcast February 19, 2005 in Dayton, Ohio.

Makebra M. Anderson, "More Companies Affected by Slavery Disclosure Laws, news.ncmonline.com, June 30, 2005.

Yardena Arar, "Artistic Freedoms vs. Political Agendas," *Dayton Daily News*.

Norman Atkins, "Marian Wright Edelman," *Rolling Stone*, Dec. 10–24, 1992, p. 130.

Jim Babcock, "Black, White Students Woven Together by Art," *Dayton Daily News*, February 12, 1992, p. Z4-1.

Ruby L. Bailey and Suzette Hackney, "NAACP seeks to unite old, new minority generations," *Dayton Daily News*, July 8, 2007, p. A28.

Joseph Barber, *Psychology Today*, July/August 1993, p. 50.

Teri Miller Barker, "We can make changes to empower ourselves," *Dayton City Paper*, August 2–8, 2006, p. 5.

Tom Beyerlein, "Banks Pressed on Loans," *Dayton Daily News*, July 9,1992, p. 1B.

Tom Beyerlein, "Expo Boosts Outlook for Minority Entrepreneurs," *Dayton Daily News*, August 1992, p. 4B.

"Black Infants More Likely to be Undersize," *Dayton Daily News*, October 1, 1992, p. 1C.

"Black Youths Blame Adults for Violence," *Dayton Daily News*, September 26, 1992, p. 4A.

Bob Blauner, *Black Lives, White Lives: Three Decades of Race Relations in America.* University of California Press, 1989.

Dwayne Bray, "City Gang Victimized 12 Whites," *Dayton Daily News*, March 14, 1992, p. 1A.

Dwayne Bray, "Wheat Agrees to Pay Penalty, Denies Allegations," *Dayton Daily News*, January 30, 1992, p. 1B.

Emma Burgin, "Disparity in cancer death rates between blacks, whites widening," *Dayton Daily News*, June 28, 2005, p. A8.

Carolyn Kleiner Butler, "Down in Mississippi," *Smithsonian*, February 2005.

"Cities Woo Black Tourists: They Want a Piece of $22 Billion Pie," *Atlanta Journal*, October 1992.

Jonathan Brinckman, "No proposal moves landfill site farther from homes," Dayton Daily News, January 30, 1993, p. 1B.

Mona Charen, *Do-Gooders: How Liberals Hurt Those They Claim to Help (and the Rest of Us)*, Sentinel, 2004.

Edwina Blackwell Clark and Timothy Gaffney, "AF cuts concern NAACP," *Dayton Daily News*, December 21, 1992, p. 1B.

Edwina Blackwell Clark, "Black Women to Take Stress Break at Retreat," *Dayton Daily News*, October 13, 1992, p. 2C.

Edwina Blackwell Clark, "Fix U.S., Lowery Tells Blacks," *Dayton Daily News*, August 10, 1992, 1A.

Edwina Blackwell Clark, "Living in separate worlds: Blacks, whites don't relate," *Dayton Daily News*.

Edwina Blackwell Clark, "School Fires 3 Administrators," *Dayton Daily News*, February 29, 1992, p. 1A.

Edwina Blackwell Clark, "SCLC Takes Aim at Drugs, Violent Death," *Dayton Daily News*, August 11, 1992, p. 1A.

"Consumers Bear Costs of Banking Regs," *Consumer Research*, October 1992.

Richard Coorsh, "Dateline Washington," *Consumer Research*, August 1992.

Michael H. Cottman, "Worrill: Firms' Apologies a Result of Pressure by Reparations Activists," blackamericaweb.com, posted June 14, 2005.

"Court Strikes Down Racial Criteria in School Diversity Plans," *NewsHour*, PBS broadcast June 28, 2007.

Jan Crawford-Greenburg and Howard Rosenberg, "Two Women Come Together to Oppose Busing: Plaintiff Crystal Meredith and Civil Rights Activist Mattie Jones Say Program Failed Their Children," June 28, 2007, http://abcnews.go.com/Nightline/story?id=3325773&page=1

CNN Money Correspondent, http:///2002/LAW/03/26/slavery.reparations/

Sara Davidson, "Face to Face with Halle Berry: Best [Supporting] Actress," *Readers Digest*, March 2005.

Dayton City Paper, January 26–Feb 1, 2005.

Bob Deans, "Riot zone in LA may not heal," *Dayton Daily News*.

"Death sweeps through LA," *Dayton Daily News*, May 2, 1992, p. 9A.

Jim DeBrosse, "Was fire at coach's home a hate crime?" *Dayton Daily News*, December 23, 2007, p. A4.

Carmen DeNavas-Walt, Bernadette D. Proctor, Cheryl Hill Lee, "Income, poverty, and Health Insurance Coverage in the United States: 2004," United States Census Bureau, August 2005.

Karen Denton, "Hate Crime Legislation: Balancing First Amendment Concerns." *ACLU Reporter.* Winter 1999.

Jim Dillon, "'Essence' Publisher Speaks at Recognition Dinner," *Dayton Daily News*, October 28, 1992, p. 4B.

Jeff Donn, "Status, race no assurance of care, study says," *Dayton Daily News*, March 16, 2006.

Thomas Byrne Edsall and Mary D. Edsall, *The Atlantic Monthly*; May 1991; Race; Volume 267, No. 5, pages 53-86.

Darryl Fears, "Seeking More Than Apologies for Slavery: Activists Hope Firms' Disclosure of Ties Will Lead to Reparations," *Washington Post*, June 20, 2005, p. A01.

FindLaw.com, March 2002.

Mary Fischer, "Change of Heart," *Readers Digest*, March 2005.

Mark Fisher, "Blacks a Priority for NASA," *Dayton Daily News*, October 22, 1992, p. 1B.

Mark Fisher, "Busing Support Erodes," *Dayton Daily News*. October 15, 1992, p. 1A.

Mark Fisher, "Math trips area students," *Dayton Daily News*, May 23, 1992, p. 1A.

"From the Medical Desk," *Time*, April 25, 2005, p. 60.

Lawrence H. Fuchs, *The American Kaleidoscope: Race, Ethnicity, and the Civic Culture*, Wesleyan University Press of New England, 1990, p. xvii.

Michael Fumento, *Science Under Siege*, William Morrow and Company, Inc., New York, New York, 1993.

Henry Louis (Skip) Gates, Jr., narrator, "America Beyond the Color Line," for PBS Wall to Wall Television, 2003.

Tim Gaffney, "CSU, Wilberforce Unity Urged," *Dayton Daily News*, March 4, 1992, p. 3B.

General Accounting Office, *Dayton Daily News*, April 7, 1992.

David Gergen, "The Two Nations of America" *U.S. News and World Report*, May 11, 1992, p. 76.

Kenneth J. Gergen, "The Decline and Fall of Personality," *Psychology Today*, November/December 1992.

Andrew Hacker, *Two Nations: Black and White, Separate, Hostile, Unequal*

Janice Haidet, "Living," *Dayton Daily News*, June 15, 1992, p. 1B.

Janice Haidet, "Make Your Successes, Malcolm X's Daughter Tells CSU Students," *Dayton Daily News*, January 29, 1992, p. 2B.

"Hair's Hot in Atlanta–The Coiffure Capital for Blacks," *Dayton Daily News*, March 15, 1992.

Lacy Harris-Lacewell, *Bill Moyers Journal*, Original PBS broadcast on May 18, 2007.

Lawrence E. Harrison, *Who Prospers: How Cultural Values Shape Economic and Political Success*, BasicBooks, A Division of HarperCollins Publishers, Inc., New York, NY, 1992.

Rosemary Harty, "Math is the Path to High-Tech Jobs, NASA Pilot Tells Patterson Crowd," *Dayton Daily News*, February 4, 1992, p. 2B.

Friedrich A. Hayek. *Law, Legislation and Liberty: Vol. 2, The Mirage of Social Justice*. The University of Chicago Press, 1976.

Ashley M. Heher, "Slave descendants try to revive reparations lawsuit," *Dayton Daily News*, September 28, 2006.

"Hidden Motives," Scientific Frontiers PBS broadcast in Dayton, Ohio on March 2, 2005.

Wes Hills, "Black firefighters' lawsuit against city dismissed in court," *Dayton Daily News*, December 16, 1993, p. 3B.

Percy Hintzen, "Empowerment, Caribbean-style," *Utne Reader*, March/April 1993, p. 127–128, as excerpted from the Pacific News Service, Nov. 16, 1992.

Robert Hughes, "Bitch, Bitch, Bitch," *Psychology Today*, September/October 1993.

Sandy Horwitt, "Racist Attitudes Alive, Youth Say," *Dayton Daily News*, August 1992.

Amy Jeter, "Court decision could affect busing policy," The Virginian-Pilot, June 29, 2007, p. 10.

Lucas L. Johnson II, "Freedom Riders, students relive landmark journey in Alabama, *Dayton Daily News*, January 1, 2007, p. 7).

Vanessa E. Jones, "Books push for change by black Americans, for black Americans," *Dayton Daily News*, February 18, 2007, p. D10.

Daniel Kahneman, *Psychology Today*, February 2005, p. 48.

Jon Katz, *Rolling Stone*, Issue 636, August 6th, 1992.

Mickey Kaus, "Yes, Something Will Work: Work," *Newsweek*, May 18, 1992, p 38.

David E. Kepple, "Race Unity Awards Honor Efforts of Ministers, Scouts," *Dayton Daily News*, June 18, 1992, p. 3B.

Raffi Khatchadourian, "Where East Met (Wild) West," *Smithsonian*, March 2005.

Les Kinsolving, "Washington Post cheerleading race reparations?" WorldNet-Daily.com, posted July 5, 2005.

"Klan vows to go after vandals," *Dayton Daily News*, December 29, 1992, p. 1B.

Natasha Korecki and Fran Spielman, "Judge says no to reparations," suntime.com, posted July 7, 2005.

Bridgette A. Lacy and James L. Patterson, Jr., "Residents Vent Anger over LA Verdict," *Indianapolis Star.*

Kevin Lamb, "Book explores shorter life expectancy of blacks in America," *Dayton Daily News*, October 26, 2006, p. D5.

Terry Lawson, "Black-themed Film Hits Built upon the Efforts of 'Race' Movie Pioneers," *Dayton Daily News*, February 16, 1992, p. 1C.

Michael Lerner, "Looters were living out the cynical American ethos"

"Literature Booming in Popularity," *Dayton Daily News*, August 1992.

Jesse McKinnon, "The Black Population in the United States: March 2002," United States Census Bureau. April 2003, viewed at www.census.gov on December 31, 2006.

From Robert McNiel's PBS documentary "Do You Speak American?", quoting Cecelia "Cece" Cutler.

"Making Amends," *ImpactWeekly*, June 22-28 2000.

Marcus Mabry and Evan Thomas, "Crime: A Conspiracy of Silence," *Newsweek*, May 18, 1992, p. 37.

Christopher Magan, "Civil rights group holds rally at Wright-Pat," *Dayton Daily News*, July 8, 2007, p. A4).

David Maybury-Lewis, *Utne Reader*, July/August 1992.

Scott Minerbrook, "A different reality for us," *U.S. News and World Report*, May 11, 1992, p. 36.

Tim Miller, "Black Power at Issue in New Voter Districts," *Dayton Daily News*, February 23, 1992, p. 3B

Lynn Minton, "Why Is There So Much Violence?" *Parade Magazine*, May 23, 1993.

"Mississippi Colleges Under Fire; Black Schools May Take Hit," *Dayton Daily News*, October 18, 1992, p. 7A.

Tom Morganthau, *Newsweek*, May 18, 1992.

Nisa Islam Muhammad, "New trillion-dollar reparations lawsuit filed," Final-Call.com, September 24, 2002.

David Mura, "Special to *Utne Reader*," July/August 1992.

Salim Muwakkil, *In These Times*, November 6, 1991.

"NAACP Called as Relevant in '92 as '42," *Dayton Daily News*, July 14, 1992, p. 10C.

"New Police Officers to Get Multicultural Training in Ohio, *Dayton Daily News*, May 8, 1992, p. 2B.

Keith A. Owens, "There'll be No National Holiday for Malcolm X," *Dayton Daily News*.

"Pacers' O'Neal says age limit suggests racism," FOXSports.com, Toronto (Associated Press) April 12, 2005.

Leonard Pitts, Jr., "Crackpots capitalizing on tragedy," *Dayton Daily News*, June 3, 2007.

Leonard Pitts, Jr., "This is how we die—we kill one another," *Dayton Daily News*, December 2, 2007.

"Poverty Among Whites Growing at Fastest Rate," *Dayton Daily News*, October 10, 1992, p. 10A.

"Race ruling reveals shallow thinking," *Dayton Daily News*, editorial board, July 8, 2007, p. A14.

"Racism's End Could Boost U.S. Economy," *Dayton Daily News*, August 2, 1992, p. 12A.

"Racial match in adoptions debated," *Dayton Daily News*, January 4, 1993.

"Race may be factor in fights," *Dayton Daily News*, December 4, 1992, p. 2B.

"Racial rage drove gunman; Notes show hatred, suburban target," *Dayton Daily News*, December 9, 1993, p. A1.

"Report: Unequal health care has blacks dying earlier," *Dayton Daily News*, p. A5, March 10, 2005.

"Report Says Black Families Fare Poorly," *Dayton Daily News*, September 25, 1992, p. 1A.

Christopher Reynolds, "Making a Connection," *Dayton Daily News*

Lolita M. Rhodes, "Heroes of Comics Played Real Role in Black History," *Dayton Daily News* February 9, 1992, p. 1E

Mike Robinson, "Bid To Revive Reparation Lawsuit Struck Down: Judge tosses effort to seek reparations from slavery-enhanced corporations," Associated Press, as reprinted at eurweb.com, posted July 7, 2005.

Eric Rose, "System Overcame Political Hysteria and Media Hype," *Dayton Daily News*, April 25, 1992.

David Rubin, AAUP-CSU Newsletter (July 15, 1992).

Ashruf H.A. Rushdy "Reflection on Jaspar: Resisting History." *The Humanist* March/April, 2000. p. 26.

"Schott: Furor over slurs is 'Berserk,'" *Dayton Daily News*, November 25, 1992, p. 1D.

Dan Seligman, *The Wall Street Journal*, November 19, 2003.

Ellen Sherman, "Friends for Life," *Readers Digest*, March 2005.

Dan Shine, "Some Blacks Feel Insulted by History Month," *Dayton Daily News*, February 16, 1992.

Greg Simms, "Blacks Defend Tyson," *Dayton Daily News*, February 5, 1992, p. 1D.

Elmer Smith, "It was a Simple Case of Picking Sides," *Dayton Daily News*, April 25, 1992.

Joanne Huist Smith, "Dayton lacks minorities in police, fire jobs," *Dayton Daily News*, July 26, 2007, p. A4.

Sister Soulja Interview, *Rolling Stone*, Issue 636, August 6th, 1992, p. 72.

Thomas Sowell, "Race and economics," August 25, 2006, as viewed at www.townhall.com, on December 31, 2006.

"Stepped-up loan-bias fight ahead," Dayton Daily News, March 6, 1993, p. 4A

Nicholas Stix, October 6, 2005, as viewed at www.theamericandaily.com on December 31, 2006.

"Survey Shows Widening Health Gap Among Racial, Ethnic Groups," *Dayton Daily News*, September 16, 1993, p. 8C, quoting from the U.S. Health Report released by the Health and Human Services department.

Tad Szulc, "The Greatest Danger We Face," *Parade*, 7/25/93, quoting Daniel J. Boorstin.

Jared Taylor, Paved with Good Intentions, Carroll and Graf, 1992.

Tom Teepen, "Is There Justice: King Jury Gave Wheel of Violence Another Bloody Shove," *Dayton Daily News*, April 25, 1992, p. 15A.

Studs Terkel "Race: How Blacks and Whites Think and Feel about the American Obsession," 1st Ed., W.W. Norton, New York, 1992.

"Tests unfair, NAACP chief says," *Dayton Daily News*, May 23, 1993, p. 6B.

"'The N word' repels, confounds, provokes," *Dayton Daily News*, editorial board, February 22, 2007, p. A22.

The National Law Journal (August 1992).

"The Price Tag: $30 Billion," *Dayton Daily News*, August 1992.

The Week, Volume 5, Issue 198, p. 19, *published in Dayton Daily News.*

Susan E. Tifft, "Out of the Shadows," *Smithsonian*, February 2005.

Nolan Walters, "Fewer Blacks Join Army; Test Scores Cited," *Dayton Daily News*, February 16, 1992.

Joseph Watras, "Misconceptions about Busing Make It More Difficult to Find Better Solution," *Dayton Daily News.*

Bernard Weinraub, "Spike Lee Asks for Black Interviewers," New York Times News Service as published in the *Dayton Daily News.*

Cornell West, Race Matters, Beacon Press, 1993.

"White Male Workers Lose Dominance," *Dayton Daily News*, August 16, 1992.

George Will, "Time to fold civil rights panel," *Dayton Daily News*, March 10, 2005.

Juan Williams, "This Time, America Must Learn the Right Lesson," *Dayton Daily News*, May 5, 1992.

Walter Williams, "Crises of 'racism' becoming cliché; how about 'racial rudeness'," *Dayton Daily News.*

Walter Williams, "Corruption of Language Cause of National Decline," *Dayton Daily News.*

Walter Williams, "No matter how you color it, racism is racism," *Dayton Daily News,* December 15, 1993.

Walter Williams, "Racial double standards threaten a civil society," *Dayton Daily News.*

Walter Williams, "Kindling for the racial bonfire," *Dayton Daily News.*

U.S. Census Bureau report on educational attainment in the United States, 2003, as viewed at www.answers.com on December 31, 2006.

"U.S. falls short of health goals," *Dayton Daily News*, June 26, 1992, quoting from the U.S. Health Report released by the Health and Human Services department.

Unknown author. Anti-Defamation League Website.

Peter Viles, for CNN Money, archives.cnn.com, posted March 27, 2002.

978-0-595-49063-9
0-595-49063-8

www.ingramcontent.com/pod-product-compliance
Lightning Source LLC
Chambersburg PA
CBHW030259290526
45785CB00001B/142

* 9 7 8 0 5 9 5 4 9 0 6 3 9 *